HISTORY OF GUILFORD.

THE OLD STONE HOUSE, ERECTED A. D. 1639.

The History of Guilford Connecticut

From

Its First Settlement
in 1639

From the
Manuscripts of

Hon. Ralph D. Smith

Heritage Books
2015

HERITAGE BOOKS
AN IMPRINT OF HERITAGE BOOKS, INC.

Books, CDs, and more—Worldwide

For our listing of thousands of titles see our website
at
www.HeritageBooks.com

A Facsimile Reprint
Published 2015 by
HERITAGE BOOKS, INC.
Publishing Division
5810 Ruatan Street
Berwyn Heights, Md. 20740

Originally published
Albany, N.Y.:
J. Munsell, Printer
1877

— Publisher's Notice —
In reprints such as this, it is often not possible to remove blemishes from the original. We feel the contents of this book warrant its reissue despite these blemishes and hope you will agree and read it with pleasure.

International Standard Book Numbers
Paperbound: 978-1-55613-323-7
Clothbound: 978-0-7884-6224-5

TO

AMOS SEWARD,

THIS HISTORY OF HIS NATIVE TOWN

IS

Respectfully Dedicated.

PREFACE.

AMONG the manuscripts left by the late Ralph D. Smith Esq., who had devoted his leisure hours during the last forty years of his life to the study of historical and genealogical subjects, was found an outline sketch of the history of Guilford, written some thirty years ago and doubtless laid aside with the hope of resuming his labors upon it when more abundant materials should have been collected for the purpose. The history of the early settlers of the town was a favorite subject of study. Although not a native, he showed an attachment to it fully equal to that ever shown by any one to the place of his birth. He was thoroughly acquainted with its records and keenly alive to everything that would add to its reputation. Had this historical sketch been filled up and completed by his own hands, it would have undoubtedly compared favorably, in accuracy and completeness, with the history of any town heretofore written. Still it seemed proper to save what he had prepared, even in its incomplete form, as something of great value to the student of local history, and as a foundation upon which future laborers might build a more complete and exhaustive history.

There is something exceedingly attractive in the history of this town and its good people, singularly reminding one of what Halleck, the Guilford poet, says in his poem *Connecticut:*

> "View them near
> At home, where all their worth and pride is placed;
> And there their hospitable fires burn clear,
> And there the lowliest farm-house hearth is graced
> With manly hearts, in piety sincere,
> Faithful in love, in honor stern and chaste,
> In friendship warm and true, in danger brave,
> Beloved in life, and sainted in the grave."

The editor has been assisted in the preparation of the manuscript for the press by Dr. Alvan Talcott, and is indebted also to Rev. Lorenzo T. Bennett, D.D., Rev. Geo. W. Banks, Hon. Edward R. Landon, and others, for occasional assistance, to all of whom he begs leave to make due acknowledgments for the same.

L. H. S.

Guilford, July 1, 1877.

HISTORY OF GUILFORD.

THE original town of Guilford, including the present towns of Guilford and Madison, stretched along the shore of Long Island sound from Branford to Killingworth, a distance on a straight line of perhaps nine or ten miles. June 16th, 1671,[1] a committee found the length of the town from south to north to be ten miles, measuring from the point of rocks at the southwest of Guilford harbor; but, as this point is north of many other points on the sound, the mean length of the town may be considered as eleven miles. The breadth diminished gradually, although irregularly, northwards until it became only about four miles and five-eighths of a mile. The mean breadth may be nearly seven miles. The western boundary, separating the town from Branford, was a straight line from the mouth of Stony creek to the centre of Pistapaug pond, where in a single monument was the corner boundary of the four towns of Guilford, Branford, Wallingford and Durham. This pond is a mile long from south to north, and a half a mile wide. The northern boundary, separating the town from Durham, ran a little north of east from the centre of this pond to the western branch of Hammonassett river. The above mentioned committee found the distance from the eastern side of the pond to this branch to be four miles, three furlongs and four rods, but as the boundary commenced in the centre of the pond the whole distance must be greater. The eastern boundary passed down the middle of this branch to the Hammonassett, thence down

---

[1] *Guilford Records*, vol. 1, page 50.

the middle of the river to Dudley's creek, whence it ran 216 rods, 50° 10' east, to West rock so called on the sound. This boundary separated the town from Killingworth. Originally it followed the Hammonassett to its entrance into Killingworth harbor, and one half of the harbor was considered as belonging to Guilford; but the legislature of the state, at an adjourned session in December, 1790, changed the line from Dudley's creek to West rock, throwing the whole of the harbor and a tract of land east of this new part of the line into Killingworth. It was provided, however, that this should not prevent the town of Guilford from regulating the fisheries of oysters and clams as fully as though this alteration had not been made.

Before the division of the town in 1826, Guilford embraced four located congregational societies, viz : Guilford First Society and the society now called North Guilford ; and East Guilford and North Bristol, now Madison and North Madison. Besides the two societies last mentioned the new town of Madison includes a narrow strip of land previously a part of Guilford First Society, running northward about two miles from the sound. The divisional line between the two towns, begins at the centre of Munger's island on the margin of the sound ; thence in a right line to the extreme point of land between the East and Neck rivers ; thence to the channel of the East river ; thence following the channel of the East river as far north as the abutment of Chittenden's landing ; thence easterly to the northeast corner of said wharf; thence northeasterly in a right line to the parish line a little south of David Dudley's dwelling house, where the centre of the road intersects said parish line ; thence on the parish lines of East Guilford and North Bristol, to the north line of Guilford. The whole original town, like others in the vicinity and country, was originally inhabited by Indians, who called it, or at least the western part of it, Menunkatuck. They were numerous on the great plains south of Guilford borough, as appears from the vast masses of shells which they brought upon it and which are mouldering to this day; and considerably numerous in other parts of the town as the harbors and shores of the sound furnished them with great advantages for fishing, and the woods back for hunting.

That part of the town which lies between Ruttawoo (East river) and Agicomook (Stony creek), constituting nearly all the present town of Guilford, was purchased of the sachem-squaw of Menunkatuck (Shaumpishuh), the Indian inhabitants consenting, Sept. 29, 1639, by Henry Whitfield, Robt. Kitchel, William Leete, William Chittenden, John Bishop, and John Caffinge, in behalf of themselves and others, who (except the said John Caffinge perhaps) had come out to New Haven the same year, and who were now resolved to make a settlement at this place. At the time of the purchase it was understood and agreed that the deed should remain in the hands of the planters, until a church should be formed in the town, to whom it should be given and under whose superintendence the lands should be divided out to those who were interested in them. The articles given for this tract were, twelve coats, twelve fathoms of wampum, twelve glasses, twelve pair of shoes, twelve hatchets, twelve pairs of stockings, twelve hoes, four kettles, twelve knives, twelve hats, twelve porringers, twelve spoons, two English coats. The Indians agreed to remove, and it was generally understood that they did remove to Branford and East Haven. An article, however, in the Guilford records suggests that a number of them were permitted to remain for a time at Ruttawoo. The English settlement commenced immediately after this purchase on the grounds now included in Guilford borough, the plain and some lands near the sound having been cleared by the natives and prepared for cultivation.

The planters had not been long in the town before Mr. Whitfield particularly, who had their prosperity greatly at heart, undertook to extend their territory eastwards, and on the 20th of September, 1641, he obtained of Weekwosh of Pashquishook [   ] a tract of land called the Neck, extending along on the sound, as it was then described, from East river to Tuckshishoag or Tuxis pond, for the consideration of " a frieze coat or blanket, an Indian coat, one faddom Dutchman's coat, a shirt, a pair of shoes and a faddom of wampum."

The right of Weekwosh to this land, however, appears to have been soon doubted, for on the 17th of Dec. following, Mr. Whitfield, Robt. Kitchel, William Chittenden, William Leete, John Bishop, John Caffinge, John Jordan, and the rest of the English planters of Menunkatuck made a purchase of Uncas, sachem of the Mohegans, which covered this land and extended northward through the township. In the deed of conveyance Uncas declared himself to be the sole owner of all these lands, denied utterly the claim of Weekwosh and all others, and accompanied his declaration with such circumstances and testimony as left little doubt that the right of sale was in his line. The consideration paid to Uncas was four coats, two kettles, four fathoms of wampum, four hatchets and three hoes.

Mr. Whitfield was desirous of extending the township still further eastward and accordingly made repeated applications to his friend Mr. George Fenwick of Saybrook, to convey to the town the tract lying between Tuxis pond and Hammonassett river, which Mr. Fenwick had previously bought of Uncas. In a letter dated Oct. 22d, 1645, Mr. Fenwick gave the tract to Guilford on condition that the planters would accommodate Mr. Whitfield with land to his content, and he was authorized to hold the land until the conditions should be fulfilled. The town accordingly made several allotments of land to Mr. Whitfield, which he accepted, and on the 20th of August, 1650, he gave to the town a deed of all the right, title and interest which he had in the lands given by Mr. Fenwick, for the consideration of £20 paid in wheat, which must be considered an addition to the allotments. On the 20th of September following he also gave to the town all his right (whatever it was) to the Neck, obtained first from Weekwosh, as the town had paid the consideration.

Uncas probably claimed the two tracts just mentioned in virtue of the conquest of the Pequots in which he assisted. They had possessed either in their own persons or by their tributaries a territory of very considerable extent. Concerning the Indians who dwelt upon this nothing certain is known. A stone with a human head and neck roughly carved, now lying in a fence half a mile northeast of Madison meeting-house, is supposed to have been used by them as an Idol. Nothing is also certainly known as to what became of them after the purchase of their grounds. They may have joined their brethren, the Menunkatuck Indians at Branford and East Haven, or the Hammonassett Indians at Killingworth, the remnants of whom remained in that town until 1739 or 1740. The latter supposition is the most probable as they appear to have been the most numerous about Hammonassett river, where they had cleared a large field which was easily cultivated and very productive. Indian bones have been found near the river and also on the Neck.

The first settlers of this town were adventurers from Surry and Kent near London, and, unlike their mercantile brethren who peopled New Haven, were mostly farmers.[1] They had

---

[1] Their first recorded act as a separate community was the Covenant, which they signed on ship-board, while on the passage, which was as follows:

COVENANT.

We, whose names are hereunder written, intending by God's gracious permission to plant ourselves in New England, and, if it may be, in the southerly part, about Quinnipiack: We do faithfully promise each to each, for ourselves and families, and those that belong to us; that we will, the Lord assisting us, sit down and join ourselves together in one intire plantation; and to be helpful each to the other in every common work, according to every man's ability and as need shall require; and we

not a merchant among them and scarcely a mechanic; and it was at great trouble and expense that they procured even a blacksmith on their Plantation. They took much pains to find land like that from which they had removed. At first they thought of Milford, but finally fixed upon Guilford, because they found it, particularly about the town plat where they first settled, low, flat and moist land agreeable to their wishes. They called the town Guilford in remembrance of Guildford a borough-town, the capital of Surry, where many of them had lived.

About forty planters came into the town in 1639, whose names in consequence of a defect in the records cannot be given with entire certainty. There were forty-eight in 1650, among which are doubtless included the original forty. Their names and the date of their admission as freemen are as follows:

  Henry *Whitfield.*
  Jno. Higginson.
  George Hubbard.
  Mr. *Sam'l Disborow,*   May 22, 1648.
  Mr. *Rob't Kitchell,*   " "
  Mr. Wm. Chittenden,   " "

---

promise not to desert or leave each other or the plantation, but with the consent of the rest, or the greater part of the company who have entered into this engagement.

As for our gathering together in a church way, and the choice of officers and members to be joined together in that way, we do refer ourselves until such time as it shall please God to settle us in our plantation.

In witness whereof we subscribe our hands, the first day of June, 1639.

Robert Kitchell,	John Stone,	Thomas Norton,
John Bishop,	William Plane,	Abraham Cruttenden,
Francis Bushnell,	Richard Gutridge,	Francis Chatfield,
William Chittenden,	John Hughes,	William Halle,
William Leete,	Wm. Dudley,	Thomas Naish,
Thomas Joanes,	John Parmelin,	Henry Kingsnorth,
John Jurdon,	John Mepham,	Henry Doude,
William Stone,	Henry Whitfield,	Thomas Cooke.
John Hoadly,		

Mr. Wm. Leete,   May 22, 1848.
Thomas Jordan,   "   "
John Hodely,   "   "
John Scranton,   "   "
George Bartlett,   "   "
Jasper Stillwell,   "   "
Alexander Chalker,   "   "
John Stone,   "   "
Thomas Jones,   May 22, 1649.
William Hall,   "   "
Thomas Betts,   "   "
John Parmelin, Sen.,   "   "
Henry Kingsnorth,   June 15, 1649.
Thomas Cook,   Feb. 14, 1650.
Richard Bristow,   "   "
Jno. Parmelin, Jr.,   "   "
John Fowler,   June 30, 1650.
Wm. Dudley,   "   "
Richard Gutteridge,   "   "
Abraham Cruttenden, Sen.,   May 19, 1651
Edward Benton,   "   "
John Evarts,[1]   Feb. 5, 1652.

The following names of planters are given in the original Records, who had not been admitted as freemen :

John Bishop Sen.,
Thomas Chatfield,
Francis Bushnell,
Henry Dowd,

---

[1] The name of John Evarts, which appears at the bottom of the list of names in 1650 was undoubtedly added afterwards, as it appears that he did not come to Guilford until the next year, being admitted a planter Sept. 4, 1651, and sworn in a freeman Feb. 5, 1652. He purchased John Mepham's allotment of Timothy Baldwin of Milford, by deed dated July 29, 1651.

Richard Hues,
George Chatfield,
William Stone,
John Stevens,
Benjamin Wright,
John Linsley,
John Johnson,
John Sheader,
Samuel Blachley,
Thomas French,
Stephen Bishop,
Thomas Stevens,
William Boreman,
Edward Sewers,
George Highland,
Abraham Cruttenden, Jr.

Among the names in the above list John Higginson, George Hubbard, John Fowler, and Thomas Betts[1] were not of the original settlers. The Rev. Mr. Higginson came from Salem, Mass., where his father Francis Higginson was the first pastor, first stopping at Hartford, afterwards at Saybrook fort, and then coming to Guilford about 1641. George Hubbard came from Wethersfield to Milford with Mr. Prudden in 1639 on the settlement of the last mentioned town and purchased the property of Jacob Sheaffe in Guilford, Sept. 22, 1648, who thereupon moved to Boston, Mass. John Fowler also came with Mr. Prudden to Milford in 1639, and is mentioned on the first list of planters made on the settlement of that town, and is supposed also to have come from Wethersfield. He came to Guilford before 1648, as he is mentioned as early as that time. John

---

[1] Thomas Betts came from Milford, where he was one of the first settlers, in 1639. He afterwards removed, 1665, or 1666, to Norwalk.

Mepham having died before the lists were made, his name is not mentioned, although he was sworn in May 22, 1648. Henry Goldam appears to have been here at this time and long afterwards but his name is omitted from the lists for some cause. Abraham Cruttenden, Sen., and Edward Benton, were among the earliest settlers, but were not admitted freemen till after the list was made out, and their names were added at the time of their being sworn, May 19, 1651. George Hubbard seems to have been received as a freeman immediately after his coming to Guilford, and Mr. Whitfield and Mr. Higginson were probably granted the privileges of freemen by courtesy, as there is no account of their being sworn in.

Of those who were only planters, John Bishop, Sen., was one of the original settlers and one of the original grantees with Mr. Whitfield and others in the deed from the sachem squaw. Thomas Chatfield and George Chatfield were brothers of Francis Chatfield (who was in Guilford as early as August, 1645, and probably some three or four years before that time), who died 1646 as appears by the settlement of his estate recorded in the first volume of the *Records*, Oct. 13, 1646. Benjamin Wright, John Stevens with his sons Thomas and William Stevens, Henry Dowd, William Stone, Richard Hues, John Johnson, Thomas French, Stephen Bishop, and Wm. Boreman appear to have been here as early as 1646. Edward Sewers and George Highland came as late as 1651 and their names must have been added to the list after it was made out.

There were many of the original planters who died or removed prior to 1650, whose names are not on the lists. John Caffinge, one of the first prominent settlers and one of the original grantees from the sachem squaw, Thomas Norton and Thomas Mills (who died 1648), John Mepham (died 1649), John Jordan (died 1649), William Somers (died 1650), William Plaine, who was here as early as 1645 and was executed about 1648, Thomas

Relf who was divorced from his wife Elizabeth Disborow in 1650, leaving the plantation so that his estate was settled as though he was dead, and his widow afterwards married John Johnson one of the early settlers, October, 1651, Thomas Dunk, who was here in 1645 but removed to Saybrook about 1650, and Francis Austin,[1] who embarked in the Lamberton ship and was lost; these are not found on the lists.

The places where most of the original settlers first located themselves are now known. The noted Stone house of Mr. Whitfield, said to have been built in 1639, erected both for the accommodation of his family and as a fortification for the protection of the inhabitants against the Indians, is supposed to be the oldest dwelling-house now standing in the United States. This house was kept in its original form until 1868, when it underwent such renovation as changed its appearance and internal arrangement to a great extent, although the north wall and large stone chimney are substantially the same as they have been for over two centuries.[2] It occupies a rising ground over-

---

[1] Francis Austin is supposed to be the ancestor of the Austins who resided formerly in the north part of North Guilford, from whom descended Stephen Austin, formerly of that village, who figured so conspicuously in the history of Texas and after whom the city of Austin was named.

[2] The following description of the old Stone house, or Mr. Whitfield's house, is taken from a note in Palfrey's *History of New England*, II, 59, furnished by Mr. Smith about 1859, and is descriptive of its appearance and condition at that time:

The walls are of stone, from a ledge eighty rods distant to the east. It was probably brought on hand-barrows, across a swamp, over a rude causey, which is still to be traced. A small addition, not here represented, has in modern times been made to the back of the house, but there is no question that the main building remains in its original state, even to the oak of the beams, floors, doors, and window-sashes. The following representations of the interior exhibit accurately the dimensions of the rooms, windows, and doors, the thickness of the walls, etc., on a scale of ten feet to the inch. The single dotted lines represent fire-places and doors. The double dotted lines represent windows. In the recesses of the windows are broad seats. Within the memory of some of the residents of the town, the panes of glass were of diamond shape.

The height of the first story is seven feet and two-thirds. The height of the

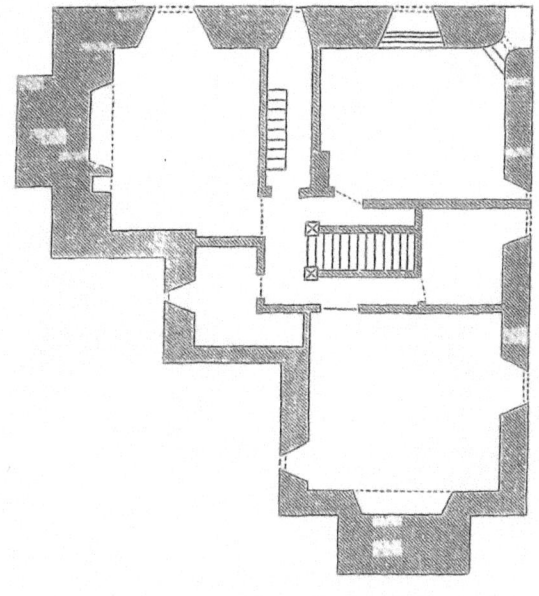

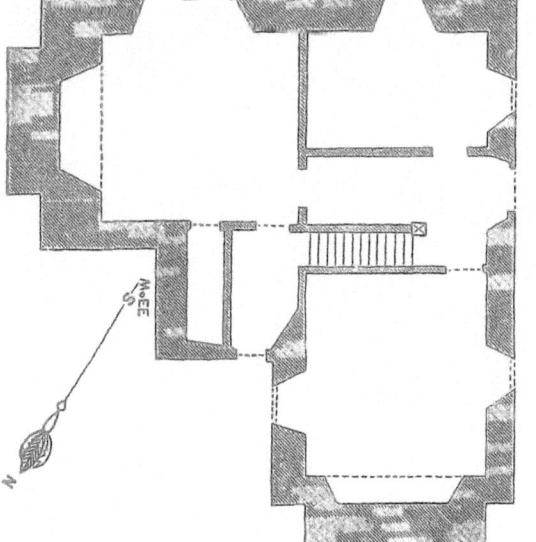

THE OLD STONE HOUSE.

Second Floor.

First Floor.

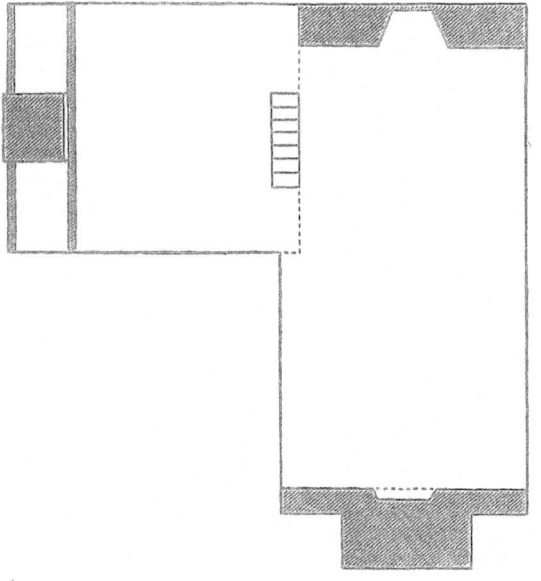

ATTIC STORY.

looking the great plain south of the village and commanding a very fine prospect of the sound. It is said that the first marriage was celebrated in it, the wedding-table being garnished with the substantial luxuries of pork and pease. According to tradition the stone, of which this house was built, was brought by the Indians on hand-barrows, across the swamp, from Griswold's rocks, a ledge about eighty rods east of the house, and an ancient causeway across the swamp is shown as the path employed for this purpose. The house consisted of two stories and an attic. The walls were three feet thick. At the southwest corner of the second floor there was a singular embrasure, commanding the approach from the south and west, which was evidently made for defensive purposes. In the attic there were two recesses evidently intended as places of concealment.

This house was undoubtedly the best in the village but not the only one built of stone. Jasper Stillwell, on the lot northward, Rev. John Higginson — son-in-law of Mr. Whitfield and subsequently of Salem, Mass., and Sam'l Disborow, the magistrate and a relative of Oliver Cromwell, all had stone houses, situated back from the street with door yards in front similar to Mr. Whitfield's. Mr. Whitfield sold his accommodations to Major Thompson of London, a man of some note during the commonwealth, in whose family it remained until a short time before the Revolutionary war, when Wyllys Elliott of Guilford purchased it.

---

second is six feet and three-quarters. At the southerly corner in the second story there was originally an embrasure, about a foot wide, with a stone flooring, which remains. The exterior walls are now closed up, but not the walls within.

The walls of the front and back of the house terminate at the floor of the attic, and the rafters lie upon them. The angle of the roof is 60°, making the base and sides equal. At the end of the wing, by the chimney, is a recess, which must have been intended as a place of concealment. The interior wall has the appearance of touching the chimney, like the wall at the northwest end. But the removal of a board discovers two closets which project beyond the lower part of the building.

Mr. Higginson lived at the southwest corner of the green on the south side of Bridge street. Mr. Disborow on the same side of the street, to the west. Mr. Leete lived on the north corner of Water and Broad streets. Mr. Chittenden on the south corner opposite, near the bank of West or Menunkatuck river. Mr. Rob't Kitchel lived on the corner of Broad and Fair streets, on the site occupied by the house of the late Judge Griffing, John Fowler on the opposite corner where Judge Fowler, one of his descendants lived in recent times.

The rich and cleared lands about the town plat, together with considerations of continual intercourse and mutual safety, induced the colonists to settle in a cluster, but as their numbers increased and as circumstances became more favorable, they gradually spread themselves into other parts of the First Society and pretty soon into Madison near the shore of the sound, and at Hammonassett. As early as October, 1646, it was " ordered that Nut plains and another plain on the east side of East river (doubtless that now called Howlett's), together with the land on the other side of said East river, both upland and marsh, should be viewed, and a survey taken of all the said parcels ; that so division might be made according as was due to every planter wanting land." In 1649 a bridge was built over East river, which makes it probable that the lands in the vicinity of this river began to be cultivated quite early, and that before the lapse of many years they began to be settled.

Dr. Bryan Rossiter joined the settlers in Guilford and was admitted and approved a planter, having purchased the estate of Mr. Disborow, the magistrate (on his leaving for England), October, 1651. He was sworn as a freeman (with Nathaniel Whitfield, who seems to have remained a few years after his father) June 8, 1654. Doctor Rossiter is said to have come over originally with five or six brothers to Boston on the first settlement of this country. In 1640 he was enumerated among the settlers of Windsor where he seems to have resided until he came to Guilford in 1651. His daughter, Johanna Rossiter, was married Nov. 7, 1660, to John Cotton, the son of the celebrated John Cotton of Massachusetts. After the marriage he preached occasionally at Guilford and at Killingworth, where he was hired for a considerable period (about 1670), as appears from the records of that town, until he finally returned to Massachusetts and was a distinguished pastor of the church at Plymouth for many years. Cotton Mather calls him one by whom not only the English but also the Indians of America have the glad tidings of salvation carried to them. He supplied the church at Guilford jointly with Mr. John Bowers, previous to the settlement of Mr. Joseph Elliott, 1664. He had two children born in Guilford.

John Meigs came to Guilford from New Haven, where he seems to have resided previously, and was admitted a planter on his buying a hundred pound allotment at Hammonassett on its settlement March 3, 1653-4. He seems to have become unpopular and removed to Killingworth on its first settlement, where he died, as appears by the Killingworth Town Records, January 4, 1671. When he first came to Guilford, his father Vincent Meigs, who appears to have been old at that time, came with him and died at Hammonassett, 1658. John Meigs, Jun., came to Guilford from Killingworth, soon after his father's death, and settled in the east part of the town where his posterity are numerous to this day.

William Seward came originally from Bristol, England, and settled first at New Haven, and, while residing there he was married to Miss Grace Norton of Guilford, April 2, 1651. He soon after removed to Guilford and took the oath of fidelity there May 4, 1654. He appears to have been a tanner, a man of considerable property and eminence in the town. For a long time he was captain of the guard in Guilford, and an anecdote is related of him, that, when the charter of the state was supposed to be concealed in Guilford, during the usurpation of Edmund Andross, by Governor Leete's family, and delegates were sent down to seize and bring it to Hartford, Mr. Seward marched his company, with their muskets loaded, down to the southeast corner of the green, where the delegates were lodged, and paraded them in front of the house to the beat of the drum. On being asked by the delegates, what they wanted? the captain informed them that he came to escort them out of town, and that he would not leave with his men until they had left, which must be as soon as possible. The delegates seeing their danger accepted the escort thus forced upon them and left. Mr. Seward died March 2, 1689, aged sixty-two years.

William Johnson, the ancestor of Dr. Johnson and a large part of the Guilford Johnsons, came to Guilford from New Haven as early as 1653. He was for many years town clerk of the plantation. He married Elizabeth, daughter of Francis Bushnell. John Baldwin came from Milford in 1651, and took the oath of fidelity, February 5, 1652. John Hill, by trade a carpenter, came from Northamptonshire, in England, as early as 1654, and settled upon the north side of the green on the place now occupied by E. C. Bishop and Tabor Smith. John Grave came from Hartford, 1657, and married Elizabeth Stillwell, daughter of Jasper Stillwell, Nov. 26, 1657. Jasper Stillwell died Nov. 8, 1656, in Guilford, without male issue, and Mr. Grave occupied his situation on the east side of South lane, now called Harbor street, two lots of land north of the stone house. He came originally from England and was for many years the town clerk. Thomas Clarke came from Milford, where he was one of the original settlers, and married Anne Jordan, widow of John Jordan, who died in 1652, and settled here 1653. He lived on the west side of South lane, nearly where William S. Kelsey now lives. Thomas Meacock, also of Milford, and one of its settlers, with Mr. Prudden in 1639, was admitted a planter of Guilford on the purchase of land from Dennis Crampton, May 14, 1660. Dennis Crampton came here prior to 1656, when he was an apprentice and was complained of, for slander and cheating, and, according to the *Records*, vol. A, page 151, not having any estate to make satisfaction by way of fine and penalty, the court ordered that he be immediately corporally punished by whipping. He afterwards, however, became a man of considerable property and some distinction in the Plantation, and his posterity remain in both Guilford and Madison to this day. He lived on the west side of South lane, and afterwards removed and settled on the Neck plain in Madison.

Nathan Bradley and Stephen Bradley came to Guilford quite early. In 1658 the former was twenty and the latter sixteen years of age, as appears by the *Records*, vol. A, page 172. Nathan Bradley settled in the eastern part of the town, and Stephen in Neck plain. Their descendants are numerous both in Guilford and New Haven at the present time. The following account of Nathan Bradley is taken from Barber's *Historical Collections of Connecticut*, page 227. He was one of a family of five or six brothers, who were staunch dissenters and came together from England. He settled and built his house about two miles and a half eastward of where the Madison Church now is, and near to the Killingworth line. He intended to have landed at New Haven but was obliged to put in at Saybrook and come across the wilderness to New Haven, there being no settlement at that time between that place and Saybrook. Mr. Bradley who was quite a hunter, was the first white person who discovered the source of the Hammonassett river, which originates in a pond still called Nathan's pond. Mr. Bradley lived to an advanced age, and is said to have killed several hundred deer while he resided in the town. In the winter, bears, wolves, and other wild animals, would resort to the sea-coast in considerable numbers. On one occasion, Mr. B., in his old age, went to see a friend who lived about a mile northerly of the meeting house. On his way he met a bear with her cubs. He endeavored to ride around her, but as he moved the bear moved, when he stopped she stopped, and sitting on her haunches, presented an undaunted front, seeming determined to oppose his further passage. Mr. B. was obliged to turn back, and in the childishness of old age shed tears that he, who had killed so many of these creatures, should be at last obliged to turn his back upon one of them.

Mr. John Collins came from Branford in 1669, and married Mary Kingsnorth, the sister of Henry Kingsnorth. He settled on Fair street, on the east side, next north of the lot on which the late Mr. Russell Frisbie's house now stands. Afterwards, in right of his wife, he came into possession of the lands of Henry and James Kingsnorth. Henry Kingsnorth came out from England, probably with the first settlers, and dying about 1660, gave his property unto such son of Daniel Kingsnorth as should come from England and claim the same, otherwise, to John Collins and his wife Mary. Accordingly James Kingsnorth appeared before the county court at New Haven and, on the exhibit of Henry Kingsnorth's will, he presented a letter from Mr. Whitfield, then in England, to Mr. Jno. Hall affirming the fact. He also showed a certificate from the rectors, church wardens and parish clerks, of Staple Hurst, in the county of Kent as to his age, whereupon he was adjudged the inheritance and resided in Guilford till his death, 1682. Not leaving any issue, by his nuncupative will he bequeathed all his real estate to either of his brothers, or either of their sons, that should come over to New England for it, and if none of them came in five years time then the inheritance to fall to his uncle and aunt Collins, they sending over to each of his brothers or their sons, a piece of plate worth three pounds in England.

His two brothers, Daniel and John Kingsnorth afterwards acknowledged the receipt of such pieces of plate, and by their deed made and executed in England conveyed the said real estate to John Collins, 1686.

Richard Hubball was admitted a planter, February 25, 165¾, on purchasing Samuel Blatchley's lots and accommodations in his stead. He appears also to have purchased the land and accommodations of John Baldwin, October 16, 1660. In 1680, however, he removed and settled in Fairfield, where his posterity are numerous to the present day. Henry Crane was a planter in Guilford about 1660, but removed to Killingworth on the settlement of that town, and is enumerated in the list of its first settlers, October, 1663. Thomas Smith came into Guilford, on the invitation of the planters, from Fairfield, in the capacity of blacksmith, 1652, and took the oath of fidelity, May 11, 1654. There seems to have been great difficulty in procuring a blacksmith and a considerable tract of land was given to induce Smith to settle here. "This was given him on condition of serving the town in the trade of a smith upon just and moderate terms for the space of five years." In 1663 Smith removed, with others to Killingworth on the first settlement of that town. John Hodgkin came from Essex, England, and was admitted to the oath of fidelity, May 11, 1654.

In 1657 or 1658 a list was made out of the freemen. It is herewith appended, with the dates of their subsequent deaths:

Wm. Leete, removed to Hartford,	died	April 6, 1683.
Robt. Kitchell, removed to Newark, 1666 or 7,	"	Oct., 1671.
Wm. Chittenden,	"	Feb., 1660-1.
George Hubbard,	"	Jan., 1683.
Mr. Bryan Rossiter,	"	Sept. 30, 1672.
Mr. John Bishop,	"	Jan., 1661.

Abm. Cruttenden Sen.,	died	Jan., 1683.
Wm. Dudley,	"	Mar. 16, 1684.
Wm. Johnson,	"	Oct. 27, 1702.
Benjn. Wright, Sen.,	"	Mar. 29, 1677
William Stone,	"	Nov. 1683.
Thomas Cooke,	"	Dec. 1, 1692.
John Stevens,	"	Sept. 1, 1670.
John Fowler,	"	Sept. 14, 1676.
John Hill,	"	June 8, 1689.
John Parmelin, Sen.,	"	Nov. 8, 1659.
John Evarts,	"	May 9, 1669.
Thomas French,		
William Seward,	"	Mar. 2, 1689.
William Stevens,	"	Jan., 1703.
Henry Kingsnorth,	"	July 28, 1668.
Richard Guttridge,	"	May 7, 1676.
Henry Doud,	"	Aug. 31, 1668.
William Hall,	"	May 7, 1669.
John Scranton,	"	Aug. 27, 1671.
Edward Benton,	"	Oct. 28, 1680.
Dan. Benton,	"	June 9, 1672.
John Meigs,	"	Jan. 10, 1671-2.
Rich'd Bristow,	"	Sept., 1683.
John Johnson,	"	Nov., 1681.
John Sheader,	"	June 1, 1670.
Rich. Hubball,	"	1692.
John Parmelin, Jun.,	"	Jan. 1687-8.
Ab'm Cruttenden, Jun.,	"	Sept. 25, 1694.
John Graves,	"	Dec. 31, 1695.
Geo. Highland,	"	Jan. 21, 1692-3.
John Rossiter,	"	Sept., 1670.
John Baldwin, left 1661 for Norwich.		
Thos. Clark,		buried Oct. 10, 1668.

Rich. Hughes,	died	July 3, 1658.
John Stone,	"	Feb., 1687.
George Bartlett,	"	Aug. 2, 1669.
Henry Goldam,	"	1661.
Nicholas Munger,	"	Oct. 16, 1668.
Geo. Chatfield,	"	June 9, 1671.
John Bishop, Jr.,	"	Oct., 1683.
Stephen Bishop,	"	June, 1690.

This list contains the names of forty-seven persons probably all freemen, as at the time the list was made out there were many others resident in Guilford and planters not named. Of the twenty-eight freemen on the former list of 1650, the nineteen mentioned again are those in italics. Mr. John Higginson, the clergyman, is not mentioned again as he was the minister, or probably had left the colony of which he was certainly not a member in 1659. Mr. Whitfield, Mr. Sam. Disborough and Mr. Thomas Jordan had returned to England. Thomas Betts had removed to Norwalk in Fairfield county, 1656 or 1657. Alexander Chalker had removed to Saybrook as early as 1654. Thomas Jones had probably removed to England with Mr. Thomas Jordan, who went back two years after Mr. Whitfield in 1654. Mr. Whitfield took one of his sons (John Whitfield) back with him, the other Nathaniel remained and was admitted a freeman as before stated, June 8, 1654. He returned to England about the same year and became a distinguished merchant in London and was agent of Mr Disborow in that city in 1664. Mr. Thomas Jones left Mr. William Chittenden as his agent here, as did the others who went back to England. He also left a son or nephew, Samuel Jones, and, on the sale of his lands by his said agent, March 4, 1667 to John Meigs, it is stated that " the alienation was made with the free consent of the said Samuel Jones who laid some claim to the lands as being the heir thereto." Jasper Stillwell had died Nov., 1656. John Evarts, the only other freeman mentioned on the former list was admitted, as before stated, Feb. 5, 1652. Of the other names on the list of 1650, which were then not freemen, seven are not named on the list of 1657 or 1658, viz.: Thomas Chatfield, Francis Bushnell, John Linsley, Samuel Blatchley, Thomas Stevens, Wm. Boreman and Edward Sewers. Thomas Stevens was not yet admitted to the oath of freeman, but he evidently continued a resident of Guilford until about 1665 when he removed to Killingworth. His name is never mentioned among the freemen of Guilford. Thomas Chatfield had sold out his property in Guilford and removed to "East Hampton in the East Riding of Long Island," as it was then called. Francis Bushnell, who had kept the town mill since the death of Thomas Norton, 1648, removed to Saybrook about 1659-60 and upon the solicitations of its inhabitants erected a corn mill on Oyster river, being the first erected in that town, for which the proprietors gave him a farm on condition that a mill should be kept there continually and that the inhabitants should have equal privileges in regard to grinding, which farm is held by his descendants on these conditions at the present time. John Linsley, becoming disaffected on account of the results of a lawsuit for slander in favor of Richard Goodrich and his wife, sold out all his allotments in Guilford to William Hall and removed to Branford, 1654. Samuel Blatchley appears to have died previous to 1660. Edward Sewers appears to have remained for awhile, and then to have removed to Stony creek, Branford. William Boreman, died about 1652 and his allotments were sold by Nathan Harman, attorney, to Daniel Butcher, brother-in-law of said Boreman, of Hawkhurst in Kent, England, 1663. The remaining thirteen were all admitted freemen from 1650 to 1660, Jno. Johnson, Feb. 7, 1652-3, Dr. Bray Rossiter June 3, 1654.

John Rossiter came in company with his father Dr. Rossiter and took the oath of fidelity with him, May 11, 1654. Thomas

Stevens, Thomas Cruttenden, Jno. Hodgkin and Thomas Smith took the oath at the same time; and Nathaniel Whitfield, Wm. Johnson, William Seward, William Stevens, Richard Hubball, Isaac Cruttenden (son of Abraham), Samuel Kitchell (son of Robert), Thomas Chittenden (son of William), Dennis Crampton, Daniel Benton (son of Edward, one of the freemen of the list just given), Andrew Benton and Daniel Evarts (son of John), took the oath of fidelity May 4, 1654; John Bishop Jr., Stephen Bishop (sons of John, Sen.), Geo. Highland, Geo. Chatfield, Wm. Boreman, Nicholas Munger, Edward Sewers, Abm. Cruttenden Jr., in 1652; Benjamin Wright Sen., Richard Hughes, Abm. Cruttenden Sen., and John Sheader as early as 1645, as also Hy. Dowd and Wm. Stone, John Stevens and his son William Stevens and Thomas French, who although not among the first settlers came very early.

About 1660, the Rev. John Bowers came to Guilford and purchased an estate, and supplied the pulpit for three or four years until Mr. Joseph Elliott was settled. He afterwards removed to Branford, and as late as 1670, to Derby where he settled.

In 1672, a third division of land was voted among all the then planters according to their lists of that year. The proprietors numbered something over one hundred, although the number of resident planters must have been much smaller. The list of freemen made out about the same time numbered about sixty-three. It contains the names of Joseph Clay, Josiah Wilcox, Obadiah Wilcoxon and Joseph Hand who had settled between 1660, and that time. Joseph Hand came from East Hampton, Long Island, and settled in the east part of the town. About the same time Jonathan Hoyt from Windsor, came and also settled in the east part of the town, as also Thomas Meacock from Wallingford. Edward Lee settled in the town about 1675, Mr. James Hooker, a man of considerable note and afterwards the first judge of the court of probate came from

Farmington about 1692, Peter Tallman from England, about 1684, Thomas Griswold from Wethersfield, about 1695, John Baily, John Sergeant, Mathew Bellamy and Ephraim Darwin, came earlier. Andrew Ward (grandson of Andrew Ward, one of the first settlers of Wethersfield, and one of the first judges of the county court, in Hartford, and son of Andrew Ward who removed from Stamford, and married Tryal Meigs, the daughter of the first John Meigs who became a settler of Killingworth, in 1668), came to Guilford with his mother, Tryal Ward about 1690. Charles Caldwell came first from Evain, Scotland, to Hartford, and removed to Guilford about 1710. Shubel Shelly arrived about 1714; Comfort and Jehosaphat Starr, from Middletown, about 1690 or 1700. Comfort Starr was a tailor and purchased, 1692, the home lot of John Collins, on Crooked Lane, now State street, nearly opposite to where Abraham S. Fowler recently lived. *Stephen Dodd* was admitted a planter Dec. 14, 1676. *Samuel Baldwin* was invited by the inhabitants to come from Fairfield, his former residence, to settle as a smith, 1675, and was admitted a planter on condition of his serving them as a smith, Feb. 8, 1675–6. Such was the need of the inhabitants for some one to serve in his trade that they granted him liberty " to take up one-half an acre of land upon the green, between John Bishop's barn and the saw-pit all along against the front of said Bishop's home lot according as it is now laid out to him," being in front of nearly all the east side of the green. Mr. *Thomas Robinson* bought out the land, which was originally owned by John Caffinge, as early as 1666, and afterward became one of the wealthiest of the settlers. He was noted for a long and very expensive lawsuit with the town, originating from his taking up land on the front of his lot, which was claimed by the town. The suits which grew out of this act were appealed eventually to the legislature, and finally were adjusted and settled by the interposition of a com-

HISTORY OF GUILFORD.   29

mittee therefrom. *Ephraim Darwin* was a man of considerable property and resided near the rocks at the head of Fair street, which have derived their name of Ephraim's rocks from him. He came to Guilford as early as 1670, but his family became extinct in the next century. *John Hodgkin* from Essex, England, came as early as 1665, *Mathew Beckwith*, in 1667, but apparently did not remain long in the colony, and *Edward Park* from Killingworth, was admitted a planter, May 28, 1671. The latter was by trade a tailor, becoming afterwards one of the first settlers of Cohabit (North Guilford). *Jonathan Hoyt*, of Windsor, was granted, Dec. 9, 1671, liberty to stay over the winter and if he behaved himself well that in that time he may procure a certificate according to law. He afterwards became one of the first proprietors of the society called E. Guilford, now Madison, where his descendants still reside. John Bayley and Thos. Tinkard, came to Guilford about 1680, Henry Wise and Jacob Everest were admitted Nov. 9, 1680, but none of their name are now residents within the limits of the ancient town. John Hodgkin, from Essex, England, was admitted as early as 1670, but his descendants gradually modified the name into Hotchkin and Hotchkiss, although some of the older people still pertinaciously employ the old name in common conversation.

When the patent was granted from the governor and colony of Connecticut, Dec. 7, 1685, there were, according to actual investigation some time afterwards, eighty proprietors inhabitants and ten deceased, whose heirs are mentioned, and one widow Susanna Bishop, all from the families previously named, although some persons who appear to have died previously or who remained without any interest in the town are not mentioned in the patent. Abraham Kimberly came from West Haven as late as 1700, Jasper Griffing from Southhold, Long Island and Joseph Pynchon from Springfield at subsequent periods.

Those names in italics in the list of 1650, and mentioned heretofore as late settlers, have become extinct in Guilford; from the other settlers a large proportion of the present inhabitants have descended, as also many families in Madison, Killingworth, and other parts of the country.

North Guilford was surveyed and divided in 1705. Soon after this, members were accustomed to go up from the First Society on Monday of each week to clear their lands and to return on Saturday. From the circumstance of their dwelling together through the week, the place began to be called Cohabit, a name which it long retained and which is occasionally applied to it at present. Their numbers, however, so increased that at the close of 1719, they had liberty to become a distinct society. Among the early settlers were Timothy and Nathaniel Baldwin, George and Daniel Bartlett, Ebenezer and Joseph Benton, Ebenezer and Samuel Bishop, Joseph Clark, John and Daniel Collins, Wm. Dudley, Samuel and Joseph Fowler, William Hall, Samuel Hobson, John Hubbard, Benjamin Leete, Jon" Robinson, Josiah and Joshua Stone and Nathaniel Parks, all of whom excepting the last named, who was from East Guilford, were from the First Society. Theophilus Rossiter from the same society was also an early settler; and Ebenezer Talman from the First Society, Joseph Chidsey from East Haven, and the ancestors of some other families moved into this section of the town some time after the settlement began.

The population of the town, including East Guilford, has gradually increased from the beginning, notwithstanding constant emigration. In 1670 there were two hundred and fifty-five inhabitants, comprising one hundred and thirty-five males and one hundred and twenty females, as ascertained at the time of making the third division of the lands in the town. At the time of the fourth division in 1690, there were one hundred and eight taxable persons. Supposing these were one-fifth part of the inhabitants, there must have been a population of five hundred and forty souls. In 1730, at the time of the sixth division of lands among the proprietors, three hundred and twenty-six persons were taxed, giving according to the same rate of calculation one thousand six hundred and thirty, as the entire population. The following enumerations made by public authority give

1756	2322
1774	2930
1800	3597
1810	3845
1820	4131, the last census before the division.
1830	4153, in the two towns, Madison and Guilford,

giving an increase for ten years of only twenty-two. The population of Guilford was then two thousand three hundred and forty-four, and of Madison one thousand eight hundred and nine. In the census last mentioned sixty-seven persons were found in the families living on the strip of land mentioned on page ten, which in 1820 belonged to Guilford First Society. Had no alterations been made in the societies by the division of the town, their population at the two periods would have stood as follows:

	1800	1820	1830
Guilford First Society,	1629	1918	1863
	[in the borough 1,097, without 821]		
North Guilford,	540	581	548
Madison First Society,	939	1079	1262
North Madison,	489	553	480
	3597		

Population in 1840 — whole town,   2421
The population according to the census of 1850 was,
   Guilford First Society,   2158
   North Guilford,   495
                        Total 2953

By the census of 1860

 Guilford First Society,   2101
 North Guilford,   523

         Total 2624

By the census of 1870

 Guilford First Society,   2079
 North Guilford,   496

         Total 2575

In the borough 1850, 1115; 1860, 1232; 1870, 1300. The emigrations from the town cannot be precisely and fully stated. When Branford was first settled in 1644 some persons, as has been previously stated, removed thither. Mr. Whitfield, Mr. Desborough, Mr. Thos. Jordan, John Hodely, Messrs. Nathaniel and John Whitfield (sons of the clergyman) and perhaps some others returned to England, 1651. When Killingworth was settled in 1663 and 1664, some families removed to that town, and about the same time, as previously stated, several removed to Saybrook. Near the commencement of the last century several families planted themselves in Durham and, in connection with others, commenced the settlement of that place; not long after this some planted themselves in Middlefield and Westfield, parishes of Middletown. About 1750 numbers moved to Litchfield, Washington, Goshen, Salisbury, and Canaan, in Litchfield county, where the names of Stone, Norton, Fowler, Elliott, and Baldwin mark their descendants at this day. Ten years thereafter numbers from Guilford joined together and took a prominent part in the settlement of Richmond and Stockbridge, in Berkshire county, Massachusetts. Guilford, Vt., as well as Chittenden county were settled to a considerable extent and derived their names from this place about 1674. Claremont and Charleston, New Hampshire, were also settled from Guilford about 1786, and about the same time some emigrated and settled Greenville, New York. More recently some have settled at Paris, Westmoreland and Verona in that state, in the Connecticut Western Reserve, Ohio, and still more recently at Fairfield and other parts of Illinois.

[In addition to these emigrations of families, many a fireside in distant states has been graced and made happy by the presence of the daughters of Guilford, who have carried with them to their husband's homes the rich dower of truth, gentleness and Christian character, attained in their New England home. Under their fostering care

> "Minds have been nurtured, whose control
> Is felt even in their nation's destiny;
> Men who swayed senates with a statesman's soul,
> And looked on armies with a leader's eye;
> Names that adorn and dignify the scroll
> Whose leaves contain their country's history."]

It has been already noticed that the first settlers were almost universally farmers. Their descendants have very generally followed the same occupation. Some mechanic arts, however, besides the manufacture of the common articles of use in a family, have been pursued. Mr. Daniel Hubbard conducted an extensive carriage-making establishment until the commercial embarrassments of 1837. A site for a clothier's works on West river, northwest of the borough, one of the first in the state, was granted to Samuel Johnson, 1707. The most that this establishment could do was to full the cloth sent to it, "a large proportion of which was worn without shearing or pressing." Cloth dressing at this establishment was carried on by the family of Samuel Johnson for many years, being even prosecuted by a great grandson of the same name within the memory of many of the present inhabitants.

Vessels have been occasionally built in this town. Many of these owned by the inhabitants have been and are employed in the coasting trade, and in former days some were employed in the West India trade. Formerly large quantities of shoes were made in the town and sent to the southern states for market.

[In   a joint stock company was organized, for the manufacture of steam-engines, machinery of various kinds, iron-castings, etc., by some of the prominent and well-to-do citizens of the town. The location of the factory was near Jones's bridge. It gave employment to a large number of persons and bid fair to be eminently successful, but eventually failed. The property and manufactured articles on hand, as well as the machinery, were sacrificed at a fraction of their value, and the building itself was removed to a lot on the west side of the green, where it is now known as Music hall.

In   Oliver B. Fowler opened an iron foundery on Fair street, which was afterwards purchased by Spencer & Sons, and has been a prosperous establishment, affording remunerative employment to many of the citizens and profitable returns to the proprietors. Since the death of Mr. Spencer, his sons have carried on the business with great prudence and energy, and to the advantage of the town.

In 1868, J. W. Schermerhorn of the city of New York, commenced the manufacture of school furniture in a building erected for the purpose of a lock factory, and were for some years very successful. Their manufactures were sought after from all parts of the union, wherever an ardent interest in education created a demand for the best possible furniture for the school-room, but financial embarassments in 1877 put a stop to the operations of this enterprising firm.]

Most of the trade of the present town of Guilford is transacted in the borough or village, pleasantly situated between the West river and East creek, north of the great plain, or rather on the northern section of the great plain itself. It was incorporated October 1815, and includes within its present limits that part of the First Society which lies between those streams, or nearly so, being the great plain and village grounds contained in the west part of the deed from the queen sachem, Shaumpishuh, extended north and south, from the sound, back about the distance of a mile and a quarter or a mile and a half, being from three-fourths of a mile to a mile and a half in breadth within these limits. Within the village (in 1838) there were one hundred and eighty-three dwelling houses, generally two stories in height, and all of wood except the noted stone house, two churches, one Congregational, one Protestant Episcopal, and two churches in process of erection, for the Episcopal and Methodist churches respectively. There were also, at that time, a town hall, an academy, post office (established in 1789), three taverns, (including the Point House), thirteen stores, six shoe shops, one carriage factory, and two cabinet shops.

The first newspaper published in Guilford, *The Shoreline Sentinel*, made its appearance March 8, 1877. It is a large sheet, handsomely printed and carefully edited by W. F. Hendrick, independent and neutral in politics, appearing weekly on Saturdays, and being the only newspaper published on the Shore line, between New Haven and New London, is likely to command a large circulation and generous encouragement.

The Guilford Savings Bank, incorporated at the May session (1875) of the general assembly, was organized October 1, 1875, and declared its first dividend July 1, 1876. Its officers are Hon. Edward R. Landon, president, Alfred G. Hull, vice president, Beverly Monroe, treasurer, Henry C. Fowler, secretary.

Within the limits of the borough is the town mill, which was established near its present location, very early after the settlement. The first mill was built about 1643 or 1644, and completed in 1645. At a meeting of the inhabitants, as early as Aug. 14, 1645, the "finishing of the mill was concluded." The first agreement was with Mr. Whitfield, to construct a tide mill upon the bay, and a certain lot was appropriated on which the mill was to be constructed for the town for a certain toll. It was afterwards concluded with Mr. Robert Kitchell in 1645, to take charge of the mill and pay for the building of the same. The mill was kept here for a number of years, and finally, the plan of a tide mill not succeeding, it was permanently built where it now is on West river. The cost of the first mill was ascertained 1646, to have been £75.

Without the borough there were, in 1838, in the First Society, one hundred and nineteen dwelling houses, four taverns, two merchants stores, two sawmills and a building containing the waterworks, blacksmithing and other parts of the carriage making establishment of Mr. Hubbard, two fulling mills, and two tanneries. According to the census of 1870, there were in

	Houses.	Families.	Population.
Guilford borough,	286	322	1,300
Out of borough,	168	177	779
First Society,	454	499	2,079
North Guilford,	119	126	496
Total,	573	625	2,575

In North Guilford there were, in 1838, ninety-nine dwelling houses, two taverns, two merchant's stores, two grain mills, two saw mills, one clothier's establishment and two tanneries.

And in the same year there were residing in the three hundred and two houses in the First Society three hundred and thirty-three families, one hundred and ninety-five in the borough, and one hundred and thirty-eight without; and in the ninety-nine houses in North Guilford, there resided one hundred and five families, making in all four hundred and one houses and four hundred and thirty-eight families.

One of the hotels in the First Society is by the water-side at Guilford point, and is called the Point House. It is only open in the summer season, when its accommodations are fully tested by the fashionable and valetudinarian guests from Connecticut and other states, who are tempted by the attractions of sea food and the hygienic luxuries of sea bathing and sea air.

The list of the town as taken in 1825 was as follows: First Society, $25,252, North Society, $8,891, Madison, $11,278, North Madison, $4,755, making in all the original town $50,176. In 1831 it was as follows: First Society $22,320, North Guilford $8,390, Madison $13,097, North Madison $5,208, making a total of $49,015. In 1850 the list of Guilford was $34,006; in 1860, $1,263,031; and in 1870, $1,430,128. The great increase of the town list between 1850 and 1860 is explained by the fact that at the former date property was placed in the list at three per cent of its assessed value, and at the last date at its full assessed valuation.

The village or borough was intended to have been laid out after the form of New Haven, for which the settlers had great regard, although it presents but an imperfect resemblance. The green or open space in the centre is much smaller than that of New Haven. Its length on the western side is sixty-seven and one-half rods, on the eastern sixty-six and one-quarter, on the northern thirty one and one-half; and on the southern twenty-eight and one-half, and it contains eleven and three-quarter acres and eight rods.[1] The ground was originally uneven and disfigured with numerous basins or pond holes, the central part had been injudiciously used for a grave yard, like the western portion of the public square of New Haven. Some sixty or more years ago the pond-holes were filled up and the ground partially leveled. The gravestones and monuments were removed to the new cemeteries laid out in 1817, about a mile on either side

---

[1] These measurements are those given by the committee, consisting of William Stone, Samuel Stone, Ebenezer Talman, and Michael Hill, who measured "the square or green in said Guilford where the meeting house of the Old Society in said town stands," August 4, 1729.— *Guilford Fourth Book of Deeds*, 120.

east and west of the village. The public buildings which formerly incumbered the green have all been removed, the last being the old Episcopal church which was taken down in 1838. The ancient Congregational church was removed in 1830, and the Town-house and the Academy about the same time. The inhabitants then planted the elms and other shade trees which now so suitably embellish the green. In 1837 the green was enclosed with a simple white railing for which a private subscription of $350 was raised. The green is now an object of attraction to all, and surrounded as it is with comfortable and elegant houses, large and commodious churches, it presents a picture of village beauty equal to any in New England. Its location is in the plain at the bottom of the valley which is overlooked by Long hill, Clapboard hill, Hungry hill, and other eminences in the neighborhood. Its distance is sixteen miles from New Haven, thirty-four south from Hartford, and thirty-six from New London by Saybrook, and about thirty-four by Essexborough. [A society of ladies, formed in 1874, under the name of *United Workers for Public Improvement*, has greatly interested itself in the general beautifying of the borough, by the erection of lamps in the green and along the different streets, and by securing general attention to such ornamentation as will increase the attractions of the place to the citizen and the stranger.]

The road through Guilford was formerly much used by travelers from New York to Boston. In May 1794 it was made a part of the great mail route from Georgia to Maine.

A line of stages was run upon it for many years until the introduction of steam boats on the sound rendered it unprofitable. About the year 1832 the stages were nearly all discontinued, but in 1837 a daily line from Norwich to New Haven was established, furnishing Guilford the advantages of a daily mail. This was destined to continue only until the much more convenient accommodations of rail cars should be introduced.

[The general assembly of Connecticut, at the May session 1848, chartered the New Haven and New London Railway Company to construct a railway from New Haven, "thence extending easterly through the towns on the shore of Long Island sound, across the Connecticut river" to New London. This company contracted in 1851 for the construction of the road, which brought Guilford in direct communication by rail with both New Haven and New London. The first passenger train was run over the road from New Haven to the river, July 1, 1852. The company was afterwards united with one authorized to construct a road from New London to Stonington, and was then known as the New Haven, New London and Stonington Railroad Company. At a later date it was reorganized as The Shore Line Railroad Company. In November, 1870, its road was leased by this company to the New York, New Haven and Hartford Railroad Company, for the sum of one hundred thousand dollars a year, which company now runs regular trains over the same, supplying great facilities for the transportation of passengers and freight to and from Guilford, and giving it direct communication with New York and Boston.]

Besides the cemeteries already mentioned, one was laid out at Leete's island at an early period, one at Moose hill in 1801, and another at Nut plains in 1817. In North Guilford there is also a cemetery, doubtless laid out at the settlement of that society.

The health of Guilford is evinced by the longevity of a large proportion of its inhabitants, of which examples are given in the ages of the ecclesiastical and civil officers mentioned in this work. From a bill of mortality kept by John Burgis, Esq., from Jan., 1746 to 1799, a period of fifty-three years, it appears that there were in the whole town 2024 deaths, which makes the average annual number of deaths a fraction over thirty-eight. The greatest mortality was in 1751, 1769, 1776, 1794 and 1795, being in these years 110, 70, 70, 67 and 60. The disease prevalent in 1751, is called "an awful epidemic," but its appropriate name is not mentioned; that in 1769 and 1776 was the dysentery. In the latter year, from the rapidity with which it spread among those who went into the army, it was usually called "the camp distemper." A large proportion of deaths in 1794 was among the children, many of whom died of scarlet fever. In 1795 nine died of the small pox contracted from persons who had left the pest-house in Haddam in a filthy condition. Nearly two-thirds of the deaths in those sickly years, were in the First Society. The deaths occurring in its numbers from 1799 to January, 1832, during thirty-three years, are 895, a fraction over twenty-seven annually. Supposing the average population during this period to have been 1850, the deaths were nearly as one to sixty-nine. In North Guilford the average annual deaths were a fraction over eight in an average population of about 570, so that the general state of health in the two societies is nearly the same.

The mortality from

	Guilford.	North Guilford.	Total.		
1830—1840 was	311,	78,	389, or	1.613	per cent.
1840—1850	323,	82,	405, "	1.672	" "
1850—1860	357,	81,	438, "	1.651	" "
1860—1870	398,	104,	502, "	1.913	" "
1870—1875	168,	38,	206, "	1.4	" "

It should have been mentioned before that in 1837, a granite quarry was opened at Sawpitts, about a mile southeast of the village. It is on the original farm of the Rev. Henry Whitfield, about half a mile east of the stone house. The Leake and Watts Orphan Asylum, in the twelfth ward of New York city, was built of this granite, and other public buildings have obtained building material from this quarry, since its opening.

Quite recently a very large quarry of excellent granite has been opened at Leete's island, which has been extensively worked by the proprietor, John Beattie.

For half a century or more after the settlement was begun, medicines were purchased by the town and used as common stock. The first settlers seem to have had quite as much faith in the efficacy of quack medicines as some individuals manifest at the present time. It is recorded in the *Town Records*, vol. B, 75, that a special town meeting was holden July 3, 1679, " to consider whether the inhabitants would buy Mrs. Cosster's Physic and Physical drugs." " And was answered by a unanimous vote that they would buy them." And in such repute were the good lady's drugs holden that at the same meeting it was considered as follows, viz : " The question was further taken whether they would pay for them by a free contribution, or by a town-rate, and it was given the town also to understand that the payment for it must be by wheat and peas and some beef, if the beef were suitable, and some flax, if the market for flax did stand, and half the payment to be made the next spring, and half the payment the next spring following." " To this it was answered by a unanimous vote, except one person, that it should be paid by a town rate, and in the specie and time proposed."

And in a subsequent town meeting, August 28th, 1679, " Lieut. Wm. Seward was chosen and appointed to fetch or procure the Physic and Physical drugs bought of Mrs. Cosster, brought to Guilford and deliver them into the hands of Mr. Joseph Elliott for the town's use."

The first physician of whom there is any notice in the records of Guilford, is Bryan Rossiter, or Bray Rossiter as he is sometimes called. He came from Windsor to Guilford on the departure of Mr. Samuel Disborough, and was admitted a planter in 1651, having purchased Mr. Disborough's large estate. The following list comprises all the regularly educated physicians who have practiced in the town:

Bryan Rossiter,	died at Guilford,	Sept. 30, 1672.
Anthony Labore,	" " "	March 19, 1712.
Nathaniel Ruggles,	" " "	Oct. 16, 1794, aged 82.
John Redfield,	" " "	May 16, 1813, " 78.
Thomas Ruggles Pynchon,	" " "	Sept. 10, 1796, " 36.
Jared Redfield,	" " "	1821, " 50.
Seth H. Rogers,	" " "	Feb. 6, 1807, " 35.
Lewis Collins,	removed from Guilford.	
David Marvin,	" " "	to Hackinsack, N. J., 1811.
Anson Foote,	" " "	May 2, 1841, " 57.
Elias Shipman,	removed from Guilford to New Haven.	
Lyman Strong,	" " "	to Hebron and Colchester.
Joel L. Griffing,	died at Guilford, June 15, 1825, aged 36.	
Joel Canfield,	settled in Guilford 1824, died April 9, 1877.	
Elisha Hutchinson,	" "	1838, removed 1849, d. Aug. 20, 1862.
Alvan Talcott,	" "	1841.
Gideon Perry Reynolds,	" "	1870.

The following physicians have been settled in North Guilford:

—— Hosford,	moved away	
David Brooks,	removed to New York,	died Jan. 1826.
Samuel Fitch,		" Aug. 8, 1847, aged 71.
Julius Willard,	removed to Avon.	
Joel Canfield,	" to First Society, 1825.	
George Kirtland,		died Nov. 5, 1825, " 25
Richard Dennison,	moved away.	
Justin W. Smith,	removed to Stony Creek.	

The lands included in the borough, on which the people first settled (the southern part of a black loam and the northern gravelly) are very admirably adapted to the culture of grain, corn, and grass. The natural richness of the soil on the great plain is much increased by the marine shells which the Indians brought upon it and which have been left to decay in the course of ages, as is also true of the soil of the other necks and points of land towards the sound. The English also made much use of these shells, as well as of rockweed, and seaweed; and the present inhabitants more recently have employed white fish and other olea-

HISTORY OF GUILFORD. 43

ginous fish in enriching the soil. The reasons have been already given why the English selected these lands and confined their attention pretty much to them for years. Another circumstance that prevented them from spreading rapidly abroad was the fact that they did not understand the proper method of subduing forests. A law was made quite early that every planter should clear up half an acre yearly. This they did at first, as was the custom in other parts of Connecticut, by digging up the trees by the roots. John Scranton, one of the early settlers, at length cleared an acre in a different manner, and astonished the people by gathering from it twenty bushels of wheat, and from this the practice of clearing the land by cutting down the trees spread through the colony.

A large proportion of the land west of West river and south of the post road to New Haven, is poor. Some of it is very stony, containing many rocky ledges, and some is swampy, although more particularly about Leete's island and Sachem's head there are limited tracts of very strong, productive soil The soil of Moose hill, a moderate elevation, extending into the town of Branford, is well adapted for grazing. The same is true of Long hill, extending on the west side of West river northward into North Guilford. Clapboard hill, east of the borough, running northward between East creek and East river, is clayey and fertile, and less liable to injury by drought than the lands generally in the neighborhood. Most of the other lands in the First Society are of an indifferent quality.

The soil in North Guilford is generally gravelly and better adapted to grazing than for the growth of grain, although about Bluff head there is some clayey and sandy soil.

There is nothing in Guilford which merits the name of a mountain except the bluff just mentioned. This is the northeastern extremity of Totoket or Branford mountain, which extends for several miles into North Guilford, and nearly crosses its northwest corner. The bluff itself is very steep and bold. It is the southern extremity of the secondary region of country, extending south along both sides of the Connecticut. A high, rugged hill, or rather succession of steep and broken basaltic cliffs, stretches south along the western shore of Quonapaug pond, terminating in North Guilford. The change in the appearance of the country, as you proceed south towards the sea shore, is sudden and striking. Instead of the sand hills and the traprocks of the region just passed, you meet only with the rigid features of granite and gneiss rocks and a hard compact soil, while the great plain is of an alluvial character, bearing impressive marks of the sea upon it. This is also true of other portions along the shore, setting back into the land like bays and harbors.

Formerly wheat was raised abundantly in this town. The First Society has always been famous for the cultivation of corn. As much as a hundred bushels have been raised to the acre, and instances have occurred of a hundred and ten, but forty bushels is considered a good yield. Great quantities of flax were formerly raised of a good quality. The other principal productions of the land are rye, oats, potatoes and grass, while latterly turnips and onions, especially in the borough, have been found to afford remunerative crops.

In consequence of the hilly or stony character of considerable portions of Guilford, much woodland remains, though this is being gradually cleared off for home consumption and exportation as fuel, for rail road ties, and for ship timber. Latterly anthracite coal has become the principal fuel employed in the borough, being delivered at the Guilford harbor at low rates of transportation, and it is gradually being introduced instead of wood throughout the town. Originally, there were considerable quantities of cedar, white pine, and whitewood in Guilford, but the prevailing kinds of wood now to be found are hickory of several varieties, the oaks and chestnut.

Menunkatuck or West river, repeatedly mentioned in this work, rises in Quonepaug pond in North Guilford, runs south and passing along the west border of Guilford borough, empties into Guilford harbor. The pond which gives rise to this stream is about two miles long from north to south, and from a fourth to a half a mile wide. It is said to be sixty feet deep in some places. In a spring, a few rods above this pond, at the foot of Bluff head, a stream rises which runs northward through Durham into Middletown, which is also called West river.

The interval along these streams furnishes a fine location for a road constructed as far as Durham street, where the Guilford turnpike strikes the road from New Haven to Middletown. This turnpike was granted in 1824, and was called the Guilford and Durham turnpike. It's length is thirteen and a half miles from Guilford green, and seventeen and half miles from Sachem's head on the sound. The capital stock of the company was $5100, or divided into fifty-one shares of $100 each.

There has never been any turnpike company formed on the great thoroughfare from New Haven to Saybrook, but the road has always been very good.

East creek, a small stream, or rather brook, noticed as the eastern boundary of the borough, rises in the limits of the First Society and empties into the East river near its mouth.

East river, or Ruttawoo, rises in several brooks, the principal of which is Stillwater brook, in the north and northwestern parts of North Madison. It takes a southwestern course and discharges its waters into Guilford harbor. Near its mouth are two wharves called the Sawpits-quarry wharf and Farmers wharf, both convenient for the navigation of the river; further up are the two wharves on the east side of the river at East river bridge, which are at the head of sloop navigation.

Guilford harbor affords but an indifferent station for vessels. It has six feet of water on the bar at its entrance at low, and twelve feet at full tide. On the flats adjacent round and long clams of a very superior quality are taken by the inhabitants, and Guilford oysters, taken from the channel of East river, are noted as among the best in Connecticut. Their flavor is peculiarly agreeable and readily recognized by the epicure. They are, however, taken in but small quantities and held at a high price. Oysters are also taken in West river, but they are of a different species and inferior in quality.

An application was made to congress in 1837 for an appropriation for the building of a breakwater, which would probably have been obtained had it not been for the critical condition of the commercial affairs of the country, which so crippled its resources that no new harbor improvements could be undertaken. The application has not been renewed.

Two miles west of Guilford harbor is a small but good harbor land-locked or rather *rock-locked* on all sides except the southwest where the entrance is narrow. This is known as Sachem's head. It has a small wharf with considerable depth of water. About fifty rods from this stood the celebrated Sachem's Head House, which was for many years a fashionable summer watering place. The house was large and commodious, adapted for the accommodation of several hundred guests, and supplied with grounds, beautifully laid out for the amusement of visitors. Destroyed by fire in June, 1865, it has not since been rebuilt.

Sachem's head received its name from the memorable battle with the Pequots in 1636. A Pequot sachem with a few of his men, having crossed the Connecticut river, was flying westward. In attempting to secrete himself on the point of land south of this harbor he was pursued by Uncas, sachem of the Mohegans, and his men, aided by some English soldiers. The Pequots swam across the mouth of the harbor but were seized as they came to the opposite bank. The sachem was ordered to be shot. Uncas executed the sentence with an arrow, then cut off his head and stuck it up in the fork of a large oak tree, directly at the head of the harbor, where the skull remained for many years. This harbor was formerly much used as a station for night by vessels traversing the sound before light houses were erected, especially in the cold and stormy seasons of the year. Before the revolutionary war it was also a favorite place for the shipping of cattle for the West India trade, driven hither not only from this town but from towns on the Connecticut river, particularly from Middletown.

A little southwest from this harbor and to the east of Leete's island is another, not much used, called Great harbor. It is shallow and not convenient for vessels. Formerly shad and bass were sometimes caught within its limits in considerable quantities in the spring of the year.

A little east of Sachem's head is a place called Bloody cove, where a skirmish occurred and some blood was shed in a battle fought between the Indians, before the capture of the Pequot sachem just mentioned. This was prior to the settlement of Guilford by the English.

Although the Indians at Guilford removed from the town immediately after the purchase from Shaumpishuh, the Indian sachem queen, with the exception of some few infirm Indians and their families, to whom the privilege of remaining on the land of their fathers was specially reserved in the original deed, yet such were their numbers at Branford and East Haven, that the English at Guilford, as well as other towns, were obliged to take the precaution of keeping a constant watch for a long period, from which none were privileged. Several houses were palisaded, the house of worship was guarded on the Sabbath, and the people were convened for public service by the beat of the drum. Eventually this became a custom and was afterwards adopted as a means of convening the people for public worship in East Guilford and North Guilford. A bell was not purchased until about 1715 or 1720, after the second meeting house was completed.

There seems not to have been that hostility between the first settlers of Guilford and the Indians which existed in other parts of the country, and there are no accounts of skirmishes or battles with them in this vicinity, such as occurred so frequently and sometimes with such disastrous consequences in other places.

In 1676, during the memorable war against King Philip, the town voted to fortify two houses, one of which was that of their clergyman, Mr. Joseph Elliott, on the south west corner of the green, and to bear in common all damage done by the enemy. Some of the inhabitants were called into actual service in 1685, and the town " granted ten acres of land to every soldier that served in the Indian war" under Robt. Treat or Mr. John Talcott.

In 1676, it was also agreed in town-meetings which were held March 9, 13 and 28, by unanimous votes, that after the first day of April then next ensuing, whatever damage should come to the housing of any individual, either within or without the fortification, should be borne and made up by the town in general.

In 1745, Col. Andrew Ward of Guilford commanded a company in the expedition against Louisburg, capital of Cape Breton, and some of the inhabitants accompanied him.

During the second French war, many persons from Guilford went into the army, of whom an unusually large number died by sickness, though there is no notice of any falling in battle. In one campaign, perhaps in more, Gen. Ward, the son of Col. Andrew Ward just mentioned, commanded a company, having Mr. Enos Bishop of North Bristol as his lieutenant. In another campaign, Col. Ichabod Scranton of East Guilford commanded a company with Abraham Tyler (afterwards Col. Tyler of

Haddam) as his lieutenant. In the revolutionary war several attempts were made by the enemy to injure the town.[1] In June, 1777, the house of Solomon Leete of Sachem's Head was burned by a party from a British ship in the sound, whose tenders had come into that harbor. On the 18th of June, 1781, a party of British with some refugees [about 150 men], as was supposed, landed [from two brigs and a schooner] at Leete's island and burned a house with two barns belonging to Daniel Leete, but were prevented from destroying other property by the rallying of the people. In a skirmish, which took place at that time, two men, Simeon Leete the head of a family, and Ebenezer Hart, were mortally wounded and died soon after.

---

[1] [The following extract, from the *Connecticut Journal*, contained in Barber's *Connecticut Historical Collections*, pp. 219-220, gives an account of a military expedition from Guilford during the revolutionary war :

Guilford, May 29th, 1777.

General Parsons having received intelligence that the enemy had collected, and were collecting, large quantities of forage, at Sagharbor, on Long Island, last Friday, about 200 of the continental troops who had previously redezvous'd at Sachem's Head, in Guilford, embarked on board a number of whale boats, commanded by Lieut. Col. Meigs, to destroy it ; at about six o'clock, afternoon, they arrived at the beach, this side of Plum-gut, and transported their boats about fifty rods, over the beach, where they again embarked, and landed several miles from Sag Harbor, where (after leaving a suitable guard to protect the boats) they marched with such secrecy, as not to be discovered till within a few rods of the sentry ; they soon set about destroying the forage, etc. As the enemy stationed there, were entirely off their guard, our troops met with little opposition ; an armed schooner of twelve guns, which lay not far from the shore, kept an incessant fire on them, but happily did them no damage. Our people returned the fire with their small arms, but whether with effect is not known ; five or six of the enemy on shore, were destroyed, and three or four made their escape, the others were made prisoners. Our people set fire to the hay (about 100 tons) which was on board transports, and on the wharves, which was entirely destroyed, with ten transport vessels, mostly sloops and schooners, and one armed vessel of six or eight guns, two or three hogsheads of rum, etc. Our troops are all returned, having performed their expedition in 24 hours.

Return of prisoners taken at Sag Harbor. One captain, two commissaries, three sergeants, fifty-three rank and file, ten masters of transports, twenty-seven seamen, in the whole ninety-six. Our people brought off fifty muskets. One of the commissaries above mentioned, is Mr. Joseph Chew, formerly of New London.]

An attempt was made in another instance by the crew of a whale boat, to do mischief at Leete's island, but the enemy was repulsed by the guard stationed there, and one of their number being killed was left dead on the shore.

The persons who have been just mentioned, viz: Simeon Leete and Ebenezer Hart, together with Capt. Phinehas Meigs of East Guilford and a Mr. Ludington, who fell at East Haven heights, and an Indian who fell in some other part of the country, are said to have been the only persons belonging to Guilford who were killed in the revolutionary war, although quite a number died of exposure and camp-diseases.[1]

[During the recent civil war, Guilford contributed 300 men to the national army, of whom sixty laid down their lives before its close. In commemoration of their patriotism and bravery,

---

[1] [The whole number of citizens of Guilford who died during the revolutionary war, either from wounds received in battle, or from camp-diseases, exposure, etc., was twenty. Their names and ages are as follows:

Timothy Barnes,		32.
David Field,	son of David,	48.
William Fairchild,	" Lewis,	17.
Lewis Fairchild,	" "	19.
Joseph Hotchkin,	" Thomas,	17.
Ebenezer Hart,	" Thomas,	24.
Eber Hall,	" Hiland,	41.
Abner Leete,	" Roland,	23.
Timothy Ludington.		
Simeon Leete,	son of Peletiah,	28.
Seth Morse,	" John,	26.
Capt. Jehiel Meigs,	" Jehiel,	33.
Bridgeman Murray,	" Jonathan,	20.
Wait Munger,	" John,	49.
Capt. Phineas Meigs,	" John,	73.
Samuel Stevens,	" Nathaniel,	22.
Abel Saxton,	" Simeon,	20.
Daniel Stone,	" Daniel,	40.
William Sabine.		
Samuel Ward, son of Thelus,		17.

A. T.]

it is proposed to erect a monument on the village green, for which a handsome sum of money has already been secured. The corner stone was laid on decoration day, May 30, 1877, at which time an appropriate address was delivered by Rev. W. H. H. Murray of Boston.]

Guilford was the third town settled in the ancient colony of New Haven, of which it remained a part until its union with the colony of Connecticut in 1664. Milford and Guilford were both settled during the year 1639, the former in February, and the latter in September. Guilford was settled at its commencement entirely by the followers and personal friends of Mr. Desborough and Mr. Whitfield, but in Milford, as in most of the other towns, Mr. Prudden brought with him, in addition to those who accompanied him from England, many who united themselves with his fortunes in this country. Mr. Whitfield with his followers were not at the celebrated meeting at Mr. Newman's barn in New Haven, June 1639, described by Dr. Trumbull, in the *History of Connecticut*, and by most others who have written of that period of the history of New Haven colony. At that meeting the Scriptures were formally acknowledged as the rule of procedure in civil as well as ecclesiastical affairs, in which all power was lodged in the church, and professors of religion only were allowed the privileges of freemen and to hold office in the community. These general principles were, however, recognized in the rules adopted for the government of Guilford. Mr. Desborough, Mr. Leete and Mr. Whitfield did not subscribe to the constitution adopted by the New Haveners because they did not then consider themselves a part of that community, yet they recognized the same principles in the policy of the colony which they founded, and to perpetuate them they entered into the compact by which, in 1643, the jurisdiction of the colony of New Haven was established. The chief principle of the "combination," as it was sometimes called, and in which it materially differed from the colony of Connecticut, was that all power was placed in the hands of the church. To this rule no plantation appears to have adhered more rigidly than Guilford; and although the adoption of this mistaken system of policy seems to have occasioned much inconvenience and disquiet in Milford, Stamford and Southold, yet none is recorded in the records of this plantation.

It has already been mentioned that the six persons who purchased the land in behalf of the planters were to hold it in trust for them until a church should be formed to whom the power should be committed, but in fact until that time only four persons were intrusted with civil power, viz: Robt. Kitchel, William Chittenden, John Bishop, and William Leete, for the administration of justice and the preservation of the peace. When the church was formed in 1643, the purchasers from the Indians accordingly resigned the deed to it, and these four persons declared that their power had ceased by the formation of the church. It was then expressly agreed that the body of freemen should consist of church members only, and that they should be the sole electors of magistrates, deputies and other officers of importance. Notwithstanding this agreement, however, in town meetings called for the purpose of dividing lands, constructing roads, etc., all the planters were permitted to attend and participate.[1]

The government of the New Haven colony, after the formation of the jurisdiction or combination in 1643, was vested in a general court for purposes affecting the whole community, which court consisted of two branches; one composed of the governor, deputy governor and three or more magistrates selected from those most distinguished for their talents, integrity and patriotism, by the general voice of the freemen annually; the other consisting of deputies elected, in some of the towns semi-annually, but in Guilford annually, to meet in the spring and fall of each year. This court, in its collective and public capacity, was sometimes called the legislature of the colony, but much oftener " the general court for the jurisdiction."

The supreme executive power, both civil and military, was in the hands of the governor and deputy governor, the judiciary in that of the governor and the magistrates. Under this general government each town had a government of its own, for the management of its individual affairs, peculiar to itself. This originated from the circumstance that the individual towns, at their settlement in 1638-39 and 40, were separate independent governments and plantations by themselves, and, on their uniting in a jurisdiction or combination for mutual defence, they retained their individual forms of government except so far as the general policy of the whole was concerned.

The method by which the rating of the individuals in a town was effected, for the support of a plantation and as a part of the jurisdiction, was the same as the modern method of assessment, and those appointed to make a valuation of the property were styled assessors. The method of listing the property, which was so long in use afterwards, was borrowed from Connecticut.

The deputies to assist in the general court for the jurisdiction were chosen annually in the month of May or June, and the other officers, such as townsmen, plantation magistrates or assistants, secretary or clerk, treasurer, marshal, assessors, etc. were chosen at the same time or at annual meeting held a few weeks later. The deputies or assistants to the magistrate, who sat with him in the particular courts were two, three, and sometimes four in number. They met with the chief magistrate of the plantation, who was also one of the magistrates of the combination, quarterly on the first Thursday in September, December, February and May of every year. In these courts the presiding magistrate resided in the town. They had cognizance of civil matters and lower felonies. Their power extended also originally to the probate of wills, to granting letters of administration, and to the division and settlement of estates. The probate of wills, etc., was transferred to the judiciary of the combination.

Mr. Desborough was the first person appointed magistrate for Guilford, and his earliest assistants, chosen by the freemen of the town, were Wm. Chittenden, Wm. Leete and Robert Kitchel, and soon after Mr. John Bishop. Mr. John Jordan sometimes supplied the place of one of these, and later Mr. Geo. Hubbard and Mr. John Fowler were occasionally chosen. Mr. Desborough continued chief magistrate till 1651, when Mr. Wm. Leete was chosen and continued until the union of the governments of Connecticut and New Haven. It is said that the assistants were confirmed by the legislature, but of this there is not any certain proof with regard to Guilford, although it seems to have been true of Milford and Stamford.

One of the rules adopted by the first settlers of Guilford was that no man should put more than £500 into the common stock for purchasing and settling the town, and that no man should sell or purchase his rights without leave of the town. It was further ordered that every planter, after paying his proportionate share of the expenses arising from buying out and settling the plantation, should draw a lot or lots of land in proportion to the money or estate expended in the general purchase and the number of members in his family. These rules were evidently intended to prevent too great disparity in the circumstances of the people.

The first settlers were most of them gentlemen of some rank and estate in their native country, and came over for the purpose of enjoying the exercise of their religious feelings in their own way, as well as what they considered political and moral freedom. For this they were willing to sacrifice all the endearments and privileges of their native land and to exchange the home of their fathers for a distant and uncultivated wilderness.[1] It has often been said that they fled from religious persecution and intolerance, and that it was strange that after they had experienced so much from this spirit in their own country, they should show similar feelings towards the Quakers, and others holding sentiments dissimilar to their own, who came among them. But a moment's reflection will convince us that the course they pursued was not singular. We, living amid all the luxuries of cultivated society, and enjoying the freedom and homes which they procured for us, are ill-fitted to conceive the extent of their sacrifices of not only natural but also civil and artificial privileges. They had not only to tame the forest, and encounter the wild beast and savage, but also to weave anew the bonds of government and bind the broken links of society. And it has been truly said that their governments for the first fifty years after the settlement of New England, were though secure, held together as with a rope of sand which was liable to be broken away by the first political disturbance. The New Haven colony, indeed, during the whole period of its existence as a separate plantation, had no distinct and positive charter as a constitution for their government. Besides the first settlers fled from their native land, not to escape religious intolerance

---

[1] " And who were they, our fathers ?' In their veins
  Ran the best blood of England's gentlemen ;
  Her bravest in the strife on battle plains,
  Her wisest in the strife of voice and pen ;
  Her holiest, teaching, in her holiest fanes,
  The lore that led to martyrdom ; and when
  On this side ocean slept their wearied sails,
  And their toil-bells woke up our thousand hills and dales,

  Shamed they their fathers ? Ask the village spires
   Above their Sabbath homes of praise and prayer ;
  Ask of their children's happy household fires,
   And happier harvest noons ; ask summer's air,
  Made merry by young voices, when the wires
   Of their school cages are unloosed."— *Halleck's Connecticut.*

but to practice their own system of religious and civil freedom apart by themselves. Mr. Whitfield's company, on their first settlement in Guilford, drafted a constitution for their government, in which they say that "the mayne ends which wee propounded to ourselves in our coming hither and settling down together are that wee may settle and uphold the ordinances of God in an explicit *Congregational church way* with most *purity, peace* and *liberty* for the benefit both of ourselves and posterities after us." Such undoubtedly were the views of most of the settlers, civil freedom and religious, to those of their own sect who had been so much persecuted in England. They were willing to leave their homes and friends for this purpose, and for this too they were willing to take up a part of the desolate wilderness far away from civilized society, but in exchange they promised to themselves that they would form for themselves a home of their own in which those of similar views might have a home and society, and hence they left the other portions of the wilderness, without their own territorial limits, to those dissenters, who suffered similar intolerance to that which they had suffered in their own country but whose opinions and sentiments differed from theirs. For this reason, as has been said, they provided in the language of the constitution just quoted and added. "We do now therefore all and every of us agree, order and conclude that only such planters as are also members of the church *here* shall be and be called freemen, and that such freemen only shall have power to elect magistrates, deputies and other officers of public interest, or authority in matters of importance concerning either the civil affairs or government here from amongst themselves and not elsewhere and to take an account of all such officers for the honest and faithful discharge of their several places respectively," thereby making their government strictly republican and making those in office directly responsible to the freemen collectively. That justice might be speedily administered, they further agreed that the judges should check all crimes and misdemeanors immediately. And that they might bind themselves together under this constitution, which they had formed, and which certainly contains many of the best principles of our present palladium of liberty, they further agreed freely to submit themselves to the magistrates, deputies and other officers to be chosen "yearly from time to time," providing also that no laws or orders be by them made except *before all the planters* then and there inhabiting and residing [whether freemen or not] due warning and notice of the meeting being made, so that what is to be done may be understood and known, that thus all weighty objections may be duly alluded to and considered, and according to righteousness satisfyingly removed. And it was afterwards concluded and ordered that in all general courts (consisting of the magistrates and deputies who were also appointed to keep particular courts) all orders shall be made by the major part of the freemen, and all actions in particular courts shall be sentenced by the major vote of the magistrate and deputies, except that the magistrate have a casting vote when equally divided. From which it appears that they were willing that dissenters of any other sect should settle in the new country which they had chosen, provided they would not interfere with their individual policy. They had been persecuted and driven from their native country because they were Congregationalists and Puritans, and they wished to enjoy their sentiments here unmolested by those who had no sentiments in common with them, who endeavored to destroy the religious and political bonds by which they had bound their new society and government together.

They wished also, and they succeeded with no inconsiderable success, in transmitting their principles to their posterity. Doctor Dwight says in his *Travels* (vol. 11, p. 514), "that the inhabitants of this town more than most others in this state have retained the ancient manners of the New England colonists Parents are regarded by their children with a peculiar respect derived not only from their domestic government and persona character, but in a considerable degree from the general state of manners. Old people are in a similar degree revered by the young, and laws and magistrates at large. Private contentions have heretofore been rarely known, and lawsuits so rare that no lawyer till lately has ever been able to acquire a living in town. The weight of public opinion has been strongly felt, and diffused a general dread of vice." No inhabitant has ever suffered capital punishment.

Paupers were formerly distributed about in different families, where they were boarded at the expense of the town. About 1795, the practice was adopted of employing a family to take them all in a body into a house and to provide for them, charging for the articles consumed. In 1814, a building with a lot of land was purchased in the west part of the borough, with a view to the forming of an alms house establishment, for $1600; which sum with that required to build an addition to the house amounted to $2080. In this house the poor of the town, varying from twenty-five to thirty in number, were supported until the division of the town. A family was procured to live in the house to take charge of the paupers, the cost being somewhat under one thousand dollars per year. By this arrangement there was a saving of some hundreds of dollars annually. Upon the division of the town, the public property was also divided, and Guilford took the town mill, while the alms house building fell to the share of Madison. After this division the poor were kept for some years in private families. [In 1850, however, a house and lot, east of the village, were purchased from the heirs of Timothy Seward, at a cost of $1,650, and an alms house for the town paupers was reëstablished. The building, becoming dilapidated and in great need of repairs, was sold, and the present alms house purchased for $1,800, in 1868, from the heirs of George Parmelee.]

A system of public policy for the regulation of the government and the civil affairs of the town does not appear to have been established until the church was gathered, " the nineteenth day of the fourth month, 1643," or according to the modern mode of reckoning, June 19, O. S., or June 29, 1643, N. S., and until that day, as previously stated, power of all kinds was provisionally vested in the hands of Robert Kitchel, William Chittenden, John Bishop and William Leete, or in the language of the constitution before mentioned " into their hands we did put full power and authority to act, order and dispatch all matters respecting the public weale and civile government of the plantation until a church was gathered among us, which the Lord in mercy having now done according to the desire of our hearts, the said four men at the public meeting having resigned up their trust as most safe and suitable for securing of those mayne ends for which we come hither, " thereupon the civil polity of the plantation was formed.

The earliest record was written Aug. 14, 1645. This is on the first page of the Records, vol. A, and is a minute of the doings of the particular or general court holden that day, and reads as follows :

"August 14, 1645.

" Mr. Samuel Disbrow, Richard Bristow, Thomas
" Betts, members of the church, and Thomas French,
" planter, took their oath "

from which it appears that but little had been previously reduced to record, for Samuel Desborough had always been the magistrate of the plantation from its very commencement. The following minutes on the records after this, relate to some decision of the court and to the affairs of the mill :

" At a court held January 8, 1645-6. It was ordered

that all men shall bring in from time to time, and *for the time past*, all sales, exchanges and conveyances of land to the next general court or courts held in this town after such sales or exchanges, that so what is done may remain for the benefit of posterity and the better preservation of the peace."

And afterwards the exchanges and deeds are mentioned merely and approved by the court until April 10, 1648, when a book of terryers of land was ordered to be kept and every individual in the town ordered to bring in a list of the land owned by him as well as house lots or out lots that a record might be made.

The title of the book is as follows, viz :

"A booke of the Terryers
of all the divided lands in Guilford
according as they were at first divided
whether by lots or otherwise upon
request of particular persons or upon
what considerations were thus
disposed together with all the
alienations which have since
been made by purchase
gift or exchange as
Dated Apr. the   followeth, viz."
10, Ano 1648.

And on the same title page is the following note, viz :

"Whatever is set down in the book with
a date or without mention of the date is
confirmed unto the person under whom
it is recorded as a first grant [or lot] to him
and allowed as unquestionable title to the
said lands for him and his heirs forever
unless an act be recorded
expressing particularly the alienation

of all or any parts or parcel of the same and bearing date since the first date of the book aforesaid."

The first record is of the terryer of Mr. Samuel Disborough, the chief magistrate, beginning, as is the case with all the others, with a description of his house lot, or home lot, as it is often called, and next of the arable land adjoining, next of marsh land. This land of Mr. Disborough according to the record was the lot now occupied by Mr. Ebenezer Redfield. It appears by this record that these lands were sold to Doct. Bryan Rossiter and the sale approved by the town Oct. 10, 1651, and they descended to Josiah Rossiter, afterwards town clerk and one of the magistracy and council, March 11, 1672. This terryer occupies several pages and specifies the whole terryer of Josiah Rossiter and all the conveyances and terryers to him or his father Doct. Rossiter.

The next record is to Mr. William Chittenden, and is similarly arranged, occupying four pages.

These records contain the names of all the first settlers who were living in 1648, or who, having died, left heirs. They are commenced in the handwriting of Gov. Leete and continued in that of the subsequent town clerks. The record of each parcel of land as set to the different individuals is very short, not usually more than from four to six lines. This book is called the first volume of the proprietors' records.

As there was no public record of the purchases of the lands from the Indians, the general court ordered, the next year, that such a record should be made. The first volume of the town records mentioned was first devoted to the registry of the doings, trials, pleadings and decisions of the particular courts, the meetings of the general courts of elections and the registry of earmarks, marriages and deaths, but not of deeds at full length, the constitution of the colony, and other more lengthy writings.

The second book, called and entitled, Guilford Booke of the more fixed Orders for the Plantation, therefore was ordered to be kept, and it commences thus, viz :

"January 31st 1649 " — [i. e. according to our reckoning 1650.]

"Upon a review of the more fixed agreements, " laws & orders formerly & from time to time made "The General Court here held the day & year aforesaid "thought fit agreed and established them according " to the Ensuing draft as followeth, viz —

"first we do acknowledge, ratify, confirm and allow the agreement made in Mr. Newman's barn at Quillipeáck now called New Haven, that the whole lands called Menunkatuck should be purchased for us and our heirs, but the deed, writings thereabout to be made and drawn (from the Indians) in the name of these six planters in our steads viz. Henry Whitfield, Robt Kitchell, William Leete, William Chittenden, John Bishop and John Caffinge, notwithstanding all and every planter shall pay his proportionable part or share towards all the charges and expenses for purchasing, selling, securing or carrying on the necessary public affairs of this plantation according to such rule and manner of rating as shall be from time to time agreed on in this plantation." "The drafts of which purchase or writing are as followeth viz." And then follows a copy of the deed from the sachem squaw, a like copy of the deed from Uncas of the east part of the town this side of Tuxis pond, next the letter of gift from Mr. George Fenwick of Saybrook of the land between the grant of Uncas and Hammonassett river to the town and Mr. Whitfield in particular, and Mr. Whitfield's grant of his share to the town on his leaving the plantation in 1651, etc.

The letter of Mr. Fenwick about Hammonassett is recorded at full length, and displays much of the character and firmness of the original Puritans and their fellow-feeling for each other. It contains a part of the original conveyance of Uncas the Mohegan to him, that is, that part which lies between Tuxis pond and the Hammonassett river, now forming and included in the eastern part of Madison.

The original letter is as follows:

Mr. Leet: I have been often moved, by Mr. Whitfield to enlarge the bounds of your plantation which otherwise, he told me, could not comfortably subsist, unto Athammonassett river; to gratify so good a friend and to supply your wants I have yielded to his request, which according to his request by this bearer I signify to you for your own and the plantation's better satisfaction, hoping it will be a means fully to settle such who for want of fit accommodation begun to be wavering amongst you, and I would commend to your consideration one particular which I conceive might tend to common advantage, and that is, when you are all suited to your present content, you will bind yourselves more strictly for continuing together; for however in former times (while chapmen and money were plentiful) some have gained by removes, yet in these latter times it doth not only weaken and discourage the plantation deserted, but also wastes and consumes the estates of those that remove. Rolling stones gather no moss in these times, and our conditions now are not to expect great things. Small things, nay moderate things, should content us, a warm fireside and a peaceable habitation with the chief of God's mercies, the gospel of peace, is no ordinary mercy though other things were mean. I intended only one word, but the desire of the common good and settlement hath drawn me a little further. For the consideration Mr. Whitfield told me you were willing to give me for any purchase, I leave it wholly to yourselves. I look not to my own profit but to your comfort. Only one thing I must entreat you to take notice of, that when I understood that that land might be useful for your plantation, I did desire to express my love to Mr. Whitfield and his children, and therefore offered him to suit his own occasions, which he, more intending your common advantage than his own particular, hath hitherto neglected, yet my desire now is that you would suit him to his content, and that he would accept of what shall be allotted him as a testimony of my love intended to him, before I give up any interest to your plantation, and that therefore he may hold it free from charge as I have signified to himself. I will not now trouble you further but with my love to yourself and plantation rest,

Your loving friend and neighbor,

Seabrooke, *Oct.* 22d, 1645.   GEORGE FENWICK.

If you consider John Mepham for his wife's sake and for mine, I shall take it kindly.

Mr. Whitfield, as has been stated before, sold out his right in the Hammonassett land, Aug. 20, 1650, to the plantation for £20.

All these records are in the handwriting of Gov. Leete. But a deed from Weekwash of the land in the Neck, September 20, 1641, to Mr. Whitfield (covering nearly the same grounds as the subsequent deed from Uncas, December 17, 1641), and the constitution of the plantation which follows, are in a handwriting different from that of Mr. Leete, and remarkably handsome for those times. It is supposed to have been written by

Mr. Whitfield. The deed of the sachem squaw, Shaumpishuh, seems to have had less formality than the deed of Uncas, and is as follows:

" The purchase from the Sachem Squaw.

" Articles of agreement made and agreed on the 29th of September, 1639 [O. S., October 9, 1639, N.S.] between Henry Whitfield, Robt. Kitchel, William Chittenden, Wm. Leete, John Bishop and Jno. Caffinch, English planters of Menunkatuck and the sachem squaw of Menunkatuck together with the Indian inhabitants of Menunkatuck as followeth:

Firstly, that the sachem squaw is the sole owner, possessor and inheritor of all the lands lying between Ruttawoo and Ajicomick river.

Secondly, that the said sachem squaw with the consent of the Indians there inhabiting [who are all together with herself to remove from thence] doth sell unto the foresaid English planters all the lands lying within the aforesaid limits of Ruttawoo and Ajicomick river.

Thirdly, that the said sachem squaw having received twelve coats, twelve fathom of wampum, twelve glasses [mirrors], twelve pairs of shoes, twelve hatchets, twelve pairs of stockings, twelve hoes, four kettles, twelve knives, twelve hats, twelve porringers, twelve spoons, two English coats, professeth herself to be fully paid and satisfied.

John Higginson, } Witnesses.   { Sachem Squaw, her mark.
Robt. Newman, }   { Henry Whitfield, in the
                              { name of the rest.

This deed including all the land between Stony creek or Ajicomick, and Ruttawoo or East river, from the sea northward, and the deeds of Weekwash and Uncas aforementioned, which last seem to include nearly the same territories as the conveyance of Mr. Fenwick before mentioned, which originally came from Uncas, seem to include all the limits of the old town of Guilford, that is from Stony creek aforesaid to Hammonassett river. The descriptions of the land conveyed in the deed from Uncas are more at length and are as follows :

> Articles of agreement made and agreed upon the 17th day of Dec. 1641, between Henry Whitfield, Robert Kitchel, Wm. Chittenden, Wm. Leete, John Bishop, John Caffinch, John Jordan and the rest of the English planters of Menunkatuck and Uncas the Mohegan sachem as followeth, viz :

> Imprimis. That Uncas, the Mohegan sachem aforesaid is the right true and sole owner, possessor and inheritor of all those lands lying between the East river of Menunkatuck called Moosamattuck, consisting of uplands, plainlands, woods and underwoods, fresh and salt marshes, rivers, ponds, springs, with the appurtenances belonging to any of the said lands and the river, brooke or creeke, called Tuckshishoagg near unto Muttomonossuck which belong to Uncas or any other Indians. And that he the said Uncas hath absolute and independent power to alien, dispose and sell all and every part of the said lands together with the island which lyeth in the sea before the said lands called by the English Falcon island, and by the Indians Messanaumuck.

> Secondly. That the said Uncas doth covenant with the said English planters of Menunkatuck aforesaid that he hath not made any former gift or grant, sale

or alienation of the said lands or any part of them to any person or persons whatsoever, and that he will warrant the same and make good the title thereof to the said English planters and their heirs against all men whatsoever whether Indians or others.

Thirdly. The said Uncas for and in consideration of four coats, two kettles, four fathoms of wampum, four hatchets, three hoes, now in hand paid or to be paid, doth bargain and sell unto the foresaid English planters of Menunkatuck all and every part of particulars formerly mentioned lying between the East river of Menunkatuck and Tuckshishoagg as is aforesaid, to them and their heirs forever, by whatsoever they are or have been usually called, with all the rights, privileges or royalties of fishing. And that it shall not be lawful for the said Uncas or any of his men, or any others for him, to set any trapps for deer in the said lands or any wares in the rivers for to catch fish, but to leave it wholly to the use and possession of the English planters aforesaid, so far as our bounds hereafter to be set out doth limit them.

Fourthly. In that divers Indians have seemed to lay claims to these lands aforesaid, as the sachem squaw of Quillipiack and Weekwosh through her right, the one-eyed squaw of Totoket and others. To this he saith that he hath spoken with all the Indians of Quillipiack, together with the sachem squaw, the one-eyed squaw and the rest, and they do all acknowledge that the right of the said land now sold by Uncas is Uncas his child's. He reporteth also that Weekwosh did confess to him that this land aforesaid did belong to his child. There were also at the agreement-making two sachems, the name of the one was Ashawmutt, the other Nebeserte, who also affirmed the same that Uncas his child was the true heir of said lands.

The bounds of this land which we have purchased is as followeth, viz., from the East river to Tuckshishoagg by the seaside from the lesser river as it goes as far as the marsh which is near the head which we judge to be eight miles off, from the East river where the Connecticut path goes over half a mile above the said place where we go over on a bridge or tree lying over, from thence it goes up east and by north in the woods, which bounds he is by promise to set out to us in the Spring. Uncas or Poquiam his mark.
Henry Whitfield, ⎫ Uncas squaw, her mark.
Samuel Disborow, ⎬ witnesses.
John Jordan. ⎭

We the planters of Mennunkatuck aforesaid do covenant with Uncas or Poquiam that if at any time any inconvenience or annoyance at any time shall arise to the English planters of Menunkatuck by the misdemeanors or evil dealings of the Indians which are his men or from himself, they shall and will at all times come to the English upon notice given them and make them such satisfaction as the English shall require according to right, and if any of the English planters of Menunkatuck shall do any wrong to him or any other Mohegan Indians under his Government, upon complaint made to the English Magistrates and officers there shall be made just satisfaction by them according to right.

WILLIAM LEETE, *Secretary.*

The purchase deed from Weekwosh was made a short time before this by Mr. Whitfield alone, and is as follows, viz:

"The purchase from Weekwosh."

Be it known by these presents that I Weekwosh of Pasquishunk do give unto Henry Whitfield all the land called the Neck lying beyond the East river in Menunkatuck which reacheth unto Tuckshishoagg with all the profits that do belong to the said ground. In witness of which bargain } Weekwosh,[1] his mark.
John Jordan,
Samuel Disborow,
Thomas Jordan.

Memorandum before these witnesses: Weekwosh did avow himself to be the right owner of this land and that he had true right unto it as given him by the sachem squaw of Quillipiag.

A frieze coate, a blanket, an Indian coate, one faddom of Dutchman's coate, a shirt, a pair of stockings, a pair of shoes, a faddom of wampum. In lieu of such things repaid by the town these are to witness

---

[1] Wequash, sachem of the Niantic Indians in Connecticut, died at an early period after the settlement of Lyme, and is buried at the Christian Indian burying ground on the west side of the bay near the mouth of the Niantic river His memorial stone says, "He was the first convert among the New England tribes." This may be a mistake. * * * Mr. Shepard wrote concerning this Pequot: "Wequash, the famous Indian at the river's mouth is dead and certainly in heaven. He knew Christ, he loved Christ, he preached Christ up and down, and then suffered martyrdom for Christ."—*Allen's American Biographical Dictionary.*

"One Wequash Cook, an Indian, living about Connecticut river's mouth, and keeping much at Saybrook with Mr. Fenwick, attained to good knowledge of the things of God and salvation by Christ, so as he became a preacher to other Indians, and labored much to convert them, but without any effect, for within a short time he fell sick, not without suspicion of poison from them, and died very comfortably."—*Savage's Winthrop's New England,* II, 74.

Capt. Israel Stoughton, August 14, 1637, writes to Gov. Winthrop: "For Wequash, we fear he is killed; and if he be, 'tis a mere wicked plot, and, seeing he showed faithfulness to us, and for it is so rewarded, it is hard measure to us-ward; and what is meet to be done therein, is difficult to me to conclude: I shall therefore desire your speedy advice."—*Savage's Winthrop's New England,* I, 400.

that I Henry Whitfield do freely give and make over all that right and title to the Neck of land expressed in this writing being given or sold by Weekwash the Indian unto me, to the town of Guilford to the use of them and their heirs. In witness hereof I have sett to my hand the 20th of September, Anno 1650.

HENRY WHITFIELD.

A reservation was appended to the first deed from the sachem squaw in words as follows, viz:

"The names of the Indians that are to sit down at Ruttawoo [East river] Suksqua, Quissuckquonoh his wife and two children, Commonasnock, Aquaihamish a blind Indian, Chamish a dumb old man and his wife, Aiasomut, his wife and two children, Meishunok, his wife and two children, Pauquun, his wife, one child, Mequunhut and his one child, Koukeshihu, his wife and two children, Metuckquashish and his one child Ponaim, Wantumbeourn and his one child, Assoweion and his one wife.

WILLIAM LEETE, *Sec.*

These deeds conveyed all the rights of the Indians to the land along the sea and extending back by indefinite bounds, except the deed from Uncas which extended from the sea north to where the original Connecticut path goes. The deed from Uncas to Mr. Fenwick being on the Saybrook records — this left the north part of the town subject to the claims of the Indians, descendants of the sachem squaw, Weekwosh and others.

On the 13th of January, 166$\frac{3}{4}$, Mr. Wm. Leete and Samuel Kitchel purchased of Uncas and his son Ahaddon, all the land lying north of Uncas' previous grants to the north boundary of the town, and at a town-meeting, March 11, 166⅘, Mr. Leete propounded the purchase of the land beyond the East river which Mr. Leete and Samuel Kitchel bought of Uncas, whether the town will have it and pay the price of it, and the town in the same meeting declared that they would have it and pay the price for it." Vol. 5, page 20.

This deed is recorded in vol. 6 at the back part, and is as follows, viz :

"A deed of Sale from Uncas."

Witness this writing made betwixt William Leete and Samuel Kitchel on the one part and Uncas the Mohegan and his son Ahaddon, alias Joshua, on the other part, that we the said Uncas and Ahaddon, being the rightful heirs and possessors of all the lands royalties and privileges betwixt the East river of Guilford and Athammonassett river, and having sold most part of that land to *Mr. Fenwick* and unto Guilford men long since, i.e., all beneath Connecticut path to the seaside, for valuable considerations already had and received, do now of our freewill bargain and sell all the rest of the lands royalties and privileges to us belonging, which land runs half way to Matowepesack, which right came to us by Uncas' marriage of the daughter of Sebequenach who dwelt at Athammonassett, and she was mother to the said Ahaddon. We say these lands rights royalties and privileges we do sell and deliver up unto the said William Leete and Samuel Kitchel to them and their heirs forever for and in consideration of an Indian coat worth thirty shillings and a shirt cloth worth ten shillings now had and received of the said William Leete and Samuel Kitchel : in testimony of the truth of all the premises well interpreted and understood by us we have set to our hands this 13th of January 1663.

In the presence
of
Thomas Chittenden,
John Chittenden,
Andrew Leete.

It was after the former writing agreed that Uncas or his son shall have leave to hunt in fit seasons within these tracts observing the directions of the said English and doing no hurt to them or their cattle. Dated January 13, 1663.

The mark of Uncas } Mohegan Sachem

The mark of Ahaddon
                                    alias Joshua.

Recorded by Josiah Rossiter

The above marks are rough facsimiles of rough imitations of a turtle as the mark of Uncas and a deer as the mark of Ahaddon.

The reader will probably be reminded of the allusion of the novelist Cooper in *The Last of the Mohicans* to this emblem of the tribe, when he speaks of it as the noblest among the Indian tribes, and as commanding peculiar respect when seen by the scattered relics of that once powerful tribe.

Afterwards the inhabitants not being fully satisfied with the title derived from Shaumpishuh the sachem squaw, at a town-meeting, January 5, 1686, " there was chosen as a committee Mr. Andrew Leete, Thomas Meacock, Sergt. Stephen Bradley, and Josiah Rossiter to treat with an Indian called Nausup belonging to New Haven, or any other Indian or Indians laying claim to some part of our town bounds; and if the said committee come to see and find the said Indian or Indians to be proper heirs of or to the sachem squaw formerly of Menunkatuck that the said committee are to bargain with the said Indian or Indians for the tract of land lying on the west side of our bounds for a settlement, and that if a deed of sale be made by the said Indian or Indians to the committee above appointed in their names in behalf of all the planters of Guilford they shall bear the charge and expense of the purchase." Guilford Records, vol. B, page 105. Accordingly the said committee on the 2d day of Feb., 1686, procured the following deed from the said Nausup alias Quatabacot as follows, viz :

"A deed of sale from Nausup.

Articles of agreement made and agreed upon the second day of Feb'y, in the year 1686, between Andrew Leete, Thomas Meacock, Stephen Bradley, and Josiah Rossiter of Guilford on the one part, and Quatabacot alias Nausup, Indian, of New Haven on the other part. The above said Quatabacot being son and heir to a sachem squaw formerly belonging to Guilford, which said squaw was the whole and sole proprietor of all the lands lying between a place formerly called Agicomook now called Stony creek on the western part, and Ruttawoo now called the East river on the eastern part in Guilford and so running from the sea up northerly unto Pesuckapaug which is at the north part of the bounds of Guilford, which said sachem squaw hath formerly sold a considerable part of the above mentioned tract of land unto the planters of Guilford, as will appear more fully by a written deed of sale from said sachem squaw dated the 29th of September in the year 1639.

Know all men therefore by these presents that

Quatabacot alias Nausup above named Indian of New Haven being heir to the above named sachem squaw and so right owner of all the remainder of the above mentioned tract of land, the said Quatabacot doth now fully confirm and ratify what his said mother hath formerly sold as above said, and he doth now for and in consideration of the sum of sixteen pounds merchant's pay, and 12 shillings in money in hand truly paid as he doth hereby acknowledge the receipt and thereof and therefrom doth acquit & discharge the above mentioned party & for divers other good causes and considerations him thereunto especially moving, here and by these presents doth grant bargain sell alien infeoff confirm and make over unto the above said Andrew Leete, Thomas Maycock, Stephen Bradley and Josiah Rossiter, in the behalf of them and all the planters of Guilford, and to their heirs and assigns for ever all the remainder part of the above mentioned tract of land which lyeth adjoining unto the former purchase of lands which were bought of the above mentioned sachem squaw and so now both purchases lying or adjoining together as it lyeth, bounded by the sea on the south, by Stony creek on the west, and so running up on the west side of the west pond, and from thence to the east side of Pesuckapaug pond about half a mile eastward of the said pond at the west side of a high hill there, and easterly by the East river and so adjoining to a purchase formerly bought of *Uncas sachem of Mohegans* running up on the east side, also as high as Pesuckapaug, this to have and to hold with all and singular rights, privileges, advantages and appurtenances whatsoever, together with all uplands, meadows, swamps, river, brooks and ponds of

HISTORY OF GUILFORD. 75

all sorts whatsoever, and the said Quatabacot doth hereby covenant to and with the party above named, that they and their heirs and assigns shall peaceably and quietly hold and enjoy the said premises without any manner of lett, molestation, disturbance, challenge claim or demand whatsoever, either by the said Quatabacot his heirs or any under him laying claim or pretending to any right to any part of lands or any privileges within the bounds or limits of the township of Guilford whatsoever : and before signing, the Indians here named doth testify that the said Quatabacot is the true heir unto the above named sachem squaw, and that the said squaw, mother to the said Quatabacot was the sachem squaw of Menunkatuck who formerly sold a part of the land of Guilford to the planters thereof. They also testify that the said Quatabacot's sister called Shambisqua has no right to any part of land within the bounds of Guilford and that the said Quatabacot is the true proprietor to the lands above mentioned to be hereby bargained and sold as above. To the true performance of all the premises above mentioned the said Quatabacot doth hereunto set his hand and seal dated the 2d day of February in the year of our Lord 1686, which is the second year of our majesty's reign — James the 2d.

Quatabacot   alias
Nausup his mark ———

Signed sealed and delivered in the presence of us	Memorandum Liberty of hunting fishing and fowling on agreement is reserved to the said Indians with the
Thomas Trowbridge, } Joseph Pardy.	
Nausump ; ivind Sen.,	

The Father his mark —   regulations of the
Naushuter [his mark   English.
Keyhow X his mark
Alias James the Brother.

On the day and year above written appeared before me, the said Quatabacot alias Nausup and the above written deed being distinctly read and interpreted to him and the Indians present, he said he well understood the substance of every clause of it, and the Indian witnesses said the same, and then he the said Quatabacot alias Nausup having made his mark and affixed his seal did freely acknowledge this to be his act and deed as above written before me,

WILLIAM JONES, assistant of His
Majesty's Colony of Connecticut.

Recorded, per Josiah Rossiter, *Recorder*.

This conveyance completes a full title of all and every part of the ancient town of Guilford from the original Indian proprietors.

The town seems to have rested satisfied with the title they acquired to their lands by their purchase from the Indians, and from Mr. Fenwick of Hammonassett, during the time of their connexion with New Haven and afterwards until the act of the legislature of Connecticut passed October session 1684 requiring all the towns to take out charters from the government &c., when a committee was appointed to consider the matter and draw something of their judgment about it for the town's consideration, Aug. 12, 1685, and at a subsequent meeting held the 4th of November, 1685, it was voted by the planters that they did desire twelve men as patentees in behalf of all the planters to be nominated in the town's patent, and it was also voted in the same meeting who the twelve men as patentees shall be. And Mr. Andrew Leete and Mr. William Leete, Lieut. William

Seward, Josiah Rossiter, Deacon William Johnson and Deacon William Grave, Mr. Thomas Meacock and Sergt. Stephen Bradley were chosen a committee according to the best of their ability to search the town records and do all things they shall judge necessary to prepare what shall be needful in and about the town's patent; that is, to furnish the secretary with what is needful for the premises." The charter was accordingly obtained as appears by its date the 7th of December 1685, and at a subsequent town meeting held the 9th of February 1685, " the town voted that it should be kept by Andrew Leete, Wm. Seward and Josiah Rossiter for the town's use." It is as follows, viz:

> Whereas, as the General Court of Connecticut have formerly granted unto the proprietors, inhabitants of the town of Guilford, all those lands both meadow and upland within these abutments viz. at the sea on the south and on Branford bounds on the west, and beginning at the sea by a heap of stones at the root of a marked tree near Lawrence's meadow and so runs to the head of the cove to a heap of stones there, and thence to a heap of stones lying on the west side of Crooper hill at the old path by the brook, and thence northerly to a place commonly called piping tree to a heap of stone lying at the new path, and from thence to a heap of stones lying at the east end of that which was commonly called Rosses meadow, and from thence to a heap of stones lying at the south end of Pesuckapaug pond, and so runs into the pond a considerable way to the extent of their north bounds which is from the sea ten miles, and it abuts on the wilderness north and runs from the last station in the pond east to the most westerly branch of Hammonassett river and on the east it abuts on the bounds of Kennilworth and

runs from the last station as that stream runs southerly until the said stream or river falls into the sea on the east of East end point, the said land having been by purchase or otherwise lawfully obtained of the Indian natives proprietors ; and whereas the proprietors, inhabitants of Guilford in the colony of Connecticut, have made application to the governor and company of said colony of Connecticut assembled in court May 25th, 1685, that they may have a *patent* for confirmation of the aforesaid land to them so purchased and granted to them as aforesaid and which they have stood seized and quietly possessed of for many years last past without interruption : now for a more full confirmation of the aforesaid tracts of land as it is butted and bounded aforesaid unto the present proprietors of the township of Guilford,—

Know ye that the said governor and company assembled in General Court according to the commission granted to them by his majesty in his charter have given granted and by these presents do give grant ratify and confirm unto Andrew Leete Esquire, Mr. Josiah Rossiter, Lieut. William Seward, Deacon William Johnson, Deacon John Graves, Mr. John Collins, Mr. John Stone, Mr. Stephen Bishop, Sergt. Daniel Hubbard, Mr. Abraham Cruttenden, Sergt. John Chittenden and Mr. John Meigs and the rest of the said present proprietors of the township of Guilford, their heirs, successors and assigns forever, the aforesaid tract and parcel of land as it is butted and bounded, together with all the wood uplands and meadows, pastures, ponds, waters, rivers, islands, fishings, huntings, fowlings, mines, minerals, quarries and precious stones, upon or within the said tract of land

and all other profits and commodities thereunto belonging or in any ways appertaining, and do also grant unto the aforesaid Andrew Leete Esquire, Mr. Josiah Rossiter, Lieut. William Seward, Deacon William Johnson, Deacon John Graves, Mr. John Collins, Mr. John Stone, Mr. Stephen Bishop, Sergt. Daniel Hubbard, Mr. Abraham Cruttenden, Mr. John Chittenden and Mr. John Meigs and the rest of the proprietors inhabitants of Guilford, their heirs, successors and assigns forever, that the aforesaid tract of land shall be forever hereafter deemed reputed and be an entire township of itself, to have and to hold the said tract of land and premises with all and singular their appurtenances, together with the privileges and immunities franchises herein given and granted unto the said Andrew Leete Esquire, Mr. Josiah Rossiter, Lieut. William Seward, Deacon William Johnson, Deacon John Graves, Mr. John Collins, Mr. John Stone, Mr. Stephen Bishop, Sergt. Daniel Hubbard, Mr. Abraham Cruttenden, Sergt. John Chittenden and Mr. John Meigs, and other the present proprietors, inhabitants of Guilford their heirs, successors and assigns forever, and to the only proper use and behoof of the said Andrew Leete Esquire, Mr. Josiah Rossiter, Lieut. William Seward, Deacon William Johnson, Deacon John Graves, Mr. John Collins, Mr. John Stone, Mr. Stephen Bishop, Sergt. Daniel Hubbard, Mr. Abraham Cruttenden, Sergt. John Chittenden and Mr. John Meigs and the other proprietors inhabitants of Guilford their heirs, & successors forever according the tenor of East Greenwich in Kent in free and common soccage and not in capite nor by knight service, they to make improvement of the same as they are capable according to the custom of the country, yielding rendering and paying therefor to our sovereign Lord the King his heirs and successors his dues according to the charter of the colony to be hereunto affixed this 7th of Dec. one thousand six hundred and eighty-five in the first year of the reign of our sovereign Lord James the second, of England, Scotland, France and Ireland, king, defender of the faith. ROBT. TREAT, *Gov.*

Entered in the public records of the colony of Connecticut Lib. D, fol. 144 and 145, Dec. 8th, 1685, per John Allyn secretary.

By order of the General Court of Connecticut signed   JOHN ALLYN, *Secretary.*

and recorded on the three last pages of vol. C, Guilford Records.

Schools were established probably as early as the establishment of the church, 1643. They were formerly supported like the clergyman by a tax. At a town meeting holden the 7th of October, 1646, a committee was appointed of three men to collect the *contributions* for the salaries of Mr. Whitfield and Mr. Higginson, and "it was ordered that the additional sum towards Mr. Higginson's maintenance with respect to the school shall be paid by *treasurer* yearly out of the best of the rates in due season according to our agreements."

And it was further ordered "that whoever shall put any child to school to Mr. Higginson shall not put for less than a quarter's time at once, and so all shall be reckoned with quarterly though they have neglected to send them all the time, after the rate of 4*s* per quarter by the treasurer." After the removal of Mr.

Higginson the townsmen procured from year to year teachers at the rate of 20 or £30 per annum.¹ A Mr. Joseph Fener in 1671 and a Mr. Matthew Belamy in 1671, and Mr. Jonathan Pitman in 1675 and 76. In 1682 Mr. John Collins for some years. In 1690 it was voted in town-meeting to give Mr. Thomas Higginson of Salem £30 per year, two-thirds from the treasury and one-third from the scholars, which was continued for some years. In 1694 Mr. Elliott was employed till 1700, when Mr. Collins was again appointed. In 1701 Capt. Andrew Ward was appointed. Until this time there was but one school in the town, viz.: at the centre of the present First Society. In 1702 "the east farmers from East river eastwards were granted liberty to provide a suitable person to keep school there, and that he be paid for the time he kept school not exceeding three months in the year." The next year (1703) the east farmers became a society called East Guilford. And as the other societies were set off they became also school districts, and received their own shares of the school money. A school house was built as early as 1645, repaired 1671 and a new one built in its stead in 1677. Mr. Joseph Dudley was chosen schoolmaster in 1705, Mr. James Elliott in 1706, Doct. William Johnson about 1720 for a year or two, and the school was afterwards kept in the family of Samuel Johnson for seventy or eighty years. The school records were at first kept with the town

---

¹ Rev. Jeremiah Peck (born in London, Eng., 1623, died in Waterbury, 1699), who married Joanna, or Hannah, daughter of Robert Kitchell, Nov. 12, 1656, taught school in Guilford from 1656 to 1660. He removed in the latter year to New Haven, where he also acted as school-master until Sept. 25, 1661, when he made an agreement to be the minister at Saybrook, which engagement he terminated Jan. 30, 1665-6. "Returning to Guilford, he with his father-in-law, joined Pierson and the Branford and Guilford people who settled at Newark, New Jersey, in 1666-7, where he probably preached until the arrival of Pierson, 1 October, 1667." He afterwards preached in Elizabethtown, Jamaica (L. I.), Greenwich (Conn.), and Waterbury.— *Sibley's Harvard Graduates*, 1, 569, 570.

records, but of late years they have been kept by themselves. There was but one school in the First Society down to (about) 1794, when the present system of school districts was adopted in Connecticut. Formerly, about the beginning of the present century four schools were taught in the borough for many years in one building which stood upon the Green. The removal of this building and the town house from the Green has already been noticed. They were located afterwards on the turnpike a few rods north of the First Congregational church.

In Nov., 1824, the Lancasterian method was adopted in the centre district and all the children were placed in one school (taught in the town house) excepting those in the private schools and in the academy. The latter was opened in 1825 and was under the charge of several teachers, Mr. (now Doctor) Alvan Talcott, and Samuel Robinson having charge for considerable periods.

In 1829 the Lancasterian system was given up and the children in the centre districts were divided into four classes. The first class, corresponding to the academy, was taught from 1831 to 1834 by R. D. Smith, afterwards by Luman Whedon, and thence to 1837 by Julius N. Dowd. In 1837 the district was divided into four parts and school houses built in the northeast and southwest districts, the northwest district occupying a part of the academy, the upper part of which building was occupied in 1838 by Mr. Dudley as a high school. The districts began to be set off from the centre district about the commencement of the present century, at which time the Clapboard Hill district was first set off.

[In 1876 the town consisted of eleven school districts, among which was included the union school district, a consolidation of five separate districts. The number of children between the ages of four and sixteen in the different districts, was reported in the same year as follows:

Union school district	312
North Guilford: South,	40
" " Centre,	31
" " Bluff,	13
" " North,	23
Sachem's Head,	13
Leete's Island,	47
Moose Hill,	26
Nut Plains, Upper,	15
" " Lower,	17
Clapboard Hill,	16

553]

[THE GUILFORD INSTITUTE. Mrs. Sarah Griffing, widow of Hon. Nathaniel Griffing, deeded August 21, 1854, to E. Edwin Hall, Henry W. Chittenden, Simeon B. Chittenden, Alvan Talcott, Abraham C. Baldwin, Ralph D. Smith and Sherman Graves (who had been created a body politic under the name and style of *The Trustees of the Guilford Institute*), a piece of land situated in Guilford, as also the sum of ten thousand dollars, "for the purpose of establishing and maintaining a school in said Guilford of a higher order than the district or common school." She states, in the deed, " whereas my wish is that the said school should in no sense be regarded as a sectarian institution but be open alike to all who wish to enjoy its advantages, and on the same terms, yet as it must necessarily be under some government and control, and as more harmony will be likely to prevail if all the directors or trustees are of the same religious views, my wish is that they should be of the denomination to which I belong, to wit, of the Congregational order and of that class designated and known at the present day as Orthodox or Trinitarian, of which the pastor of the First church in Guilford shall always be one, should he hold such religious views or belief." She also expresses the wish that "the Bible should always be used in said school as the foundation of all education for usefulness or happiness."

To this donation was added another of ten thousand dollars, by Hon. Simeon B. Chittenden, Brooklyn, N. Y., October 12th, 1855.

The corner stone of the building for the accommodation of the institute was laid September 13, 1854, on which occasion an address was delivered by Rev. T. D. P. Stone of the Normal school at Norwich, Conn. The building being completed, the first term of the institute was opened September 3, 1855, with suitable public exercises, and addresses by Rev. E. Edwin Hall, S. B. Chittenden, and others.

In September 1872, by an arrangement with the Union school district of Guilford, its scholars were admitted to the privileges of the institute *free*. In 1875 the institute failing to receive any interest on certain bonds constituting their investments, the trustees gave permission to the union district to occupy the building for a high school, which arrangement continues to the present time.

The following persons have acted as trustees of the institute :

	Appointed.	Termination.
Rev. E. Edwin Hall,	1854,	1855.
" "	1866,	1869.
Henry W. Chittenden,	1854,	1855.
" "	1857,	1867.
Simeon B. Chittenden,	1854.	
Alvan Talcott,	1854.	
Rev. Abraham C. Baldwin,	1854,	1857.
Ralph D. Smith,	1854,	1874.
Sherman Graves,	1854,	1875.
Edward L. Leete,	1855.	
Rev. Henry Wicks,	1856,	1858.

	Appointed.	Termination.
Rev. William S. Smith,	1859,	1865.
Eli Parmalee,	1867.	
Rev. Cornelius L. Kitchel,	1870,	1873.
Rev. Geo. W. Banks,	1874.	
Rev. T. L. Day,	1875,	1877.
Henry D. Cone,	1875.	

The following persons have been principals of the institute, the dates of their first appointment are also given:

Eli T. Mack,	1855.
Augustine Hart,	1858.
J. Wilson Ward,	1860.
Henry S. Barnum,	1862.
Joseph L. Daniels,	1863.
Winthrop D. Sheldon,	1864.
W. H. Ayres,	1865.
Edwin H. Wilson,	1865.
James P. Hoyt,	1867.
Frederic S. Thompson,	1869.
Charles E. Gordon,	1871.
John P. Slocum,	1871.
Jairus P. Moore,	1875.

In 1737 a library was formed in the towns of Guilford, Saybrook, Killingworth and Lyme.[1] The books were principally on

---

[[1] To this library the writer of *Halleck's Life* refers in the following account of his love of reading:

"Books in the days of Halleck's boyhood were less common in country towns than at present, and so, after reading everything contained in the family library, Fitz Greene had recourse to a public collection, of which he once assured me that he had read every book, as his father had done before him. The Guilford library contained, among its four hundred volumes, the works of many of the standard English poets and novelists, essayists and historians, with other volumes published prior to 1800. The old dog-eared and well-thumbed copies of Goldsmith and Gibbon, Josephus and Joseph Andrews, Pope and Plutarch, of Shakespeare and Smollet, with numerous less used and heavy volumes of still heavier sermons, by old and approved British and New England divines, are still to be seen over a grocer's shop divinity, some of them being large and valuable. In May 1787, (after many had probably been lost or worn out) these consisted of sixty folios, twenty-four quartos, and three hundred and seven of other sizes, which were appraised at £167. 7s. Many of the proprietors of this library lived in Guilford. Sometime before 1797, this company was dissolved and a new company formed in Guilford First Society, unto whose library some of the books of the former library were introduced. The young people afterwards associated and purchased another library. These libraries were united about 1820 and called the Union library, which contained in 1838 about six hundred volumes.

A public library was formed in North Guilford about 1760. In 1794, the house in which it was kept was burned and most of the books were destroyed. New books were purchased until it contained 185 volumes. This was dissolved, and a new one formed which contained in 1838 less than 100 volumes.

As the great object of the first settlers was the enjoyment of the privileges of the gospel in their own way, they very early erected a house for public worship, although it is not certainly known in what year. It was probably finished in 1643, at the time the church was gathered here. In 1645, " it was ordered that no more trees should be cut down before the meeting house." This house was of stone and stood on the northwest part of the Green. In it a gallery was built across the west end in 1668, and a porch attached to it in 1672. At a town-meeting held in January 1679–80, it was agreed to build in addition to a porch on the south side, a gallery on all sides of the house, two seats in width. In 1681, it was voted to enlarge the house extensively, the manner is not recorded. Thus en-

---

at Guilford, now quite out of date, forgotten, and fallen into disuse and covered with dust to such an extent, that plain, gilt, marble, or red-edged volumes, present one uniform dull, dingy aspect." *Wilson's Halleck*, 53, 54.]

larged it continued until June 1712. A large wooden church was then erected, sixty-eight feet long and forty-six wide three stories high, with double galleries ; and a steeple (one hundred and twenty feet high) was built at the west end and a bell furnished the same in 1726. At the same time a clock was made for it and given to the society by Ebenezer Parmelee, an ingenious mechanic. This is said to have been the first meeting house in Connecticut furnished with a steeple, bell and clock. This building was taken down in 1830 ; the present one was raised in June 1829, and dedicated May 19, 1830. It is large, beautiful and convenient, being built of wood, is eighty feet in length by sixty in width, with a projection of six feet, and cost $7,400.

[The first public meeting in reference to building a new meeting house was held Feb. 18, 1828. Previous to this a subscription paper had been circulated, and something over $5,000 had been raised in that way. It had been agreed that those, who should subscribe, might bid off pews, in the house when built, to the amount of their subscription, and that all other members of the society should have the same privilege. Objection was made by some to the owning of the pews by individuals, and the preference was for the erection of the house by a tax and the seating of the occupants by age as had been the custom in the old house. It seemed very difficult to raise the sum needed for the building, and in this position of affairs about thirty members of the society became responsible for the money necessary to complete it, taking the risk of being reimbursed by the sale of the pews. At a meeting, held Nov. 28, 1828, it was voted to proceed to the building of the house. The site selected was the Lot Benton place, at the north end of the Green, which was purchased at the price of $925. A contract was made with Ira Atwater and Wilson Booth of New Haven to build a house eighty by sixty feet for the sum of $6,500.

The corner stone was laid June 5, 1829, and a suitable address was delivered by Rev. Aaron Dutton. The raising was commenced June 10, 1829, and completed without accident June 18, the men from the different districts assisting in succession.

The meeting house was dedicated May 19, 1830, and the pews were offered for sale on the next day. They sold for more than enough to pay all the bills, and a great degree of harmony and good feeling prevailed.

The meeting house remained substantially unchanged until 1861, when extensive alterations were made, and the whole structure was improved and modernized. The pulpit and galleries were lowered, the pews made more comfortable, the walls frescoed, and the lecture room was enlarged. In 1868, a superb organ was generously presented to the society by Mrs. Mary G. Chittenden.

After the erection of the new house the pews were held as private property by the original purchasers and their heirs and assigns, and the expenses of public worship, as had always before been the custom, were provided for by a tax on the list, in the same manner as the expenses of the town. This tax in 1828, was five cents on the dollar of the assessment list (which was three per cent of the property valuation); in 1849, the last year in which a tax was laid, it was twelve cents on the dollar. In 1850, the members of the society owning pews gave them to the society by a joint deed, and the pews, that were owned by members of other societies or by persons who had moved away, were purchased at about one-half of their original cost. After which the society proceeded to make provision for the support of public worship by the annual renting of the pews, which is the method adopted at the present time. A. T.]

The people doubtless observed public worship from the beginning, as they sustained a very pious character, and Mr. Whitfield, one of their number, had long been in the ministry, having indeed been the pastor of some of them in England, but for some cause now unknown a church was not regularly formed until 1643. On the 19th day of the third month (i.e. June 29th, of our present reckoning) according to the method practiced in New Haven, seven persons were selected called pillars, viz: Henry Whitfield, John Higginson, Samuel Disborow, William Leete, Jacob Sheafe, John Mepham and John Hoadley, that to these others might be united. To whom accordingly the other professors, embracing more than half the inhabitants, were joined at that time. At this time Mr. Whitfield was the pastor and, as he had been especially ordained in England and ministerially connected with most of them in that country and with all of them here, he was not formally installed. Among the reasons, that might have partly caused the delay, may have been the fact that until this period there does not seem to have been a permanent settlement at this place, and that prior also to this period there seems to have been no regular teacher associated with the clergyman, which they seem to have considered an almost indispensable requisite. Mr. John Higginson, son of Mr. Higginson first minister of Salem, Massachusetts, and son-in-law of Mr. Whitfield, was duly called and instituted into that office. He seems to have been for several years a preacher, as he had been employed in that duty at Hartford and at Saybrook. The articles of faith or covenant originally adopted were used in the church until 1837, when they were amended in only a few particulars, although some other prior unimportant alterations were perhaps made by the Rev. Dr. Dutton. A public relation of experiences was required in order to admission into the church until 1762, when a vote was passed by the church that they would not insist upon such a relation from those who should be indisposed to give it. Since then such relations have been given generally in a private manner.

Mr. Whitfield continued here as pastor until the month of

October, 1651, when he took leave of his church and congregation, who greatly loved him and followed him to the waterside with many tears, and shipped for his native country where he appears to have finished his days in the ministry in the city of Winchester.

The character given of him by Cotton Mather in his *Magnalia*, and by Doctor Trumbull in his *History of Connecticut*, is very excellent. In point of character and talents he ranked among the first ministers in New England. His father, who was an eminent lawyer, designed him for the bar and gave him a liberal education for it at the university and afterward at the inns of court, but, being early called by grace, he was desirous of becoming a preacher of the gospel, and was encouraged to this intent by such eminent men as Doctor Stanton, Maj. Byfield and others. Entering into orders he was first stationed at Ockley in Surrey near London, where his labors were blessed to many of the inhabitants of that town and vicinity.[1] Finding his occasional labors abroad useful, and enjoying one of the best church-livings and having a large estate of his own, he employed an able and pious minister to preach to his own people and went into destitute places among the poor himself preaching the glad tidings of mercy. Though a conformist he was on the most friendly terms with Mr. Cotton, Mr. Hooker, Mr. Goodwin, and others, men of eminent piety among the non-conformists who afterwards became lights in the American church, and often entertained them in the kindest manner at his house. At length having a conference with Mr.

---

[1] During his connection with Ockley he wrote a book, the title of the second edition of which was as follows:

Some Helpes to Stirre up to Christian Duties etc., by Henry Whitfield, B. D. Preacher of God's Word at Ockley in Surrey. The Second Edition. Corrected and enlarged. London, printed for John Bartlett, and are to be sold at his shop at the Giltcup in Cheapside, 1634, pp. 228.]

Cotton and some of the other divines about church discipline, he became a non-conformist himself, and, unable to pursue his ministry peaceably in England, he now procured a godly successor and resigned his charge, sold his estate and came over, with many pious persons attached to his ministry, to this country. During his continuance at Guilford a large proportion of his property was expended in helping his people in their settlement, while he supported a numerous and expensive family. He had ten children, two of whom remained at Guilford a year or two after him, their names were Nathaniel and John Whitfield. One married Mr. Higginson, and another Mr. Fitch the minister at Saybrook and afterwards at Norwich. Most of the children, however, were dependent upon him for support. The prospect therefore was that he must suffer great embarrassment if he remained at Guilford, and he had many and pressing invitations to return to England where the change of times under the protectorate opened the way for him to resume and prosecute the ministry without molestation. His family appear for some reason or other to have remained here for some years afterwards. His son Nathaniel Whitfield, removed to New Haven, and after remaining for some years, removed thence to London, England, where he seems to have been a wealthy merchant and to have been very useful to the settlers. Mr. Whitfield's wife appears to have been here as late as 1659, and at that time she is spoken of on the records as being here and managing the estate. Mr. Whitfield was a distinguished preacher, delivering his discourses with a peculiar beauty, dignity and solemnity. He published a work entitled, *The Light Appearing More and More*, giving an account of the progress of the gospel among the Indians, etc. In consequence of what he had expended in the purchase of the town and the gift of Mr. Fenwick, numerous and valuable tracts of land were allowed him in various parts of the town, which upon his return to England he offered to sell to his people upon low terms. They, however, did not purchase them partly on account of their poverty, and partly from an expectation which prevailed for a time that they should eventually follow him. He therefore sold them to Major Robert Thompson of London, in whose family they remained, to the great detriment of the town, until Oct. 22d, 1772, when Andrew Oliver Esq., of Boston, as attorney for Thompson's heirs, sold them all to Mr. Wyllys Elliott of Guilford for £3000 of the current money of Massachusetts. They continued in his family for several years. The stone house was purchased in 1776, by Jasper Griffing, and finally passed into the possession of his son Judge Nathaniel Griffing, and the Sawpitts farm was purchased in 1837, of Samuel and Reuben Elliott by Walter Johnson Esq.

Mr. Higginson became sole pastor of the church after the departure of Mr. Whitfield, and was duly instituted into those duties, Sept. 1653. He was the son of Mr. Francis Higginson, for some time minister of Leicester, England, and afterwards first minister of Salem, Mass. His father dying soon after his settlement in Salem, Mr. John Higginson was privately educated by benevolent friends, among whom was Mr. Hooker of Hartford. He lived some time in the latter place, employed in school keeping, and probably prosecuting his theological studies. In the year 1636, he was chaplain at Saybrook fort during the Pequot war, where he labored about four years, where, in the language of another, " his ministrations were suitable, seasonable and profitable according to the present dispensation of Providence." He removed to Guilford about 1641 where he remained until 1659, when he shipped for England intending to visit his father-in-law, but the vessel being forced into Salem by contrary winds, the people wishing then to settle a pastor, he was persuaded to accept a call from the church where his father had been settled about thirty years previous. He was installed Aug. 29, 1660, and became eminent by his preaching and his exemplary life. He wrote "An Attestation to the Church History of New England by Cotton Mather," and published also a volume of sermons dedicated to the people of Saybrook, Guilford and Salem."[1] He died Dec. 9, 1708, in the 93d year of his age, having been in the ministry seventy-two years. His likeness is preserved in the Atheneum at Salem and his descendants in that town are numerous and respectable, although the name seems to have become extinct among them. The Hon. Stephen Higginson, his sole surviving male descendant died at Boston in the autumn of 1828, at the advanced age of eighty-five. He was a member of the revolutionary congress of 1778, where he distinguished himself by his talents and acquired the confidence of the most distinguished men in this country.

After the departure of Mr. Higginson, the town of Guilford was in a confused state for several years. Mr. John Cotton (H. C., 1657) who married the daughter of Doct. Bryan Rossiter was here a part of the time, and also Mr. John Bowers (H. C., 1649) from New Haven, but the latter seems not to have been generally liked by the people, and was also much opposed by Doct. Rossiter. Mr. Cotton soon removed and afterwards settled at Plymouth, Massachusetts;[2] and Mr.

[[1] Our Saviour's Dying Legacy of Peace to his Disciples in a troublesome World, from John xiv, 27. My Peace I give unto you, etc. Also a discourse on the Two Witnesses, etc; unto which is added some help to self-examination (which I drew up for myself in the year 1652). By John Higginson, pastor of the church in Salem, etc. Boston, printed by Samuel Green for John Usher near the Town House, 1686. pp. 205.]

[[2] Rev. John Cotton, born March 22, 1639-40 at Plymouth, Mass., married at Wethersfield, Conn., Nov. 7, 1660, Joanna Rossiter, by whom he had eleven children. He left Connecticut for Boston in 1663, where he was excommunicated for immoral conduct, but was restored the next month. Removed to Plymouth, Mass., 1667, remaining there until his dismissal Oct. 5, 1697. After this he was called to Charlestown, S. C., where he arrived December 7, 1698, and labored until he died September 17 or 18, 1699, of the yellow fever. — *Sibley's Harvard Graduates*, 1, 496-508.]

Bowers returned to New Haven, afterwards settling at Derby, where he remained till his death, June 14, 1687. In the fall of the year 1663, the town received a letter from Dr. Increase Mather, who gave them much encouragement of coming to settle here, but declined the call given him during the next spring.

In 1664, however, Mr. Joseph Eliot, a native of Roxbury, Mass., and graduate of Harvard college (1658), was called and happily settled. He was the second son, born Dec. 20, 1638, of the Rev. John Eliot, pastor of Roxbury, called frequently the apostle to the Indians, and was endowed by the God of nature and of grace with a liberal portion of the excellencies of his father. Before he came to this place he preached sometime in Northampton, Mass., where he was unanimously invited to settle, the health of Mr. Mather, minister of that town having declined. The settlement, however, did not take place, probably on account of Mr. Mather's recovery. As a preacher, Mr. Joseph Eliot is said to have been inferior to none in the age in which he lived, and he was a burning and shining light in this community. His religious character is well exemplified in a pious and excellent letter written by him to a brother in Roxbury, " showing how we must live in this world, so as to live in heaven," which having been published in this century served to bring his character and work afresh to remembrance. He died May 24, 1694.

The Rev. Thomas Ruggles, who was born (March 10, 1671), at the same place and educated at the same college (H. C., 1690) with Mr. Eliot, preached in Guilford during the summer after his death, and was ordained his successor, Nov. 20, 1695. His character and standing as a minister were respectable. He was a fellow of Yale college from 1711 until his death, which occurred June 1, 1728, in the 58th year of his age.

[On the 9th of June, 1728, " being the Lord's day next after the funeral," a discourse was pronounced in Guilford on Death, the Advantage of the Godly : from Philippians i, 20, by Elisha Williams, A. M., and Rector of Yale college, from which the following characteristics of Mr. Ruggles are excerpted :

" What of him first took our Thoughts, was his Comely, Serene and Majestick Aspect, his Pleasant, yet Grave and Solemn Deportment, every way becoming the great Excellencies of his Mind, always commanding our Reverence, and Attracting our Love. Most happy was he in a Meek composed, Peaceable and Pleasant Disposition. He excelled in a peculiar Sweetness and Goodness of Temper, and in a Beneficent Love to Mankind. This his Love most Diffusive, tho' especially directed to such where the Christian appeared, yet led him to do Good to all, and to the greatest distance from speaking Evil of any. He was Hearty and Real in his Affection to his Friend, Faithful to his Interest, Obliging and Sincere in the Expressions of his Friendship, and wholly Unpracticed in the Arts of Dissimulation."]

The Rev. Thomas Ruggles, eldest son of the preceding, a graduate of Yale college (1723) was ordained here, March 26, 1729 and died Nov. 19, 1770, aged sixty-five. He was a fellow of Yale college during the last twenty-four years of his life.

[The funeral sermon of Rev. Thomas Ruggles, Jr., was delivered, on the next Lord's day after his death, by Jonathan Todd, A.M., pastor of the Second church in Guilford, on " Judgment and Mercy: or Aaron dead and lamented, and Eleazer in his Office," from Numbers xx, 28, 29. Mr. Todd speaks of him as a man of sound understanding, a solid judgment, a penetrating genius, a very strong and tenacious memory. His attainments in valuable and useful learning were very considerable. The metaphysical and unintelligible jargon of the schools he always disliked. But true philosophy he loved, and was well acquainted with the principles thereof. But divinity was the chosen study to which he chiefly applied himself. * * He was a judicious, orthodox divine. He was a plain, instructive preacher. His study was not rhetoric, and the 'enticing words of man's wisdom.' Nor was he happy in his elocution. But his preaching was solid and weighty, practical and serious. " He was of a cautious temper ; an able counselor ; grave, but affable, pleasant and facetious in his converse ; he loved peace, was noted for his hospitality in his house ; was a lover of good men, and a friend to mankind. Having devoted much attention to local history, he left in manuscript a *History of Guilford*, down to 1769.]

The Rev. Amos Fowler, a native of Guilford, also educated at Yale college (1753) was ordained a colleague of Mr. Ruggles, June 8, 1757, and died Feb. 10, 1800, at the age of seventy-two.

[At the funeral of Mr. Fowler, the sermon was delivered by Thomas Wells Bray, A.M., pastor of the Third (North Guilford) church in Guilford, on " The Duty of Living and Dying to the Lord," from Romans xiv, 8. The speaker had been a fellow-laborer for almost thirty-four years, and spoke of him as " by nature of a placid, grave, patient and meek spirit ; which amiable qualities, being greatly brightened by divine grace, rendered him eminent for constant serenity and uninterrupted calmness of temper, under all trials. His whole deportment appeared to be most remote from pride, envy and ostentation. Such were his unaffected modesty and humility, that his work appeared to much greater advantage to those who improved their acquaintance with him. He was amiable for his hospitality ; his esteem of good men ; his peaceable and friendly disposition to all. He was ever cautious of speaking evil of any man ; and not only desirous of living peaceably with all, but possessed a wonderful talent of cooling down the wrath and violence of those whose passions were tumultuous. That wisdom which is from above, seemed to be eminent in him, which is first pure, etc. He was ever cool and judicious in counsel — was a man of prayer; with plainness and pertinency adapting his expressions to every case on which he was called to speak. Mr. Fowler was a constant father to the people of his charge, manifesting a readiness, in season and out of season, to spend and be spent for them, to live and die with them." Another sermon was also delivered on the occasion of Mr. Fowler's death by John Elliott, A.M., pastor of a church in E. Guilford, on 2 Kings ii, 14. " Where is the Lord God of Elijah," in which he says, Mr. F. "read with care the primitive fathers, but his system of faith was founded on the Bible."

The Rev. Israel Brainerd of Haddam became the successor of Mr. Fowler, June 11, 1800, and was dismissed June 11, 1806. [We learn from an obituary of this minister, published in a Presbyterian paper, that he was born in 1772. At the age of sixteen he made a profession of religion. His collegiate education was obtained at Yale, where he maintained a respectable position, graduating 1797 in a class containing such men as Dr. Lyman Beecher, Dr. James Murdock, Judge Henry Baldwin and others. He spent one year teaching in Albany, pursued his theological studies with Dr. Chas. Backus of Somers, and was licensed to preach in Oct., 1799. The writer says that during his ministry here, gross errors had crept into the church, and that although the influential part of the congregation " cried for smooth things," his faith in the fundamental doctrines of grace was so strong, and his sense of personal responsibility to the great Head of the church was so vivid, that he was unable to yield to their wishes, but on the other hand was earnest and bold to declare the whole counsel of God, whether men would hear or forbear. "After his dismissal from Guilford, he was commissioned by the Connecticut Home Missionary Society as a missionary to Oneida county, N. Y., and was subsequently settled in Verona, where he remained pastor for thirty years. After closing his pastoral labors in V., he served "the church as a missionary, an agent, or as a colporteur till the last week of his life." He died in Syracuse on the 5th of Sept., 1854.]

The Rev. Aaron Dutton, a native of Watertown, Conn., was ordained here Dec. 10, 1806, became the next minister in charge, remaining until his dismission, June 8, 1842. [He was the son of deacon Thomas Dutton, and was born in Watertown, May 21, 1780. His collegiate education was obtained in Yale college, where he was graduated in the class of 1803. He also received from the college the degree of A.M., but declined that of D.D., as contrary to the divine injunction in Matt. xxiii, 8. In 1825, he was elected as a member of the corporation of the college, and took part in its management until his death in 1849.

As a preacher he was plain and practical, not eloquent nor displaying the graces of oratory, but forcible and pointed in his sermons, and had the high satisfaction of knowing that his labors were not in vain. During the first three years of his ministry about one hundred and fifty persons united with the church by profession, and during the year 1821, alone, there were one hundred and eighteen. General revivals occurred in 1827, 1831, 1834 and in 1840. More than six hundred persons made a profession of religion during his ministry.

He was very kind and attentive in the visitation of the sick ; making daily visits in cases of dangerous sickness. Active and efficient in promoting the cause of education ; notwithstanding he was personally engaged in teaching a school for the higher branches, he acted as school visitor almost every year, and was able to state from personal knowledge who were efficient as teachers and successful as scholars.

He married Miss Dorcas Southmayd of Watertown, shortly before his settlement in Guilford. They had eight children : Mary who was for some time principal of Grove Hall Female Seminary in New Haven ; Dorcas S. wife of the late Rev. Edwin R. Gilbert of Wallingford, who died in 1849 ; Rev. Thomas, a graduate of Williams college, and settled for a time in Ashford ; Rev. Dr. Samuel W. S. of New Haven, so well known and so universally lamented at his death in 1866; Aaron R. Esq., of the class of 1837, a lawyer in Columbus, Ohio ; and three others who died at the ages of eleven, fifteen, and eighteen respectively.

After Mr. Dutton's dismission in 1842, he served for a time as a missionary in the west. He died in New Haven, June 13, 1849, at the age of sixty-nine.— A. T.]

[Rev. E. Edwin Hall, born April 1814, in Blanford Mass., a graduate of the University of Illinois (1838), was settled as pastor October 25, 1843, and continued in that position until July 24, 1855, when, desiring to make a visit to Europe, he was dismissed at his own request.

Rev. Henry Wickes, born Feb. 11, 1821, at Jamaica N. Y., a graduate of Marietta college (1848), was settled as pastor May 22, 1856, and, after a pastorate of two years, was dismissed July 21, 1858, by mutual consent.

Rev. William S. Smith, born July 10, 1821, at Leverett, Mass., a graduate of Amherst college (1848,) was next settled over the church as pastor, May 3, 1859, but, after continuing in that relation for more than six years, was dismissed July 3, 1865, on account of ill health.

The church remained without a settled pastor for nearly five years after Mr. Smith's resignation, during a part of which time Rev. E. Edwin Hall acted as stated supply. Finally, however, Rev. Cornelius L. Kitchel, born July 5, 1841, at Thomaston, Conn., a graduate of Yale college (1862), was settled as pastor, April 13, 1870, and remained until his resignation and dismission March 24, 1873.

Rev. Theodore L. Day, a graduate of Yale college (1867) was then engaged as a stated supply, from November 1874, remaining as such until February, 1877.]

Upon the settlement of Mr. Ruggles the younger, an unhappy separation took place which, only after the lapse of nearly a century, was healed. A large number of the church, together with many of the society, being unwilling to receive him as their pastor, withdrew and established public worship among themselves. They obtained Mr. Edmund Ward, a native of the town and graduate of Yale college (1727), who had been recently licensed to preach at New Haven, as a candidate for the ministry to preach for them, and they went forward and erected a house for the service of God. After various, unsuccessful attempts of councils and committees appointed by the legislature to reconcile them to their brethren, they were formed into a distinct society called " *the Fourth Society in Guilford,*" having the same territorial limits as the First Society, by an act of the general assembly passed May session, 1733.

The Rev. Mr. Ward was ordained Sept. 21, 1733, pastor over the new congregation, and the church organized. The ordination sermon was delivered by the Rev. John Graham, the first pastor of the church in Southbury, then a parish of Woodbury in this state. Mr. Ward remained with his church and society until sometime in 1735, when he was dismissed and deposed by a council. After this he became an Episcopalian, and united with some others in the formation of the Episcopal society in Guilford. He used occasionally to read service, but never took orders in the Episcopal church. He died, October, 1779, aged 73.

The Rev. James Sproat, D.D., of Scituate, Mass., was ordained over the Fourth Society, Aug. 23, 1743, and dismissed Oct. 18, 1768, and soon after this was installed over the Second Presbyterian church of Philadelphia. Dr. Sproat was educated at Yale college, where he graduated 1741.' He became a subject of religious exercises during his connection with that institution, under a discourse delivered by the celebrated Gilbert Tennent, his predecessor in Philadelphia. Dr. S. remained

[¹ The following articles from *The Connecticut Journal*, manifestly refers to the departure of Dr. Sproat from Guilford. They show that some of his members were animated with unfriendly feelings towards him, and that bitter controversy was stimulating those engaged in it to indulge in unseemly and abusive language :

Guilford, Aug. 18, 1769.

In the town of G—d, an under shepherd lately deserted or ran away from his flock without leave or license, either from his own or the flocks of the circuit with which he was consociated, having nothing to keep him in countenance but the advice of seven of his brethren, and the concurring yelps of four of their spaniels. When he came to them, he had neither crook, shoes nor scrip, nor two coats; but soon clothed and warmed himself with their fleeces, and very soon became a listener to the bleatings of other flocks, and nothing would stop their din from his ears, but to stuff them with the fleeces of his own purchase. He may be found in the cool of the evening rolling in his chaise, with his charming shepherdess, had on when he went away, a large Presbyterian cloak somewhat soiled, with a full bottomed wig, and five or six hundred pounds of fleece from his flock. Whoever shall secure him, or set him over a herd of goats, till his master's will shall be known, no doubt when the flocks are gathered together, will meet with an ample reward.

P. S. The reason why no inquiry has been made after him any sooner, was because he has made several rambles before, of a month or six weeks, it was not known, but he would have returned again, and as there is no signs of it at present, it is likely there will be monthly some such inquiry made.

The following appears in the next paper :

This may certify all whom it may concern, that the *art* of *barking* is taught by *Toby Ramshorn*, bell-wether of the flock of G—l—d. It is unnecessary to expatiate on the benefit arising from the noble art, let it suffice that the flock in G—l—d under the instructions and directions of old *Toby*, have regained their liberty, driving away their shepherd, and are now barking at him after he is gone. Old Toby instructs at the lowest price, in all the various ways of barking — teaches to bark by note both treble, tenor, and bass, and is preparing a treatise upon the subject of barking. He proposes for ready money, to bark either for religion or liberty, or against them ; and will bark gratis, monthly, for public good. He at present bears the bell in the flock at G—l—d, which is a fine flock, though we must confess very much *hide-bound*. A specimen of his barking may be seen in the last paper. If any man, dog, wolf, sheep, or any other kind of animal, desires to be instructed in this noble art, let him repair to aforesaid Toby, who with all possible cheapness and diligence will teach him the exercise of the *windpipe*.— *Barber's Conn. Hist. Collections*, 219.]

in his new charge until his death, which occurred Oct. 18, 1798, in the 71st year of his age. His death was owing to the yellow fever, which proved fatal not only to him, but to his wife and several of their children. In each of his two charges he spent twenty-five years, and was greatly and deservedly esteemed in both, as a man, a Christian and a minister. Doct. Ashbel Green, late president of Princeton college, who had been his colleague and successor, describes him, in a funeral sermon, as excelling in the graces of the gospel, as a good proficient in scholastic attainments, and as an eminent theologian.

As a preacher he had but few equals in his day, being highly evangelical and dwelling much on the doctrine of grace. In the early part of his ministry, his exertions were mainly directed to the extension of the great revival which then happily prevailed in our country. Throughout his whole life his labors were admirably adapted to the promotion of experimental and vital religion.

The Rev. Daniel Brewer of Springfield, Mass., also a graduate of Yale college (1765), succeeded Dr. Sproat, Sept. 18, 1771, in Guilford. Soon after this, embracing the sentiments of the Sandemanians, he was dismissed in 1775. In 1779 he removed to Newtown, Conn., and thence to Taunton, Mass., where he died in December 1825 in the 82d year of his age. He retained his Sandemanian sentiments through life, and of course never preached after leaving his charge in Guilford, as that denomination admits none as preachers but Christ and his apostles, although they allow their professors and especially their elders to remark on passages of scripture read in their assemblies, and to deliver exhortations. Mr. Brewer was an elder in his new church-connection, both at Newtown and Taunton. He was a man of good natural abilities, respectable as a scholar and apparently pious.

The Rev. Beriah Hotchkin, a native of Guilford but not a

college graduate was ordained over the Fourth Society, Aug. 17, 1785, and was dismissed March, 1789, in which year he removed to Greenville, N. Y., whither some of his people had gone before him. He was installed about 1793, and remained in connection with them until 1824 or 1825, when he obtained a dismission and removed to the county of Steuben. He continued to preach for some time, supplying a destitute congregation, and died February, 1829, aged seventy-eight. When Mr. Hotchkin, removed to Greenville, the northern parts of New York, from the Hudson to the region of Oneida county, as far west as English settlements had been extended, were almost wholly destitute of religious instruction. There was not a single Congregational minister in this region beside himself, and but few of the Presbyterian and Reformed Dutch churches. He had a very happy influence in promoting the cause of the Redeemer in Greenville and vicinity, and in other parts of the state.

Mr. Hotchkin was the last clergyman ever settled over the Fourth Society. Many of the members died, others removed or joined the First Society, until the church became extinct. In 1810, sixteen persons who had belonged to that society, were returned to the First Society by an act of the legislature, and the society was considered at an end. The circumstances that led to the formation of this church and society were very unhappy. The town and vicinity were agitated and confused, but the separation does not merit, I apprehend, all that prominence which the excellent Doctor Trumbull has given to it in the history of this state.

It has already been noticed that a large proportion of the first settlers of the town were professors of religion. A large share of their descendants, from generation to generation, are understood also to have been professors, but as no records of the First church exist of a date prior to January, 1747, it is impossible to state precisely how many belonged to this church before that period. There were then one hundred and seventy-two members. From that period onward until the death of Mr. Fowler one hundred and sixteen were added. Mr. Brainard admitted eighty-six, and Mr. Dutton about six hundred.

In 1801 some special interest in religion prevailed, and during the two succeeding years more than fifty were added to the church. In the beginning of 1808, a revival prevailed and one hundred and nineteen were soon after admitted. Another revival prevailed about the close of 1820, and the beginning of 1821, and one hundred and eighteen were added to the church soon after. In 1827, thirty-five were gathered into the church from a revival that occurred during that year, and from another in 1831, about eighty.

[The following persons have entered the ministry from the First church viz. Jared Eliot, Daniel Collins, Timothy Collins, Edmund Ward, Bela Hubbard D.D. (Ep.), Samuel Johnson, D.D. (Ep.), Thomas Ruggles, William Seward, Timothy Stone, Andrew Fowler (Ep.), Thomas Ruggles, Jun., Joy H. Fairchild, William Leete, Jr., Thomas Dutton, Edwin H. Seward, Theodore A. Leete, Beriah Hotchkin, John H. Fowler, Henry Robinson, Sherman Griswold (Bap.), S. W. S. Dutton, D.D., Martin Dudley, Henry L. Hall, Edward C. Starr, John W. Starr.]

HISTORY OF GUILFORD. 105

The following Persons have been chosen Deacons in the First Church.

Names.	Time of Election.	Deaths or Removals.	Age at death.
Nathaniel Baldwin,	unknown,	{ removed to Littlefield 1732, died 1760,	67.
George Bartlett,	probably June, 1665,	died Aug. 3, 1669.	
John Fowler,[1]		" Sept. 14, 1676.	
William Johnson,	November, 1673,	" Oct. 1, 1702,	73.
John Graves,	about 1676,	" Dec. 31, 1695,	
John Meigs,	1696,	" Nov. 9, 1713,	73.
James Hooker,	1702,	" May 12, 1742,	77.
Samuel Johnson,	1713,	" May 8, 1727,	54.
Thomas Hall,	1727,	" Feb. 1, 1753,	82.
William Seward,		" May 31, 1764,	80. d. in N. Haven.
Col. Timothy Stone,	1742,	" Sept. 9, 1765,	70.
Dr. Nathaniel Ruggles,	1751,	" Oct. 16, 1794,	82.
Ebenezer Bartlett,	1765,	" May 27, 1775,	74.
John Burgess, Esq.,	Nov. 2, 1775,	" Feb. 26, 1799,	85.
Thomas Burgess, Esq.,	Nov. 5, 1794,	" June 14, 1799,	62.
Samuel Chittenden,	June 19, 1799,	" May 27, 1802,	74.
Abraham Chittenden, Esq.,	July 2, 1799,	" March 4, 1848,	96.
David Bishop,	April 28, 1802,	{ removed to Paris, N. Y., 1807, died 1809,	52.
Ambrose Leete,	Dec. 2, 1807,	died Feb. 14, 1809,	61.

[1] John Fowler was the sole deacon from Aug. 3, 1669, to 1673.

HISTORY OF GUILFORD.

The following Persons have been chosen Deacons in the First Church.

Names.	Time of Election.	Deaths or Removals.	Age at death.
Thomas Hart,	March 29, 1809,	died May 29, 1829,	66.
Anson Chittenden,	March 29, 1809,	{ removed to Mt. Pleasant, N. Y., in 1813; died 1849,	79.
William Starr,	Dec. 1, 1813,	d. April 8, 1830,	60.
John B. Chittenden,	Oct. 3, 1823,	{ removed to Fairfield, Ill., Sept., 1831; d. 1813,	73.
Comfort Starr,	Aug. 30, 1827,	died Dec. 1, 1862,	82.
Jason Seward,	Aug. 30, 1827,	{ removed to Madison, April, 1839; died in Guilford, Oct. 14, 1874,	90.
Abraham Dudley,	Aug. 30, 1827,	died July 18, 1852,	73.
Col. Samuel Robinson,	May 3, 1832,	" Nov. 17, 1839,	77.
Albert A. Leete,	May 3, 1832.		
Edward L. Leete,	Nov. 14, 1852.		
Eli Parmelee,	Nov. 14, 1852.		
Edwin O. Davis,	Jan. 8, 1871.		
John Graves,	March 30, 1877.		
John William Norton,	March 30, 1877.		

The following Persons were Deacons in the Fourth Church.

Names.	Time of Election.	Deaths or Removals.	Age at death.
Samuel Cruttenden,	1733,	died Dec. 12, 1745,	70.
Daniel Benton,	May 29, 1740,	" Aug. 25, 1756,	61.
Seth Morse,	Dec. 30, 1755,	" June 12, 1783,	96.
Peletiah Leete,		" Oct. 13, 1768,	88.
Daniel Leete,	1766,	" Oct. 1, 1772,	63.
Joseph Bartlett,	July 28, 1768,	" Aug. 29, 1769,	70.
John Davis,	June 5, 1772,	" May 29, 1776,	63.
Peletiah Leete, 2d,	Jan., 1773,	" May 28, 1786,	74.
John Hall,	1776,	{ removed to Richmond, Mass., died 1826,	82.
Ambrose Leete,	1786,	reelected in First Church.	
James Corwin,		removed to Long Island.	61.

Within the local limits of the First Society an Episcopal congregation was embodied, September 5, 1744, by the Rev. Mr. Lyons, a missionary of " the Society for the Propagation of the Gospel in Foreign Parts," belonging to the Church of England. The conformists in January, 1746, viz: Messrs. Samuel Collins, Nathaniel Johnson, Edmund Ward, Ebenezer Bishop and John Collins, in regular meeting voted to build a church, which was raised the following year and opened by Rev. Samuel Johnson, D.D., in March, 1750, since which time the Liturgy of the Church of England has been employed by its members. The members were few in number until 1805 or 1806, when they received considerable accessions from the First Society. They enjoyed at first the occasional services of some of the missionaries from the society just named, and those of the Rev. Bela Hubbard, D.D. (Y. C., 1758), a native of Guilford, then residing in New Haven, from 1764 to 1767. During the revolutionary war it is believed that they were deprived of clerical ministration and so continued probably down to 1793. The church edifice suffered during the war greatly from plunder and decay, and the congregation became almost extinct. Indeed from the peace of 1783 to about 1793, the parish was only nominally in existence, but occasional services were rendered by Rev. Bela Hubbard, D.D. (perhaps by Rev. Andrew Fowler), and Rev. David Butler.

The Rev. Nathan B. Burgess, a native of Washington, Conn., was called in 1801 to be the rector of this church and of that formed in North Guilford, and remained until September, 1805, when his connection was dissolved by mutual consent. He afterwards settled in Glastonbury.

In March, 1807, the Rev. David Baldwin, of Litchfield, began to conduct service in Guilford, and in June, 1809, was inducted into office as the rector of the Episcopal parishes of Guilford, North Guilford and North Killingworth, in all of which he officiated until September, 1824, when he confined his labors to the two parishes of Guilford. In 1833, he resigned the rectorate of the first parish, and his place was supplied by Rev. Lorenzo T. Bennett, D.D., of New Haven, a graduate of Yale college (1825), who continued until Easter, 1835, when he resigned and became associated with the Rev. Doctor Harry Croswell over the Episcopal church in New Haven. In the same year the Rev. William N. Hawks was made rector of the Guilford parish, but in consequence of the failing of his voice he resigned in the following October. He was succeeded in the ensuing March by the Rev. Levi H. Corson (a graduate of Washington, now Trinity college, Hartford), who resigned March, 1838, and was succeeded in April by the Rev. Edward J. Darken. Mr. Darken resigned in 1840, and the Rev. Lorenzo T. Bennett, D.D., was again invited to the rectorship, which he retains to this day.

The name of the parish in Guilford is Christ Church. The church which was consecrated in 1750, was the last edifice left standing on the Green, where it attracted attention for many years, surrounded as it was with stately poplars. In 1836, the enterprise of building a new edifice was undertaken, a little east of the old building on the margin of the Green. The corner stone was laid in the usual form by Mr. Corson, the rector of the parish, June 24, 1836 (the bishop of the diocese being absent); on which occasion an elegant and appropriate address was delivered by the Rev. Dr. L. T. Bennett. The church was consecrated December 12, 1838, by the Rt. Rev. Dr. Thomas Church Brownell, bishop of Connecticut.

This edifice is a peculiarly beautiful gothic structure of granite, sixty-four feet by forty-four, and cost about 7,500 dollars. In 1872 repairs and extensive improvements were made, and a recess chancel was added, at a cost of 5,000 dollars, rendering the edifice one of the handsomest rural churches in the diocese.

The following Persons have been Wardens.

Names.	Date of Election.	Expiration of Office.	Death.	Age.
Thomas Powers,...	Nov. 11, 1799,	April 3, 1820,	Dec. 26, 1822,	80.
Charles Collins,....	Nov. 11, 1799,	April 3, 1820,	Feb. 26, 1823,	78.
Abraham Coan,....	April 3, 1820,	April 20, 1840,	Feb. 14, 1863,	88
Jedediah Lathrop,..	April 3, 1820,	April 19, 1824,	1859,	91.
Erastus C. Kimberly,	April 19, 1824,	April 4, 1825,	July 17, 1875,	80.
re-elected, ...	April 6, 1863,	April 1, 1872,		
Thomas Burgis,....	April 4, 1825,	April 8, 1833,	May 25, 1861,	90.
re-elected, ...	April 20, 1840,	April 17, 1854,		
Henry Loper,......	April 8, 1833,	April 6, 1863,	Feb. 21, 1873,	82.
John H. Bartlett,...	April 17, 1854,	April 1, 1861,	July 10, 1864,	68.
George A. Foote,...	April 1, 1861,	April 6, 1874.		
George B. Spencer,.	April 1, 1872.			
Henry Hale,.......	April 6, 1874.			
George C. Kimberly,	April 17, 1876.			

This parish has a fund $1,050, at interest devoted to the support of the gospel, of which $1000 was a legacy from Charles Collins and $50 from Miss Ruth Loyselle. It has also been the recipient of $300 from Franklin M. Hill. Wm. H. Hubbard, a native of Guilford, but for many years a resident of Richmond, Va., also bequeathed the sum of $10,000 to the parish, of which only a portion has been received, in consequence of losses experienced by his estate during the rebellion.

The parish of North Guilford, called St. John's church was organized in 1748, when a few inhabitants of North Guilford united together, and built a church, since which time they have increased considerably. In 1812 they built a new church in place of the old one which had become dilapidated. They were supplied with ministers in the same way at first as the other parish.

St. John's church has a fund about $800, given by Zadoc Hull and George Bartlett.[1]

A Baptist church was organized June 30, 1808, consisting of nineteen members. Elder Alvah B. Goldsmith was ordained,

---

[1] W. H. Hubbard also left this parish, in his will, $10,000 a portion of which has only been paid over, in consequence of the losses experienced by his estate, already mentioned.

Feb. 24, 1823, over this society, and his father Joshua Goldsmith was appointed and ordained deacon at the same time. They met for a long time in one of the rooms of the academy on Sunday.

[The Methodist Episcopal church owes its origin here to the labors of Rev. Nathan Kellogg who first preached in a private house, with a view to effect a church organization. During the winter of 1837-8, Rev. Charles Chittenden, from the New York conference, came here as a missionary, and through him a Methodist society was formed. The society commenced building a frame church, forty-eight by thirty-six feet, on the west side of the green during his pastorate. The timber used in its erection was furnished by Mr. William Hale, the pastor proceeding to the woods, along with some of the members, and helping to fell the first tree. During the erection of the church, service was held in private houses. The church was completed and dedicated during the pastorate of Rev. Hart Pease 1838-9. The original trustees were John Hale, William Hale, Henry Griffin, Samuel Leete, Samuel A. Barker, Lucius Elliot, F. C. Phelps and A. Kelsey.

Since Mr. Pease's departure, the following clergymen have been in charge, Rev. James Rawson, Rev. E. S. Stout, Rev. R. W. Wymond (he remained two years and received ninety on probation. At this time a great revival occurred in the town, some two hundred professing religion in the village), Rev. Benjamin Pillsbury, Rev. Lawson Turner, Rev. Julius Field, Rev. Chas. W. Lyon (two years), Rev. C. W. Gallagher, Rev. E. A. Blake, Rev. Douglass, Rev. John S. Wilson and R. W. Whitcomb. During the years when the church was without a regular minister, the pulpit was supplied from the Wesleyan university at Middletown, Conn.]

[The Third Congregational church. At an ecclesiastical council held in Guilford, November 23, 1843, one hundred and twenty-three persons, from the First Congregational church, were organized into the Third Congregational church of Guilford. The present house of worship was built in 1844, and dedicated to the service of God, January 1, 1845. It was remodeled in 1862, and supplied with a suitable organ in 1873. The church is connected with the New Haven East Consociation. Its membership (Sept. 18, 1876) is 228, and the Sabbath school connected with the church numbers 306. The church has been served by the following pastors :

Rev. David Root, the first pastor, was born in Piermont, N. H., June 17, 1791. He graduated at Middlebury college, Vt., and there studied for the ministry. Went to Georgia to preach about 1818, and there married Miss Almira Alden of Connecticut. About the year 1820 he became pastor of the Second Presbyterian church in Cincinnati, Ohio. Removed thence to Dover, N. H., where he married, as his second wife, Miss Mary Gordon. Next he went to Philadelphia, where he became pastor of the First Congregational church, after which he removed to Waterbury, Conn., where he was installed, in July, 1841, pastor of the First Congregational church. Having been duly dismissed in 1844 from this church, he was installed pastor of the Third church, Guilford, January 1, 1845. Being dismissed from the church, at his own request, April 6, 1851, he did not again resume ministerial labors. The remainder of his days he spent in New Haven, and with his son-in-law Horace White, Esq., in Chicago, at which latter place he died August 30, 1873. His remains were brought to Guilford, and interred in Alderbrook cemetery. The monument, marking his grave, bears this inscription :

Rev. David Root, pastor of the Third Congregational church, Guilford, 1845-1850. Born in Piermont, N. H., June 17, 1791, died in Chicago, Illinois, Aug. 30, 1873, aged 82.

A faithful and fearless servant of God the father of our Lord

Jesus Christ. A pioneer and untiring laborer in the anti-slavery cause. A man of active benevolence, and a diligent promoter of Christian education. His memory is lovingly cherished by those with whom he dwelt, and his influence remains to bless coming generations.

Rev. Richard Manning Chipman, the second pastor, was born at Salem, Mass., January 12, 1806, the eldest of twelve children of Deacon Richard M. and Elizabeth (Grey) Chipman. He prepared for college at Kimball Union academy, Moriton, N. H., and graduated at Dartmouth college, 1832. He studied for the Christian ministry in the Theological seminary, Princeton, N. J., and in the theological department of the University of New York. During the years 1833 and 1834 he was corresponding secretary of the American Peace Society, and editor of their periodical, *The Calumet*, in New York. He was ordained pastor of the Congregational church in Harwinton, Conn., March 4, 1835, and dismissed from the same March 13, 1839. In 1839 he was elected professor of theology in the Oneida (Collegial) institute at Whitesboro, N. Y., and also invited to the pastorate of the Congregational church in South Norwalk, Conn., both of which overtures he declined. He was pastor of the Evangelical (Congregational) church in Athol, Mass., from August 15, 1839 to December 23, 1851, and of the Third Congregational church of Guilford from Jan. 14, 1852 to May 19, 1858. Since then he has been acting pastor of Congregational churches at Wolcottville in Torrington, Conn., 1859–1861, at Middle Haddam in Chatham, Conn., 1861–1863, at Hyde Park, Mass., 1864-6, at East Granby, Conn., 1866–70, and from 1871 at Lisbon, Conn. In 1863-4 he was in the service of the National Freedman's Relief Commission of Salem, Mass.

Mr. C. has published among others ;

1. Discourse on Ecclesiastical Prosperity, delivered at dedication of church at Terryville in Plymouth, Conn., 1838.
2. Discourse on Free Discussion, delivered at Harwinton, Conn., 1839.
3. Discourse on Maintenance of Moral Purity, delivered at Athol, Mass., 1841.
4. Memoir of Eli Thorp, 1842.
5. The history of Harwinton, Conn., 1860.
6. The Chipman Lineage, particularly as in Essex Co., Mass., 1872.

Mr. Chipman married June 11, 1835, Mary, second daughter of Rev. Fosdic and Elizabeth (Bunnel) Harrison, then of Roxbury, Conn. His only child is Richard Harrison Chipman, born January 19, 1837.

Rev. George Ingersoll Wood, the third pastor, was born at Stamford, Conn., May, 20, 1814, being the second son of Hon. Joseph and Fanny (Ellsworth) Wood. His mother was a daughter of Oliver Ellsworth, second chief justice of the United States. Mr. W. graduated at Yale college in the class of 1833, studied law for two years with his father, spent a year in the Divinity school at New Haven, and completed his theological education in the Union Theological seminary of New York, in 1838. He was ordained pastor of the Second Presbyterian church, in Washington, D. C., May 18, 1840, whence, after two years ministry, he was called to the pastorate of the Congregational church of West Hartford, where he was installed and remained for a few years until ill-health obliged him to ask a dismission. From 1844 to 1850 he supplied the pulpit of the First Congregational church in North Branford, Conn., when he was installed pastor of the church in Ellington, Conn., June 26, 1850. A bronchial difficulty interfering with his performance of ministerial duty, and having in vain sought relief by rest and a voyage to Europe, his request for a dismission was reluctantly granted February 20, 1854. After resting for a year, he again supplied the pulpit in North Branford, Conn., for three years, at the end of which time he was called to Guilford and installed as pastor of the Third Congregational church, November 30, 1858, where he remained until October 2, 1867, when the recurrence of the bronchial trouble compelled him to resign. For eighteen months after this, he lived in St. Cloud, Minnesota, where he preached most of the time in the First Congregational church. On his return to the east he took up his residence in Ellington, Conn., supplying the pulpit of the church there for a year and a half. He now preaches occasionally in different parts of the state.

Mr. Wood married April 24, 1840, Susan T., daughter of Rev. Samuel and Clarina B. Merwin of New Haven, by whom he had four children.

Rev. George M. Boynton, the fourth pastor, was born in Brooklyn, N. Y., in 1837. He graduated at Yale college in the class of 1858, and at the Union Theological seminary in New York city in 1863. He was ordained pastor of the Presbyterian church at Riverdale, N. Y. (now included in the city of New York). He was installed pastor of the Third church, Guilford, June 24, 1868, and dismissed, December 1, 1872, from that relation to become pastor of the Belleville avenue Congregational church, in Newark, N. J., where he is laboring at the present time.

Rev. Geo. W. Banks, the fifth and present pastor, was born at Greenfield Hill, Fairfield, Conn., July 11, 1839. He graduated at Yale college in the class of 1863, and at the Yale Theological seminary in 1866. He was ordained, October 3, 1866, pastor of the Congregational church in Bethlehem, Conn., and dismissed March 11, 1874. He was installed pastor of the Third church, June 18, 1874.]

The following Persons have been chosen as Deacons in the Third Church.

Name.	Date of Election.	Death.	Age.
Asher Dudley,	December 8, 1843,	October 29, 1862,	92.
Leverett Griswold,	March 8, 1844.		
Julius A. Dowd,	March 8, 1844.		
Alfred G. Hull,	September 12, 1852.		
James D. Hall,	March 11, 1877.		
Henry E. Norton,	May 13, 1877.		

Of the three hundred and thirty-three families living, in 1838, within the bounds of the located parishes of Guilford, two hundred and twenty-three were Congregationalists, fifty-seven Episcopalians, thirty-five Baptists, four Methodists and fourteen *Nothingarians.*

[The Roman catholics first met together in Guilford, as a distinct religious body in 1854. Their first meetings were held in the old stone house, once the residence of Rev. Henry Whitfield. In 1860, they purchased a small building on Harbor street and fitted it up as a chapel, in which they continued to meet for several years. In 1876 they erected a handsome church on the corner of Harbor and High streets in which some thirty families find suitable accommodations, and where public worship is statedly maintained.]

The people in North Guilford, having been incorporated as a society by an act of legislature passed in May 1720, went forward and built themselves a house of worship in 1723. Their second house was erected in 1814. Mr. Samuel Russel (Y. C., 1712), son of the Rev. Samuel Russel minister of the church in Branford, one of the founders of Yale college and son of the Rev. John Russel for some time a minister at Wethersfield and afterwards at Hadley, Mass., where he became so distinguished as a protector of the regicides, Judges Goffe and Whalley — was the first clergyman of this parish. Bearing the character of a faithful and worthy minister of the gospel, he died Jan.

19, 1746, in the fifty-third year of his age. The number admitted by him to the church is unknown.

The Rev. John Richards of Waterbury, who, as well as Mr. Russel was a graduate (1745), of Yale college, and his successor and son-in-law, was ordained at North Guilford, Nov. 2, 1748, and dismissed, at his request, by the consociation Dec. 25, 1765. After his dismission he resided sometime at Watertown, where he had no charge, when he removed to New Concord in the town of Chatham, New York, where at length he gathered a church and was installed its pastor 1771, but was dismissed at the close of the year 1773. He removed afterwards to Piermont, New Hampshire, where he gathered another church and was soon after again installed its pastor. In advanced life he was dismissed a third time. He then retired to New Hampton in the same state, where he died in 1811, aged eighty-five. He admitted eighty-five persons to the church in North Guilford.

The Rev. Thomas Wells Bray, a native of Branford, who had spent most of his youth in Farmington, also a graduate (1765), of Yale college, was ordained minister of this parish, December 31, 1766, and died April 23, 1808, in the seventieth year of his age. Mr. Bray was a man of good judgment and examplary piety, a plain, serious preacher. He admitted one hundred and fifty-two members to the communion, and fifteen more were admitted in the interval between his death and the ordination of his successor.

The Rev. William Fowler Vaill, of East Haddam, was ordained pastor December 21, 1808. Mr. Vaill was a graduate (1866), of Yale college, and fitted quite a number of young men for that institution. In April 20, 1820, Mr. V. being invited to take charge of the missionary station at Union, in Arkansas territory, he accepted and removed there soon after, where he remained until 1833, when he returned to the east and preached in various portions of the state. He died at

Wethersfield, Ill., in the year 1865. During his ministry here and previous to the ordination of his successor thirty-four persons were admitted to the church.

The Rev. Zolva Whitmore was settled here Sept. 5, 1821. He was a native of Rutland, Vermont, and a graduate of Union college. [At his own request, in the twenty-fifth year of his ministry, he was dismissed August 31, 1846. He removed first to Great Barrington, Mass., thence to Vermont, where he was in charge of a church for two years, thence to North Becket, and Chester Factory, Mass., where he died Aug. 5, 1867.

After Mr. Whitmore's dismissal the church was supplied until January 1848, by Messrs. Hoadley, Gurnsey, Grosvenor, Taylor and Smith.

Rev. John L. Ambler, was the acting pastor during the year 1848. He was followed by the Rev. Henry Eddy (Yale college, 1832), as acting pastor from January 1849, to March 1851. Mr. Eddy took the degree of Doctor of Medicine in 1851, and is now engaged in the practice of that profession in Bridgeport, Conn.

Rev. Fosdic Harrison was the acting pastor from November, 1851 to November 1854. During his ministrations there was a revival in the summer of 1853, and eleven were added to the church by profession.

Rev. Abraham C. Baldwin (Bowdoin college, 1827, and A. M. of Yale college 1843), acted as pastor from December 10, 1854, to October 28, 1855. During his service the church edifice was repaired and the interior entirely renewed at a cost of $1,100.

Rev. Thomas Rice Dutton (Yale college, 1837), was the acting pastor from December 9, 1855, to May 1, 1859. His ministrations were zealous and faithful, and thirty-seven were added to the membership of the church, twenty-four of whom

HISTORY OF GUILFORD.   119

were the result of a revival during the spring and summer of 1858.

Rev. Richard Crittenden (Oberlin college,) acted as supply from July 16, 1859, was ordained pastor August 1, 1860, remaining until April, 17, 1864, and was dismissed September, 1864. Mr. C. was very active in the Sunday school.

Rev. William Howard acted as supply from August, 1864, was installed December 20, 1865, and dismissed September, 1875, when he removed to Northfield, Litchfield county, Conn. His ministry was exceedingly acceptable to his people and eminently successful.

Rev. William B. Curtis (Yale college, 1840), has been acting pastor since July, 1875.

A revival took place in the summer and autumn of 1808, while Mr. Vaill was laboring here as a candidate, which was followed by the admission of thirty-eight persons to the church in that and the two following years. A similar revival in 1820–21, was followed by the admission of seventeen. From the revival of 1827 an equal number was received, and from that of 1831, eleven persons.

The following Persons have been chosen Deacons of this Church.

Names.	Time of Election.	Deaths.	Age.
George Bartlett,	probably June, 1725,	Sept. 23, 1765,	67.
William Dudley,	probably June, 1725,	Feb. 28, 1761,	77.
Theophilus Rossiter, Esq.,	October 5, 1760,..	April 9, 1771,	75.
Simeon Chittenden, Esq.,	October 25, 1760,..	April 12, 1779,	74.
Selah Dudley,	Feb., 1763,	Oct. 14, 1797,	84.
John Bartlett,		March 13, 1801,	66.
Robert Griffing,		Nov. 6, 1796,	77.
Joel Rose,		March 27, 1831,	91.
Levi Chittenden,		Nov. 11, 1835,	73.
Timothy Rossiter,	June 14, 1810,	Feb. 26, 1835,	80.
Benjamin Rossiter,	Nov. 14, 1825,	Nov. 20, 1866,	76.
Wm. R. Collins,	Dec. 11, 1825.		
Samuel W. Dudley,	May, 1856.		
John R. Rossiter,	May, 1856.,		

The members of this society have (1838) a fund for the support of the gospel of about $1700, derived from the sale of lands given by the proprietors of lands in Guilford.

In 1838, of the one hundred and five families in North Guilford, sixty-one were Congregationalists (six of which attended worship in Northford, a parish of North Branford, as being more convenient), thirty-two Episcopalians, four Methodists, and the rest of no denomination.

A number of residents and natives of Guilford have been distinguished in civil life, and brief biographical sketches of a few of these are herewith appended.

Samuel Disborough,[1] one of the first settlers of the town and one of the seven pillars of the church at its first formation here, has been already mentioned as a magistrate, and as holding courts in the town with three or four deputies appointed by the freemen for that purpose. He was associated with Gov. Eaton, Gov. Leete and other distinguished men in forming and establishing the combination and government of the New Haven colony in 1643, and, while in this country as one of its magistrates and the civil father of one of its towns, shared some of its highest honors. Upon his return to England with Mr. Whitfield, says President Stiles in his *History of the Judges* (p. 35) quoting from Noble, he became one of the commissioners of the revenues, and in the same year represented the city of Edinburgh in parliament at a council held at Whitehall, May 4, 1655. He was appointed one of the nine counsellors of the kingdom of Scotland, and the same year keeper of the great seal of that

---

[1] Samuel Disborow was born on the manor of Ettisley in Cambridgeshire, on the 30th of November, 1619, and was the third surviving son of James Disborow, Esquire, and a younger brother of the famous Major General John Disborow who married Jane Cromwell a sister of the Lord Protector Oliver Cromwell, and was a member of several parliaments and one of the judges appointed to try Charles I. Mr. Samuel Disborow studied law with his brother John Disborow, who in early life was a barrister.]

nation and allowed £2000 annually. The year following he was returned a member of the British parliament for the sheriffdom of Midlothian, and was continued in all his employments under the Protector Richard. Burton, who kept a diary of the doings of Cromwell's parliament, of which he was a member, makes frequent and honorable mention of Samuel Disborough as one of the most active and talented members of that body. "This shows him," says President Stiles, "a man of political abilities to sustain so many and such high betrustments with the reputation and acceptance with which he discharged them."

William Leete, also one of the first settlers of the town, and one of the pillars of Mr. Whitfield's church, received the highest honors which the colony of New Haven, and, after the union of that colony with Connecticut, which the united government, could give. He was bred to the law in England, and served as a clerk for a considerable time in the bishop's court at Cambridge, where observing the oppressions and cruelties then practiced on the conscientious and virtuous Puritans, he was led to examine more thoroughly their doctrines and practice, and eventually to become a Puritan himself and to give up his office. Coming over to New England with Mr. Whitfield, he enjoyed his religion and had an opportunity to serve his brethren in his station, for which his ability and education happily fitted him. From 1651 until 1658, he was the magistrate of the town, and one of the court of magistrates for the jurisdiction of the New Haven colony for a much longer period. In 1658 he was chosen deputy governor and continued in that office until 1661, when he was elected governor of the colony, which dignity he held until the union with Connecticut in 1664. Upon this union he was elected magistrate, and then in Connecticut from 1669 until 1676, deputy governor, when he was chosen governor, which office he held until his death. "For forty years," says Doctor Trumbull, "he was magistrate, deputy governor or governor of one or other of the colonies. In both colonies he presided in times of the greatest difficulty, yet always conducted himself with integrity and wisdom so as to meet the public approbation." He was the chief magistrate of the county court of New Haven county, after its formation in 1664, and held that office until his removal to Hartford on his election to the office of governor. After that time he remained there managing the affairs of the government of the whole colony until his death, April 16, 1683, full of days and full of honors. His tombstone was discovered somewhere about 1830 at Hartford, on removing some earth that had been allowed to accumulate in the ancient burial yard of that place.

Governor Leete left a numerous family in Guilford, where many of his descendants still remain, while others have removed to other parts of the state. His eldest son John, who died Nov. 25, 1692, aged about fifty-three, is said to have been the first white person born in Guilford. Governor Leete's first wife came from England with him. Her name was Anna Leete. The stone cellar in which the governor kindly secreted and nourished Genls. Whalley and Goffe, so particularly described in President *Stiles's History of the Judges* [1] still remains. It is

---

[1 " The governor's house was situated on the eastern bank of the rivulet (West river) that passes through Guilford. He had a store on the bank a few rods from his house, and under it a cellar remaining to this day, and which I lately (1793) visited and viewed with attention. It is, as I have said, still in the general and concurrent tradition at Guilford, that the judges were concealed and lodged in this cellar several nights, most say three days and three nights, when the governor was afraid to see them. A daughter of Governor Leete afterwards married in New Haven to Mr. (John) Trowbridge. It is an anecdote, still preserved in the family, that she used often to say, when she was a little girl, these good men lay concealed some time in this cellar of her father's store; but that she did not know it till afterwards : that she well remembered that at the time of it, she and the rest of the children were strictly prohibited from going near that store for some days, and that she and the children wondered at it and could not conceive the reason of it at that time, though they knew afterwards. Tradition says that they were however constantly supplied

on the west side of the borough, near the bank of the West river, and on the property formerly owned by Timothy Stone, Esq., and now by his daughters. The site is now covered by a barn and other out buildings.

Andrew Leete, Esquire, son of the preceding, possessed a liberal portion of the excellencies of his father. He was early appointed commissioner or justice of the peace, and had principal concern in managing the affairs of the town. In 1677 he was elected an assistant in the colony, and annually re-elected until his death Oct. 31, 1702. He is said to have had the principal agency in recovering the charter of the colony, during the time Major Andross usurped the government, and that he kept it for a season in his house. He appears to have been a man of infirm health, most of his life subject to fits of epilepsy, which impaired his usefulness. For a number of years he was one of the justices of the county court for New Haven county. He married a daughter of Thomas Jordan, Esq., one of the principal settlers, and, after the return of his father-in-law to England about 1660, occupied his estate and dwelling-house, on the northwest corner of the green.

Josiah Rossiter, son of Doctor Bryan Rossiter, for many years town clerk and one of the principal men in the town, was elected an assistant in 1701, and annually reelected to that station afterwards until May, 1711. He died January 31, 1716.

Abraham Fowler, Esq., sustained the same station as Mr. Rossiter from 1712 to 1720, and was also one of the justices

---

with victuals from the governor's table sent to them by the maid, who long after was wont to glory in it, that she had seen those heavenly men." *Stiles's History of the Judges*, page 92. The time of this concealment must have been between June 11, and 20, 1660. "Here and at Mr. Rossiter's they spent above a week, while it was deliberated whether the surrendery could or could not be put off, or at least deferred. Finally, their friends would not suffer them to surrender at this time; and it was concluded that they should retire again to their concealment."— *Stiles's Hist.*, page 45.]

of the county court for New Haven county, in which position he was distinguished for his firmness and good judgment. He died December 5, 1720.

Abraham Bradley 3d, who was at one time deputy post master general, was born in Guilford, December 11, 1731. In a letter written to Medad Stone (who kept the stage house and post office on the public square), dated Washington city, August 15, 1812, he states that he had been born at the lower end of Crooked lane, had been a resident in six different states of the Union, and had then resided a little more than a year in Washington. He also encloses some verses, which are as follows:

An Address to Guilford.

How shall I sing with becoming grace
The high respect due to my native place?
To thee, O Guilford, gratitude is due,
In thee, at first the vital air I drew;
In thee I first received the visual ray,—
Therefore to thee I will due homage pay.

The keen sensations nature has designed
To form impressions on the tender mind,—
The childish sports, the pure and playful joys
Which give a relish to the taste of boys,
Leave grateful traits which to the man adheres,
Inseparable through revolving years,
And which, though busy life may disengage,
Again recur in the decline of age.

The Indians there had unknown ages dwelt —
Men, who the softer passions seldom felt,
To whom were arts and sciences unknown;
Who knew no common interest nor their own.
Wild flesh, wild fruits, their food, but oft'ner fish
And clams and oysters their more common dish,
Skins of wild animals for raiment served;
They oft with cold and oft with hunger starved.

These sons of nature held the right of soil,
On which, however, they disdained to toil;
Void of invention, iron they had none —

Their edge tools all were made of shell or stone.
Menunkatuck was the Indian name,
When to the English they transferred their claim,
On contract fair their right they did assign,
September, sixteen hundred, thirty-nine.

Pleased with the site, they now enjoyed the purchase,
Cleared up the ground, built fences, houses, churches,
Soon did the savage howl and yelling cease,
Succeeded by religion, love, and peace,
And 'tis among their heirs and their assigns
Now happiness resides and virtue shines.

The rapid changes of the human race
Every day and moment taking place,
Must, while a full half century has run down,
Make me a stranger in my native town,
For my coevals now are chiefly gone,
To distant bournes, perhaps to worlds unknown,
Except some few whom fate denied the boon
Of a removal into Heaven so soon.

Meanwhile a younger race, a different age,
Has risen up to occupy the stage.
Yet oft I think of Guilford with delight,
And feel full half way there while this I write.

Though edifices elegant and new
Present themselves to the spectator's view,
And tho' the old are levelled with the ground
And rarely any vestige to be found,
And tenements and tenants change their name,
The ancient landscape still must be the same.

E'en now my recollection brings to view
The scenes long past and people once I knew,
Their simple manners and their social glee,
Philanthropy to all, good will to me,
Morals humane, pacific, mild and just,
(Tho' some too much to doubtful faith might trust),
Virtues, in which they might indulge more pride
Than those of any other spot on earth beside,
And tho' the produce of their grav'ly soil
But ill renumerates the farmer's toil,
Economy and commerce lend their aid
So they're as blest as under Eden's shade.

Crooked Lane.

And still I feel an impulse to maintain
The ancient honors of old Crooked Lane,
A people whom the arts ne'er taught to stray
Among the stars or climb the milky way.
Here enterprise was ever a recluse,
And dormant slept the genius and the muse.
Here proud ambition never fixed his throne
And maddening politics were little known.
The gilded demons, wealth, and power, and fame,
To them were but the whistling of a name.
No flags have they in distant seas unfurled,
Nor sought the subjugation of a world,
Content at home as foxes in their holes,
Nor pride nor envy fired their souls,
But when tobacco smoke perfumed their noses,
Felt wise as Solomon, and meek as Moses.
In erudition sought no greater glory
Than of some witch to hear and tell the story.
The way their fathers trod, supinely bred to tread
Without enquiring to what goal it led.
Honesty, banished from the proud and great,
Set up in Crooked Lane her humble seat.
'Tis thought they stood as good a chance for Heaven
As Mary Magdalene purged of her seven.

When now Thanksgiving takes her yearly circuit,
It is a merry farce the way they work it.
Molasses they must have and quick in search on't
Each with his jug runs nimbly to the merchant;
And if this noblest luxury can be had
Their eyes are lively and their face how glad!
If not they must adjourn for that same reason
The giving thanks unto another season.
For pies and puddings sweet, as well as tarts,
The great incentives are to thankful hearts,
And they were never brought to such a pass as
To celebrate this feast without molasses.

A sunday coat held good, unnumbered years,
However oft meanwhile the fashion veers:
May be transferred, from father down to son,
As long as grass shall grow, or water run.

> 'Tis on this spot, this paradise of earth,
> (Pardon my arrogance), I boast my birth.
> Though this indeed it were not need confest,
> For so, who reads these lines would sure have guessed.
> Now what I write I let my readers know
> Relates to facts of seventy years ago.
> If any change for better or for worse
> Has since occurred — pray what is that to us —
> Some rising bard may in a fitting strain,
> The present state depict of Crooked Lane.

James Hooker, Esq., first judge of the court of probate for the district of Guilford, was a native of Farmington and removed here about 1700. He married the daughter of William Leete, Jr., and held a distinguished place in the esteem of the people until his death, March 12, 1740.

Colonel Samuel Hill was a native of this town, and during his life time one of the principal regulators of its affairs. He was chosen town clerk in 1717, and was afterwards made clerk of the proprietors of the town until his death. In 1720, at the formation of the probate court for Guilford district, he was chosen clerk, and, on the death of Judge Hooker, in 1740, judge of that court, which position he held until his death in 1752. He was also, for a considerable period, judge of the county court for the county of New Haven, and one of the principal magistrates of the town. He always sustained a high character for integrity, uprightness, firmness and perhaps sternness of principle. His son Nathaniel Hill and grandson Henry Hill, were both eminent men in the town, county and state, and each in his day was clerk and afterwards judge of the probate court for this district, for a great length of time.

Nathaniel Hill, Col. Timothy Stone, Gen. Andrew Ward, Nathaniel Rossiter, and Nathaniel Griffing, Esq., were justices of the county court for the county of New Haven for considerable periods, and for many successive years enjoyed the highest honors in the gift of the town.

Abraham Baldwin was a native of North Guilford. He graduated in Yale college, 1772, and was a tutor from 1775 until 1779. His attention was first directed to theology; he became a candidate for the ministry, and was a chaplain in the Continental army through several of the last years of the revolutionary war. At the close of the war, at the request of a friend, Gen. Greene, he removed to the state of Georgia, where he relinquished the ministry and entered the profession of law, in which he rose to great eminence as also in his civil career. His talents and patriotism were too conspicuous to remain unnoticed even among strangers. He was soon elected a representative to the legislature of his adopted state, and in 1784, a member of the old congress, continuing in that situation until the national constitution superseded the system of government then in existence. He was a distinguished member of the convention which formed the present constitution of the United States and, upon the organization of the new government, was chosen a member of congress under the same, and so continued without interruption until he was promoted by the citizens of the state to a more exalted station, being chosen member of the United States senate, in which office he continued until his death, March 4, 1807, at the city of Washington, in the 53d year of his age, in the midst of his usefulness and surrounded with honors. It is a remarkable circumstance, and an instance of assiduity almost without a parallel that, during his long congressional life, he was never known to be absent a single hour during the session of congress, on account of indisposition or any other cause, until the week preceding his death. He was a man of great industry and talents, and his distinguished patriotism, learning and public services shed an honor on his native state as well as on that of his adoption. In 1785, he was placed at the head of the system of education then adopted in Georgia, and was the founder of a college at Athens, in that state, of which he was president for some years. He was a man of extensive benevolence, living in an eventful and important period of our history and filling such high and responsible stations in the forming and maturing of our general government as well as of the government and literature of Georgia, he will descend to posterity among the names of the most illustrious men of our country. Baldwin county, including Milledgeville the capital of Georgia, derived its name from him.

The Rev. Samuel Johnson, D.D., son of Samuel Johnson and grandson of William Johnson, one of the principal settlers of the town, was a native of Guilford, being born Oct. 14, 1696. He was a graduate of Yale college in 1714, and was tutor in the same institution from 1716 to 1719. In 1720 he was ordained at West Haven, the south parish of Orange in this state, being the first minister settled over that church. In 1722 he declared for Episcopacy, and was distinguished as the first convert to that denomination in Connecticut. Soon after, and during the same year, he was dismissed from his charge and sailed for England in company with Mr. Cutler, president of Yale college and Mr. Browne one of its tutors, together with Mr. Wetmore of New Haven, where they obtained ordination according to the Episcopal form. Mr. Johnson returned to Connecticut and was employed by "the society for the propagation of the Gospel in foreign parts" as the missionary to Stratford in this state. He entered the field of labor assigned him in 1723, and continued in the same until his election to the presidency of King's (now Columbia) college in the city of New York, in 1754, preaching to the Episcopalians of Stratford and its vicinity, and occasionally in his native town. He discharged the duties of president of King's college from 1754 until 1763, when he resigned and returned to Stratford, resuming his former charge and continuing in the same until his death in his chair, epiphany, January 6, 1772, in the seventy-sixth year of his age. Dr.

Johnson was distinguished for his literary and popular talents and acquirements, was genteel and engaging in his manners, and of great personal worth. It is said by a gentleman of his church that the whole course of Dr. Johnson's life, was a practical commentary on the beneficial influence of a firm adherence to principles.

Thomas Chittenden, the first governor of Vermont, was also a native of this town. His father's name was Ebenezer Chittenden, grandson of William Chittenden, one of the first settlers of the town. His father removed to East Guilford in the early settlement of that town. He married the daughter of Samuel Johnson and sister of the Rev. Dr. Samuel Johnson of Stratford. His eldest son Ebenezer Chittenden 2d, who settled in New Haven, possessed great mechanical genius. He invented a machine for bending and cutting card teeth with a single movement, and one or two other curious machines. The late celebrated Eli Whitney had an exalted opinion of his skill and judgment as a mechanic. Thomas Chittenden, brother of the last mentioned, was born in 1730 and, at the age of twenty-one years, removed to Salisbury in this state, where he remained until 1773, when he removed a second time to Williston on Onion river in Vermont. While in Salisbury, although he had enjoyed only the advantages of a common education, his good sense secured him the esteem and honors of his fellow-citizens, who repeatedly elected him representative to the legislature, and from whom he held the office of justice of the peace and commissions in the militia of that region through the various ranks up to the command of a regiment. After his removal from Salisbury to Williston, the troubles and dangers connected with the revolutionary war rendered it necessary for him again to remove. He purchased an estate at Arlington, where he resided until 1787, when he returned to Williston, where he spent the remainder of his days. When the general convention was held at Westminster, January, 1777, which declared Vermont an independent state," he was the only person among the members, who had ever before sat in the capacity of a legislator. He was on the committee to report to congress, the proceedings of the inhabitants, and to solicit the admission of their district into the American union. The next year he was elected governor of the state, and was re-elected each succeeding year, except one, until his death, August 24, 1797, in the sixty-eight year of his age. During the early years of his administration the state had to contend with great difficulties. It was threatened with invasion by the British forces from Canada, and its independence was not yet acknowledged by congress. He had the wisdom to pursue a course of measures, which saved the state from invasion and secured its admission finally into the union. At the time of this admission General Washington observed, in 1791, that Gov. Chittenden deserved well of his country for the wisdom, patriotism and firmness he had displayed in managing the affairs of his adopted state.

Governor Chittenden was clearly a man of superior natural abilities, of keen discernment, well acquainted with human nature, uncommonly skilled in reconciling discordant parties, and capable of forming and accomplishing important designs. He was a great blessing to Vermont and saw it rising up under his government from a small beginning to strength and importance. He was kind and liberal to the poor and distressed, and a sincere professor of the religion of Jesus Christ. In his manners and personal appearance he was rough, blunt and uneducated, yet his bluntness was so seasoned with frankness and benevolence that he was universally beloved wherever he was known, and the citizens of his adopted state have named one of their counties after him in honor of his memory.

William Todd, Esquire, was a native of East Guilford. He was the son of Doctor Jonathan Todd, and grandson of the

Rev. Jno. Todd, the second clergyman of that parish. He graduated at Yale college in 1806, and was admitted to the bar in 1809. [After practising his profession for almost a quarter of a century in Guilford, and securing the confidence and esteem of his fellow-citizens, he died October 8, 1831.]

[Fitz-Greene Halleck, the poet, was born in Guilford, July 8, 1790. His father was Israel Halleck, who married Mary Eliot, a descendant of the Rev. John Eliot, "the apostle to the Indians." He began to make verses at an early age, and several poems are still extant written at the age of ten. At fifteen he entered a store in Guilford as clerk, where he remained until 1811, when he became a clerk in the banking-house of Jacob Barker in New York. In 1822 he made a visit to Europe, during which he enjoyed the opportunity of meeting some of the most distinguished literary men of that country. After eighteen years connection with the house of Barker, he left the same and devoted himself for a short time solely to literary pursuits. In 1832, however, he entered the counting-house of John Jacob Astor, where he remained for sixteen years, until the death of the latter. Mr. Astor left Mr. Halleck an annuity of two hundred dollars, to which his son, William B. Astor, added a gift of ten thousand dollars. Early in the year 1849 he returned to Guilford, and made it his home until his death, which occurred Nov. 19, 1867. For many years his residence was the house, now occupied as a hotel, opposite the southwest corner of the green. He was buried in Alderbrook cemetery, and a monument, erected to his memory by his friends and admirers, was formally dedicated July 8, 1869, on which occasion an oration was pronounced by Bayard Taylor, and the following original sonnet read by his friend and brother-poet George Hill:

> "In thee no gorgeous capital, no mart,
> Known whereso'er a wave rolls, though we see,
> Yet Guilford, even thine no humble part

> In memory's pageant henceforth e'er shall be.
> The earth that heaps thy relics, Halleck, where
> No name more famed sepulchral shaft shall bear.
> Full many a pilgrim-band from many a shore
> Shall wend to greet, till time shall be no more;
> The spot, henceforth to genius ever dear,
> Shall gladly hail nor quit without a tear;
> Some strain of thy imperishable lyre
> Recall, and, ere reluctant he retire,
> Exclaim, " In thee, O Fame's lamented son,
> A thousand poets we have lost in one."

In 1837, Mr. Halleck received the honorary degree of master of arts from Columbia college, New York.

The following poem written for the occasion by Oliver Wendell Holmes, was also read by Gen. James Grant Wilson, through whose instrumentality mainly the money for the monument had been collected :

> Say not the poet dies !
> Though in the dust he lies,
> He cannot forfeit his melodious breath,
> Unsphered by envious death;
> Life drops the voiceless myriads from its roll ;
> Their fate he cannot share,
> Who, in the enchanted air
> Sweet with the lingering strains that echo stole,
> Has left his dearer self, the music of his soul.
>
> We o'er his tomb may raise
> Our notes of feeble praise,
> And carve with pious care for after eyes
> The stone with " Here he lies ;"
> He for himself has built a noble shrine,
> Whose walls of stately rhyme
> Roll back the tide of time,
> While o'er their gates the gleaming tablets shine
> That wear his name inwrought with many a golden line.
>
> Call not our poet dead,
> Though on his turf we tread !
> Green is the wreath their brows so long have worn,
> The minstrels of the morn,
> Who, while the orient burned with new born flame,

> Caught that celestial fire
> And struck a nation's lyre!
> These taught the western winds the poet's name;
> Their's the first opening buds the maiden flowers of fame.
>
> Count not our poet dead!
> The stars shall watch his bed.
> The rose of June its fragrant life renews,
> His flushing mound it strews,
> And the tuneful throats of summer swell
> With trills as crystal clear
> As when he moved the ear
> Of the young muse that haunts the wooded dell
> With songs of that " rough land " he loved so long and well.
>
> He sleeps; he cannot die!
> As evening's long drawn sigh,
> Lifting the rose leaves on his peaceful mound,
> Spreads all their sweets around,
> So laden with his song, the breezes blow
> From where the rustling sedge
> Frets our rude ocean's edge
> To the smooth sea beyond the peaks of snow,
> His soul the air enshrines and leaves but dust below.

Halleck was the first American poet, to whom was awarded the honor of a bronze statue in a public place. This is of heroic size, representing him seated, holding a thin roll of manuscript in his left hand and a pen in his right. It was presented to the city of New York by some of Halleck's admirers, and occupies a prominent position in the Central Park near the statues of Shakspeare and Sir Walter Scott. The ceremony of its unveiling took place May 15, 1877, when the venerable poet William Cullen Bryant presided, and, after making a brief speech full of pleasant memories of his old companion, introduced Gen. Rutherford B. Hayes, president of the United States, who formally presented the statue, in the name of the subscribers, to the city of New York, through its mayor, Hon. Smith Ely, Jr. A eulogy was then pronounced by William Allen Butler, Esq., of New York, and the following poem, written for the occasion by John Greenleaf Whittier of Massachusetts, was read :

Among their graven shapes to whom
    Thy civic wreaths belong,
O, city of his love ! make room
    For one whose gift was song.

Not his the soldier's sword to wield,
    Nor his the helm of state,
Nor glory of the stricken field,
    Nor triumph of debate.

In common ways, with common men,
    He served his race and time
As well as if his clerkly pen
    Had never danced to rhyme.

If, in the thronged and noisy mart,
    The Muses found their son,
Could any say his tuneful art
    A duty left undone ?

He toiled and sang ; and year by year
    Men found their homes more sweet,
And through a tender atmosphere
    Looked down the brick-walled street.

The Greek's wild onset Wall street knew,
    The Red King walked Broadway ;
And Alnwick Castle's roses blew
    From palisades to bay.

Fair city by the sea ! upraise
    His veil with reverent hands ;
And mingle with thy own the praise
    And pride of other lands.

Let Greece his fiery lyric breathe
    Above her hero-urns ;
And Scotland, with her holly, wreathe
    The flower he culled for Burns.

O, stately stand thy palace walls,
    Thy tall ships ride the seas ;
To-day thy poet's name recalls
    A prouder thought than these.

> Not less thy pulse of trade shall beat,
>   Nor less thy tall fleets swim,
> That shaded square and dusty street
>   Are classic ground through him.
>
> Alive, he loved, like all who sing,
>   The echoes of his song;
> Too late the tardy meed we bring,
>   The praise delayed so long.
>
> Too late, alas! Of all who knew
>   The living man, to-day
> Before his unveiled face, how few
>   Make bare their locks of gray!
>
> Our lips of praise must soon be dumb,
>   Our grateful eyes be dim;
> O, brothers of the days to come,
>   Take tender charge of him!
>
> New hands the wires of song may sweep,
>   New voices challenge fame;
> But let no moss of years o'er-creep
>   The lines of Halleck's name.

[George Hill, the poet, was born in Guilford Jan. 29, 1796. He graduated at Yale college in 1816, was afterwards employed as a clerk in one of the departments in Washington. In 1827 he entered the navy as instructor in mathematics and, during his term of service, made a cruise in the Mediterranean. On his return to the United States he was appointed librarian of the state department. Subsequently he was appointed United States consul for the southern portion of Asia Minor, and, on his resignation in consequence of ill health, was again made a clerk in one of the departments in Washington. He resumed his residence in Guilford, about 1856, and died December 15, 1871.]

Ralph Dunning Smith, son of Richard and Lovine (Hebert) Smith, was born in Southbury, Conn., October 28, 1804. On the father's side he was a descendant of John Smith, who with his wife Grace came to Milford about 1640. His mother was a daughter of Ebenezer Hebert, of Wyoming, Pa., and was born at Easton, Pa., during the flight of her mother from the great massacre at Wyoming.

He was fitted for college at the Weston (now Easton) academy, under the superintendence of its principal, John Hiram Lathrop, LL.D. He graduated at Yale in 1827, in a class of which the Rev. Dr. Horace Bushnell, N. P. Willis, Judge Henry Hogeboom the Rev. Dr. Wm. Adams, the Rev. Dr. Theron Baldwin and others, whose names have attained a national reputation, were honored members.

After the completion of his collegiate course he adopted the profession of law as the pursuit most congenial to his tastes, and prosecuted his studies under the direction of the Hon. Edward Hinman, of Southbury, and Heman Birch, Esq., of Brookfield, completing his course of preparation in the law school attached to Yale college, then under the care of Judges Daggett and Hitchcock. He was admitted to the bar at New Haven in 1831, and in November of the same year located in Guilford, where he spent the remainder of his life.

During the probationary period, through which every young professional man must past, he occupied himself for some years in teaching a select school in the place of his adoption, at which some of the most prominent men of his state were prepared for college.

He married, October 13, 1837, Rachel Stone Seward, daughter of Amos Seward, of Guilford, who is left to mourn his loss. They had four children, viz : Sarah Spencer, who married Dr. Lewis H. Steiner, of Frederick city, Md. ; Mary D., who died when two years of age; Walter Hebert (Y. C. 1863), died Nov. 27, 1863, and Richard Edward (Y. C. 1866), died December 18, 1868.

In January, 1844, he was appointed judge of the probate court, which office he held until July 4, 1850, filling the duties of the office with great skill, care and judgment. In 1859 he was elected a representative of the town of Guilford in the general assembly of Connecticut, and during its sessions acted as chairman of the committee on judiciary, and as a member of other important committees.

" From 1848 to 1854 he was engaged in chartering and conducting the New Haven and New London rail road, and the New London and Stonington rail road, performing several years of severe and continuous labor as secretary, treasurer, director and attorney in originating and building these roads, and in the subsequent management thereof."

Prior to, during and subsequent to, his labors in connection with these rail roads, Judge Smith was actively engaged in the duties of his profession, acquiring a well merited reputation as a thorough office lawyer and a sound practitioner, distinguished for his conscientious devotion to the interests of his clients and for his hesitation in taking charge of a case until he was absolutely satisfied of its justness. Judge Munson, of Seymour, spoke of him, at the bar-meeting called in honor of his memory, as one " who knew the law better than any lawyer within the acquaintance of the speaker, as a walking text-book, who only needed to be reminded of the principle involved in a case to tell at once its name" and to give a reliable opinion of the same. Another colleague, at the same meeting, spoke of him " as a thoroughly honest lawyer, preparing his case with great care and never employing questionable means or using questionable efforts to secure a result in his favor," and of " the genial qualities which made his counsel and pleasant words go deep into the hearts of the young as well as the old." Resolutions offered by Judge Edward R. Landon, a former student of Judge Smith, were adopted by the same meeting.

But although devoted to the study and practice of his chosen profession with an earnest zeal rarely excelled by its honored practitioners, he still found time to cultivate the fields of elegant literature, history, biography, and genealogical research. He studied the old English writers with a zest that could only spring from a genuine love of the beautiful and true. His memory was richly stored with the choicest English poetry, which was always at his command whenever needed for illustration. He took great pleasure in English and American history, and his calm, unprejudiced mind enabled him to pronounce exceedingly accurate judgments upon the lives and motives of whose who had figured most prominently upon their pages. But his love for research led him to investigate the obscure corners and nooks of history and biography, which other and more superficial students were in the habit of passing by unnoticed. And thus he was brought into the fields of genealogical research by a sort of inevitable necessity. Here, however, he found an ample scope for the exercise of his habits of careful research and untiring labor.

Shortly after his location at Guilford he was attracted by the rich materials for study furnished by its early history, and beginning with a careful study of its early records from 1639, he found the field of his investigation becoming wider and wider as his untiring spirit zealously pursued its labors. Old records, old tombstones and monuments were favorite subjects for study, indeed everything that could elucidate its history became of special interest to the enthusiastic student. Necessarily his investigations took a still more and more extensive range until everything connected with the genealogy of New England became attractive to his inquiring spirit, and his shelves began to fill up with books devoted to local and family history, while his manuscript collections increased until they became mines of wealth to younger investigators.

Another subject of special interest was the biography of the early graduates of Yale college. To this he devoted himself with great care and painful assiduity, and completed a series of sketches of the lives of the same extending from the first graduate down the class of 1767 inclusive.

His manuscripts are very voluminous, comprising: (1) A sketch of the history of Guilford with the genealogy of its principal families. This would probably make two volumes of some 600 pages; (2) A Biographical Record of the Class of 1827, Yale College, consisting of full and accurate sketches of the lives of all its members; (3) The Biographical Sketches of Yale Graduates from 1702–1767; (4) A catalogue of the Connecticut Election Sermons; (5) Fragmentary sketches of the early history of the First and Fourth Congregational Societies of Guilford, etc., etc., etc. Some of these may hereafter be put in a more permanent form should the way be opened for their publication.

Judge Smith was a modest, retiring man, avoiding as far as possible public life but delighting in the company of his friends, the genial attractions of his literary and professional studies, and in imparting information from his richly stored memory to any seeker after knowledge. Indeed no one ever approached him with an appeal for aid or assistance, whether pecuniary, professional or literary, without obtaining the same if it were in his power to furnish it. The results of his genealogical labors he delighted to impart to every inquirer, and was always very happy when he could aid a brother genealogist in his researches. A fellow-laborer writes that he was the most generous man with his collections he ever met, or that he could imagine to exist. And another closes a warm eulogy with the statement that he "has not left behind him any one so conversant with the general family history of the state."

He was a Congregationalist from choice and conviction, and attached to the First church of Guilford, but his religion was of that catholic nature which recognizes those, of whatever name, who love Jesus Christ, as brethren. The loss of his sons, shortly after they had graduated with distinction, and when careers of great usefulness were seemingly before them, for a while detached him from his favorite pursuits, but as grandchildren grew up around him he learned to sympathize in all their joys and sports, and he again resumed his former studies with some of the ardor he had shown in earlier days.

During the spring and summer of 1874, however, he gradually laid by his favorite pursuits, and seemed to suffer from symptoms of the painful disease which finally terminated his earthly labors on the 11th of September. On the 15th his funeral was attended by a large concourse of his fellow-townsmen, who felt that they had lost their most important citizen, and by many friends and professional brethren who had come from a distance to show respect to his memory. The Rev. Leonard Bacon, D.D., an old and valued friend, pronounced the funeral discourse, after which the remains of the accomplished scholar and veteran lawyer were deposited in the Alderbrook Cemetery, Guilford.—*From the N. E. Hist. and Gen. Reg. for July, 1875.*

Centennial Celebration, July 4, 1876.

[With the view of paying respect to the memory of its deceased citizens and of recalling some incidents of its past history as well as of honoring the grand event which gave birth to the United States, July 4, 1776, Guilford held a celebration on the centennial anniversary of the nation. This was largely attended by her citizens and many visitors from distant parts of the country. At sun rise one hundred guns were fired, as a salute, by the Guilford Light Battery, Lieut. Wm. H. Lee, commanding. At nine A.M., there was a grand procession that moved through the different streets of the village, and at eleven A.M., the special exercises of the day were held on the Green, Judge Edward R. Landon in the chair as president of the day.

The music was furnished by the New England band, composed of citizens of the town.

The exercises consisted of the reading of the Proclamation of the president of the United States, recommending the celebration of the day, by Rev. John Wilson, Scripture selections by Rev. Theodore L. Day, prayer by Rev. Geo. W. Banks, address of welcome by Rev. Lorenzo T. Bennett, D.D., reading of the Declaration of Independence by Gen. E. M. Lee, a Historical address by Dr. Alvan Talcott, and a poem by Samuel W. Loper Esq., of Durham. After an intermission of an hour, the audience was called upon to hear brief addresses in response to sentiments announced from the stand: that to the president and congress of the United States" was responded to by Hon. Simeon B. Chittenden, representing the third district of the state of New York in congress, to " the state of Connecticut" by Judge H. Lynde Harrison, to " the town of Guilford " by Judge Robt. E. De Forrest of Bridgeport, to " the soldiers and statesmen of 1776 " by Gen. E. M. Lee, and that to " the ladies " by Hon. Lewis H. Steiner of Maryland. A poem by Andrew J. Benton was then read by Rev. John Wilson, and the audience was dismissed with the benediction by Rev. Henry Robinson. At night there was a general illumination throughout the village, and fireworks were exhibited on the Green and in the grounds of some of the citizens.]

The probate court for the district of Guilford was established, October session, 1719, being one of the first districts separated from the counties in this state. The probate of wills, etc., was made in the particular courts, from the establishment of civil order in the colony, 1643, till the formation of the county courts, 1666, where it continued until the probate districts were formed. The first probate district for Guilford included the towns of Guilford, Branford (except Northford), Killingworth and Saybrook (Durham was joined with Middletown, Haddam and a part of Chatham and a part of Berlin in forming the district of Middletown in 1752). Killingworth and Saybrook were set off in 1780, into the district of Saybrook, and in 1834, Madison (formerly East Guilford) and Killingworth were each formed into separate districts, which left the probate district of Guilford to include Branford, Guilford and the First Society of North Branford, from which Branford was set off as a separate probate district in 1850.

HISTORY OF GUILFORD.

The names of the several Judges and Clerks are as follows:

	Date of appointment.	Death or removal.
James Hooker (Guilford),...	............May, 1720,	.March 12, 1740.
Samuel Hill, clerk.		
Col. Samuel Hill (Guilford),.	...............June, 1740,	............1752.
Henry Hill, clerk,..........	...............June, 1740,	...July 27, 1751.
Nathaniel Hill, clerk,......	 1751,	............1752.
Col. Timothy Stone (Guilford),	 1752,	....Sept. 9, 1765.
Nathaniel Hill, clerk,......	 1752,	............1765.
Nathaniel Hill (Guilford),...	..........September, 1765,	...Nov. 16, 1771.
Samuel Hill, clerk.		
Aaron Elliott (Killingworth),	...............June, 1772,	............1780.
Ebenezer Parmele Jr., clerk,.	...............June, 1772,	......Feb., 1780.
John Elliott, clerk,.........	.............Feb., 1780,	...Aug. 22, 1780.
Samuel Barker (Branford),...	 1780,	..December, 1781.
Elizur Barker, clerk, ...	 1780,	.....April, 1782.
John Elliott, clerk,.........	..............April, 1782.	
Col. Edward Russel (Branford),	 1782,	............1810.
John Elliott, clerk,.........	....	....August, 1796.
Henry Hill, clerk,..........	............August, 1796,	............1810.
Henry Hill (Guilford),......	 1810,	............1820.
William Todd, clerk,........	 1810,	......July, 1820.
Reuben Elliott (Guilford),...	 1820,	............1834.
George Griswold, clerk,....	.............July, 1820,	............1834.
Maj. Sam'l Fowler (Guilford),	 1834,	............1835.
Ralph D. Smith, clerk,.....	...............June, 1834,	......June, 1835.
Reuben Elliott (Guilford),....	 1835,	............1838.
George Griswold, clerk,.....	...............June, 1835,	......June, 1838.
Joel Tuttle (Guilford),......	 1838,	............1842.
Ralph D. Smith, clerk,......	...............June, 1838,	......June, 1842.
George Griswold (Guilford),..	 1842,	... Feb. 7, 1843.
Alvah B. Goldsmith, clerk,..	.... 1842.	
John R. Wilcox (Madison),..	(acting judge), Feb. 7, 1843,	...June 5, 1843.
Alvah B. Goldsmith, clerk.		
George Landon, ...	1843,	............1844.
Alvah B. Goldsmith, clerk,..	....	.....June, 1844.
Ralph D. Smith,............	..............June, 1844,	............1846.
E. R. Landon, clerk.		
George Landon,............	 1846,	............1847.
Alvah B. Goldsmith, clerk.		
Ralph D. Smith,............	1847,	............1850.
Edward R. Landon, clerk.		
George Landon,............	1850,	............1854.
Alvah B. Goldsmith, clerk.		
Edward R. Landon,........	1854	
Sylvanus Clark, clerk.		

HISTORY OF GUILFORD.

The following is believed to be a correct List of the Magistrates and Justices of Guilford, although they may not be arranged exactly in the order of appointment, beginning 1644 or 1645.

Name	Appointed	Notes	Died	Age
Samuel Disborough,	1644,	Returned to England, 1651.		
Guv. William Leete,	"	Removed to Hartford, 1676,	died April, 1683.	
George Hubbard,	October 5, 1670,		Jan. 1683.	
Andrew Leete,	Commissioner, June, 1676,	Assistant, April, 1678,	Oct. 31, 1702,	aged 59.
Josiah Rossiter,	Justice 1698.	" April, 1701,	Jan. 31, 1716,	" 70.
Abraham Fowler,	" 1705,	1712,	Dec. 5, 1720,	" 68.
James Hooker,	" 1712,		March 12, 1742,	" 77.
Col. Samuel Hill,	" 1734,		May 28, 1752,	" 75.
Capt. Andrew Ward,	" 1716,		Aug. 7, 1756,	" 86.
Col Timothy Stone,	" 1748,		Sept. 9, 1765,	" 70.
Nathaniel Hill,	June, 1762,		Nov. 16, 1771,	" 55.
Samuel Robinson,	" 1753,		March 6, 1776,	" 80.
Dr. Nathaniel Ruggles,	" 1753,		Oct. 16, 1794,	" 82.
Joseph Pynchon,	" 1752,		Nov. 23, 1794.	
Samuel Brown,	" 1772,		June 4, 1814,	" 89.
Gen. Andrew Ward,	" 1778,		Jan. 10, 1798,	" 70.
Deacon John Burgis,	" 1774.		Feb. 26, 1799,	" 85.
William Starr,	" 1781,		Nov. 30, 1816,	" 76.
Deacon Thos. Burgis, Jun.,	" 1780,		June 14, 1799,	" 62.
Henry Hill,	" 1792,		Dec. 21, 1827,	" 77.
Deacon Abram Chittenden,	" 1794.		March 4, 1848.	
Nathaniel Rossiter, Esq.,	" 1800,		1835,	
Nathaniel Griffing,	" 1802,			
Col. Samuel Robinson,	" 1800,		Sept. 17, 1845,	" 79.
Maj. Samuel Fowler,	" 1807,		Nov. 17, 1839.	" 77.
Joseph Elliott,	" 1815,			" 1836.
William Todd, Esq.,	" 1818,		Jan. 11, 1829,	" 62.
Timothy Stone, Esq.,	" 1819,		Oct. 8, 1831,	" 49.
Reuben Elliott,	" 1818,		Dec. 11, 1846,	" 78.
			Oct. 18, 1844,	" 76.

List of the Magistrates and Justices of Guilford (continued).

Abraham Coan,	Justice 1818,	died Feb. 14, 1863,	aged 89.
William Spencer,	" 1819,	" July 31, 1857,	" 83.
George Griswold,	" 1819,	" Feb. 7, 1843,	" 62.
George Landon,	" 1821,	" Oct. 8, 1866,	" 79.
Samuel Elliott,	" 1830,	" Sept. 12, 1843,	" 79.
Deacon Comfort Starr,	" 1832,	" Dec. 1, 1862.	" 82.
George Hart,	" 1833,	" May 25, 1848,	" 54.
Samuel Scranton,	" 1833,	" March 28, 1860,	" 66.
Col. George A. Foote,	" 1834.		
Ralph D. Smith, Esq.,	" 1834,	" Sept. 11, 1874.	" 70.
Doctor Anson Foote,	" 1835,	" May 2, 1841,	" 57.
Henry Loper,	" 1835,	" Feb. 21, 1873,	" 82.
Samuel C. Spencer,	" 1835.		
Joel Tuttle,	" 1838,	" May 1, 1855,	" 63.
S. C. Johnson,	" 1838,	" Nov. 11, 1872,	" 80.
Amos Seward,	" 1838.		
Dr. Joel Canfield,	" 1838,	" April 9, 1877,	" 76.
A. S. Fowler,	" 1838,	" Nov. 6, 1875,	" 87.
John Burgis,	" 1840,	" Nov. 6, 1864,	" 66.
Reuben Stone,	" 1841,	" April 8, 1863,	" 73.
Walter Osborn,	" 1842.		
Alvah B. Goldsmith,	" 1842,	" June 12, 1863,	" 70.
Elisha Hutchinson,	" 1842,	" August 20, 1862.	
Horace Norton,	" 1842.		
Daniel Chittenden,	" 1842.		
S. A. Barker,	" 1843.		
William Kelsey,	" 1843.		
J. H. Bartlett,	" 1843,	" July 10, 1864,	" 68.
Samuel Robinson,	" 1844,	" April 7, 1866,	" 71.
Henry W. Chittenden,	" 1844,	" Oct. 30, 1867,	" 72.
Edward R. Landon, Esq.,	" 1844.		

List of the Magistrates and Justices of Guilford (continued).

Albert B. Wildman,	Justice 1844.	
Noah Fowler,	" 1845,	died June 10, 1850, aged 55.
William Hale,	" 1845,	" March 19, 1870, " 63.
John Bartlett, 2nd,	" 1846,	" Sept. 12, 1864, " 66.
Sam. E. Stone,	" 1846,	" March 5, 1876, " 63.
Franklin C. Phelps,	" 1846,	" Dec. 29, 1873, " 70.
Rufus N. Leete,	" 1846.	
W. C. Dudley,	" 1846.	
Eber S. Hotchkiss,	" 1846.	
Wm. W. Baldwin,	" 1848.	
Albert A. Leete,	" 1848.	
Henry R. Spencer,	" 1848.	
Russell Frisbie,	" 1849,	" March 28, 1866, " 84.
James A. Norton,	" 1849,	" Jan. 31, 1875, " 60.
Leverett Griswold,	" 1850.	
John Hale,	" 1850,	" April 2, 1872, " 61.
Robert Hunt,	" 1850,	" April 4, 1870, " 74.
Russell Benton,	" 1851,	" April 2, 1869, " 67.
Horace Norton,	" 1851.	
Jasper Monroe,	" 1852,	" August 5, 1869, " 76.
Alferd G. Hull,	" 1854.	
Erastus L. Ripley,	" 1854.	
William T. Wilcox,	" 1856.	
Amos N. Benton,	" 1858.	
Leverett C. Stone,	" 1858.	
William Tyler,	" 1858.	
John A. Stanton,	" 1862.	
Edward L. Leete,	" 1864.	
Alvah Kelsey,	" 1864.	
Lewis Griswold,	" 1864.	
T. D. Hotchkiss,	" 1866.	

HISTORY OF GUILFORD.

List of the Magistrates and Justices of Guilford (continued).

H. B. Griswold,	Justice 1866.	
Richard E. Hart,	" 1866.	
Almon O. Wilcox,	" 1866,	died Sept. 16, 1874, aged 66.
Amos Griswold, Jr.,	" 1866.	
Richard Bartlett,	" 1868.	
U. N. Parmalee,	" 1868.	
J. A. Dowd,	" 1868.	
Henry Fowler,	" 1870,	" Oct. 1, 1875, " 56.
Chas. W. Miller,	" 1870.	
William E. Weld,	" 1870.	
Alvord A. Stone,	" 1872.	
H. Lynde Harrison, Esq.,	" 1876.	
Henry E. Norton,	" 1877.	
John Beattie,	" 1877.	
Edward M. Lee,	" 1877.	
Geo. C. Griswold,	" 1877.	

HISTORY OF GUILFORD.   149

Justices in North Guilford Parish.

Samuel Hopson,	1750,	removed to Wallingford, 1760.	died February 28, 1761, aged 77.
William Dudley,	1740,		" April 9, 1771, aged 80.
Deacon Theophilus Rossiter,	1749,		" May 20, 1781, aged 70.
Oliver Dudley,	1772,		" April 12, 1789, aged 74.
Deacon Simeon Chittenden,	1769,		" " 30, 1814, aged 70.
Gen'l Augustus Collins,	1800,		" Nov. 3, 1832, aged 77.
Nathan Chidsey,	1814,	removed to Worthington, O.,	" 1834.
Thomas R. Bray,	1818,		
David S. Fowler,	1820,		" Sept., 1849, aged 80.
Jared Scranton,	1820,		" March 15, 1853, aged 82.
Henry Elliot,	1829,		" Dec. 20, 1864, aged 82.
Col. Abel Rossiter,	1830,		" July 24, 1845, aged 75.
Richard Fowler,	1832,		" May 14, 1863, age 70.
Samuel W. Dudley,	1836,		
Wyllys Elliott,	1836,		" Feb. 25, 18..., aged 76.
Alfred Norton,	1836,		" March 27, 1850, aged 59.
Victor Fowler,	1839,		" Aug. 29, 1868, aged 69.
Wm. M. Dudley,	1840,		
Ammi Fowler,	1841,		" Nov. 20, 1866, aged 76.
Benjamin Rossiter,	1845,		
John R. Rossiter,	1847,		
Augustus E. Bartlett,	"		
Whitney Elliot,	1848,		" Jan. 20, 1875, aged 72.
Nathaniel Bartlett,	"		
Timothy Rossiter,	1849,		" Dec. 8, 1865, aged 57.
Edmund M. Field,	"		" Aug. 26, 1869, aged 67.
Stephen Fowler,	1850,		
John G. Johnson,	1852,		" Nov. 17, 1869, aged 69.
Grove Hubbard,	"		
Sam. F. Hubbard,	"		

Justices in North Guilford Parish (continued).

Martin C. Bishop,	1858.	
George Hill, 2d,	1860.	
Stephen R. Bartlett,	1864,	died Nov. 27, 1869, aged 59.
Louis Fowler,	1868.	
Joseph A. Scranton,	"	
Edwin W. Bartlett,	"	" April 6, 1876, aged 50.
Jerome Coan,	1877.	

At the first settlement of the town no form of government seems to have been adopted, probably because they were in doubt for a year or two whether they should remain or not. It is said in the "Review of the more fixed agreements, laws and orders made from time to time from the settlement up to 1649," that the church was gathered June 19 (O. S.) 1643, and that the feoffees in trust of the plantation resigned up their right, into the hands of the church, of all the lands purchased from the natives; and those four men of their number also, which had been chosen to the exercise of civil power, did also express that their trust and power for that purpose was terminated and ended. Whereof notice being taken at the public meeting, it was propounded, agreed and concluded that whereas, in times past there being no church gathered, the power was put in the hands of four men, that now the affairs being settled the town and church should be organized, etc.

The power was entrusted to the hands of the four to whom reference has been made, at a public meeting (not a general court) Feb. 2 (Feb. 12, new style) 1641–2, in the form following, viz: "It is agreed that the civil power for administration of justice and preservation of peace shall remain in the hands of *Robt. Kitchel, William Chittenden, John Bishop,* and *William Leete* formerly chosen for that work, until some may be chosen out of the church that shall be gathered here. In the hands of these men the power seems to have been placed without limitation until June, 1643. They may hence be considered magistrates and committee from September, 1639, to June 29, 1643.

At the meeting of the planters, held June 29, 1643 (N. S.), the church was accordingly gathered, and the constitution adopted, by which the choice of officers was regulated as also the first division of land, and probably the first town magistrates and other officers were chosen. *Mr. Samuel Disborough* and

Mr. William Leete were chosen to meet the court at New Haven and the *Combination* of the jurisdiction of the New Haven colony was planned. Accordingly, we find on the 6th of July (16th N. S.), 1643, or about seventeen days after that, Mr. Disborough and Mr. Leete were admitted members of the court at New Haven for Menunkatuck, and "received the charge of freemen of this court," and at the same meeting " it was ordered that £5 from Stamford, £5 from [Menunkatuck] Guilford and £2 from Yennicock [Southold, L. I.], shall be raised and paid into the treasury of New Haven toward the charges about the *Combination*." And at the same meeting

" *Menunkatuck* was named *Guilford*."[1]

At the organization of the *Combination* in the month of October, 1643, Stamford was the first annexed to New Haven in terms following, viz : that the settlers pay the New Haven plantation the expenses of purchase from the Indians and other charges expended amounting to £33 " and join in *one jurisdiction* with New Haven upon certain considerations, propounded at the first settlement of the plantation but since perfected in a fundamental agreement settled for this jurisdiction *October*, 1643, as by that record more particularly may appear ; and upon their desire their plantation is called *Stamford*."

And immediately after Guilford is admitted as follows, viz : " Menunkatuck, formerly purchased and planted by Mr. Whitfield and his company, was also admitted into this jurisdiction upon the same fundamental agreement as Stamford ; and upon their desire that plantation is called *Guilford*."

" Milford the neighboring plantation to the westward was also admitted into this jurisdiction upon the same fundamental agreement in *October*, 1643."

---

[1] *New Haven Town and Colony Records*, vol. 1, page 47.

HISTORY OF GUILFORD. 153

"Totoket [also] a place fit for a small plantation, between New Haven and Guilford, and purchased from the Indians, was granted to Mr. Swayne and some others of Wethersfield, they repaying the charges which are between £12 and £13 and joining in *one jurisdiction* with New Haven and the forenamed plantations upon the same fundamental agreement in *October*, 1643, which they duly considering readily accepted."

This year for the first time the general court at New Haven is distinctly recorded and distinguished by the title of the governor, deputy governor, magistrates and deputies.

The *fundamental agreement*, spoken of above, is given at length in Appendix A to this History, and was adopted at the first organization of the government for the whole jurisdiction, October 27, 1643, at which meeting, *William Leete* and *Samuel Disborough* were the deputies from Guilford, and *Samuel Disborough* was recognized as the *magistrate* for Guilford, which office he held 1651. The deputies associated with him for that particular court are not mentioned until 1645 when they were

	William Leete.
	John Mipham.
	John Hodely.
1646	Willliam Chittenden.
	William Leete.
	Thomas Jordan.
1649	William Chittenden.
	William Leete.
	Robert Kitchell.
1650	William Chittenden.
	Robert Kitchell.
	Thomas Jordan.
	George Hubbard.

William Leete was chief magistrat from 1651 until the union

20

with Connecticut. In 1661, John Fowler was chosen in place of William Chittenden deceased and George Bartlett in the room of Thomas Jordan, continuing until the union with Connecticut colony in 1664, and two years later until the organization of the judiciary in 1666, when the county court for New Haven county was organized and commenced its first session at New Haven, June 13 (O. S.), 1666, with the following magistrates;

Mr. William Leete, Chief Magistrate.

Mr. William Jones,
Mr. Benj. Fenn,   } Assistants.
Mr. Jasper Crane,

Alex. Bryan,   } Commissioners.
James Bishop,

Since then the magistrates of the town have been the assistants and the justices of the peace.

The Deputies for the several years were as follows:

1643.	First and Second Sessions,	Samuel Disborough.
		William Leete.
1644.	" " "	William Leete.
		Jacob Sheafe.
1645.	" " "	William Leete.
		John Mipham.
1646.	First Session, May,	William Leete.
		John Mipham.
1646.	Second Session, Oct.,	William Leete.
		William Chittenden.
1647.	First and Second Sessions,	William Leete.
		William Chittenden.
1648.	" " "	William Leete.
		William Chittenden.
1649.	" " "	William Leete.
		William Chittenden.
1650.	" " "	Robert Kitchell.
		William Chittenden.
1651.	" " "	William Chittenden.
		Thomas Jordan.
1652.	" " "	Thomas Jordan.
		George Hubbard.
1653.	" " "	William Chittenden.
		Thomas Jordan.
1654.	Several extra sessions,	William Chittenden.
		Thomas Jordan.
1655.	Whole year,	William Chittenden.
		George Hubbard.
1656.	" "	William Chittenden.
		Robert Kitchell.

1657.	Whole year.		William Chittenden.
			George Hubbard.
1658.	" "		William Chittenden.
			George Hubbard.
1659.	" "		William Chittenden.
			George Hubbard.
1660.	" "		William Chittenden.
			George Hubbard.
1661.	First and second sessions,		Robert Kitchell.
			John Fowler.
1662.	" " "		Robert Kitchell.
			George Hubbard.
1663.	Whole year.		Robert Kitchell.
			George Bartlett.
1664.	Extra session, Jan.,		John Fowler.
			John Scranton.
1664.	Summer session,		John Fowler.
			George Bartlett.

[After which time the colonies of Connecticut and New Haven being united, the delegates were chosen twice a year to Hartford until May, 1701, when it was ordered, "at a court of election holden at Hartford," that the May terms should thereafter be held in Hartford and the October terms in New Haven. In 1818, however, when the present constitution of the state was adopted, provision was made for but one stated session of the general assembly, to be holden in each year, alternately at Hartford and New Haven, on the first Wednesday of May, and at such other times as the general assembly shall judge necessary; the first session to be holden at Hartford; but the person administering the office of governor, may, on special emergencies, convene the general assembly at either of said places, at any other time. And in case of danger from the prevalence of contagious diseases, in either of said places, or other circumstances, the person administering the office of governor may, by proclamation, convene said assembly at any other place in this state. "In accordance with the requirements of this amendment, delegates were after 1818 chosen annually.

In 1873, an amendment to the constitution was adopted by the inhabitants of the state, which provided for only one capital, and is as follows: "All annual and special sessions of the general assembly shall, on and after the first Wednesday of May, 1875, be held at Hartford; but the person administering the office of governor may, in case of special emergency convene said assembly at any other place in this state."

In 1875, another amendment was adopted, requiring the stated session of the general assembly, next following the May session of 1876, to be held on the Wednesday after the first of January, 1877, and that thereafter, annually, stated sessions should be held in Hartford on the Wednesday after the first Monday in January.]

Deputies to the General Court from Guilford.

1665.	First Session,	....	George Bartlett.[1]
			John Fowler.
"	Second "	....	George Hubbard.
			William Johnson.
1666.	First "	....	John Fowler.
			Thomas Cook.
"	Second "	....	George Hubbard.
			John Fowler.
1667.	First "	....	John Fowler.
			William Johnson.

[1] The name of *George* Bartlett does not appear on Col. Rec., and the name of John Fowler's associate is given as *John* Bartlett.

1667. Second Session,............ John Fowler.
　　　　　　　　　　　　　　　　William Johnson.
1668. First　"　　............ John Fowler.
　　　　　　　　　　　　　　　　William Johnson.
　"　　Second　"　　............ Dea. Jno. Fowler.
　　　　　　　　　　　　　　　　Sergt. Wm. Johnson.
1669. First　"　　............ Dea. Jno. Fowler.
　　　　　　　　　　　　　　　　Sergt. Wm. Johnson.
　"　　Second　"　　............ William Johnson.
　　　　　　　　　　　　　　　　John Scranton.
1670. First　"　　............ John Scranton.
　　　　　　　　　　　　　　　　John Graves.
　"　　Second　"　　............ Dea. Jno. Fowler.
　　　　　　　　　　　　　　　　William Johnson.
1671. First　"　　............ Ens. John Graves.
　　　　　　　　　　　　　　　　William Johnson.
　"　　Second　"　　............ Dea. John Fowler.
　　　　　　　　　　　　　　　　Ens. John Graves.
1672. First　"　　............ Dea. John Fowler.
　　　　　　　　　　　　　　　　Ens. John Graves.
　"　　Second　"　　............ Dea. John Fowler.
　　　　　　　　　　　　　　　　Ens. John Graves.
1673. First　"　　............ Dea. John Fowler.
　　　　　　　　　　　　　　　　Ens. John Graves.
　"　　Second　"　　............ Dea. John Fowler.
　　　　　　　　　　　　　　　　Lieut. Wm. Seward.
1674. First　"　　............ Dea. Wm. Johnson.
　　　　　　　　　　　　　　　　Ens. John Graves.
　"　　Second　"　　............ Lieut. Wm. Seward.
　　　　　　　　　　　　　　　　Dea. John Fowler.
1675. First　"　　............ Ens. John Graves.
　　　　　　　　　　　　　　　　Dea. John Fowler.

1675. Special Session,............... Dea. John Fowler.
                                      Ens. John Graves.
  "   Second   "   .... Mr. Andrew Leete.
                                      Dea. John Fowler.
1676. First   "   .... Mr. Andrew Leete.
                                      William Johnson.
  "   Second   "   .... Mr. Andrew Leete.
                                      Ens. John Graves.
1677. First   "   .... Mr. Andrew Leete.
                                      Mr. William Leete.
  "   Second   "   .... Mr. Andrew Leete.
                                      Ens. John Graves.
1678. First   "   .... Mr. Andrew Leete.
                                      Mr. William Leete.[1]
  "   Second   "   .... Ens. John Graves.
                                      Dea. William Johnson.
1679. First   "   .... Dea. William Johnson.
                                      Ens. John Graves.
  "   Second   "   .... Mr. William Leete.
                                      Dea. William Johnson.
1680. First   "   .... Mr. William Leete.
                                      Dea. William Johnson.
  "   Second   "   .... Mr. William Leete.
                                      Dea. William Johnson.
1681. First   "   .... Mr. William Leete.
                                      Ens. John Graves.
  "   Second   "   .... Mr. William Leete.
                                      Ens. John Graves.
1682. First   "   .... Dea. William Johnson.
                                      Ens. John Graves.

---

[1] Mr. Andrew Leete having also been chosen Assistant, Mr. William Leete was the sole Representative.

1682.	Second Session, ...	Mr. William Leete.
		Ens. John Graves.
1683.	First "	Lieut. William Seward.
		Mr. Josiah Rossiter.
"	Second "	Mr. William Leete.
		Lieut. William Seward.
1684.	First "	Mr. Josiah Rossiter.
		Ens. John Graves.
"	Second "	Lieut. Wm. Seward.
		Ens. John Graves.
1685.	First "	Lieut. William Seward.
		Dea. William Johnson.
"	Second "	Lieut. William Seward.
		Dea. William Johnson.
1686.	First "	Dea. William Johnson.
		Dea. John Graves.
"	Second "	Dea. William Johnson.
		Dea. John Graves.
1687.	First "	Dea. William Johnson.
		Dea. John Graves.
"	Second "	Dea. William Johnson.
		Dea. John Graves.
1688.	First "	There was no meeting of the Assembly, in consequence of the usurpation of E. Andross, and no delegates chosen.
"	Second "	
1689.	First, and Special Session,	Dea. William Johnson.
		Dea. John Graves.
"	Second Session, ...	Mr. Josiah Rossiter.
		Dea. William Johnson.
1690.	First and Special Session,...	Mr. Josiah Rossiter.
		Dea. William Johnson.

1690.	Second	Session,	....	Mr. Josiah Rossiter.
				Capt. John Graves.
1791.	First	"	....	Dea. William Johnson.
				Capt. John Graves.
"	Second	"	....	Mr. William Johnson.
				Capt. John Graves.
1692.	First	"	....	Capt. John Graves.
				Lieut. Stephen Bradley.
"	Second	"	....	Capt. John Graves.
				Lieut. Stephen Bradley.
1693.	First	"	....	Capt. John Graves.
				Lieut. Stephen Bradley.
"	Second	"	....	Capt. John Graves.
				Lieut. Stephen Bradley.
1694.	First	"	....	Mr. Josiah Rossiter.
				Lieut. Stephen Bradley.
"	Second	"	....	Mr. Josiah Rossiter.
				Dea. William Johnson.
1695.	First	"	....	Mr. Josiah Rossiter.
				Mr. Thomas Meacock.
"	Second	"	....	Mr. Josiah Rossiter.
				Mr. Thomas Meacock.
1696.	First	"	....	Mr. Josiah Rossiter.
				Mr. John Eliot.
"	Second	"	....	Mr. Josiah Rossiter.
				Lieut. Stephen Bradley.
1697.	First	"	....	Mr. Josiah Rossiter.
				Mr. John Elliot.
"	Second	"	....	Mr. Josiah Rossiter.
				Mr. Abraham Fowler.
1698.	First	"	....	Mr. Josiah Rossiter.
				Ensign Abr. Fowler.

1698.	Second Session,		....	Capt. Stephen Bradley.
				Lieut. Abr. Fowler.
1699.	First	"	....	Mr. Josiah Rossiter.
				Lieut. Abr. Fowler.
"	Second	"	....	Mr. Josiah Rossiter.
				Lieut. Abr. Fowler.
1700.	First	"	....	Mr. Josiah Rossiter.
				Capt. Stephen Bradley.
"	Second	"	....	Mr. Josiah Rossiter.
				Capt. Stephen Bradley.
1701.	First	"	....	Capt. Stephen Bradley.
				Lieut. Abr. Fowler.
"	Second	"	....	Capt. Stephen Bradley.
				Lieut. Abr. Fowler.
1702.	First	"	....	Lieut. Abr. Fowler.
				Ens. Nathaniel Stone.
"	Second	"	....	Lieut. Abr. Fowler.
				Mr. James Hooker.
1703.	First	"	....	Capt. Abr. Fowler.
				Mr. James Hooker.
"	Second	"	....	Capt. Abr. Fowler.
				Mr. James Hooker.
1704.	First	"	....	Mr. Joseph Dudley.
				Lieut. John Seward.
"	Second	"	....	Capt. Abr. Fowler.
				Mr. Joseph Dudley.
1705.	First	"	....	Lieut. John Seward.
				Mr. James Hooker.
"	Second	"	....	Capt. Abr. Fowler.
				Sergt. Joseph Dudley.
1706.	First	"	....	Capt. Abr. Fowler.
				Mr. James Hooker.

1706. Second Session, ... Capt. Abr. Fowler.
                                     Mr. James Hooker.
1707. First   "   .... Capt. Abr. Fowler.
                                     Mr. James Hooker.
 "   Second "   .... Capt. Abr. Fowler.
                                     Mr. James Hooker.
1708. First   "   .... Capt. Abr. Fowler.
                                     Mr. James Hooker.
 "   Second "   .... Capt. John Seward.
                                     Mr. James Hooker.
1709. First   "   .... Mr. James Hooker.
                                     Mr. John Seward.
 "   Second "   .... Capt. Abr. Fowler.
                                     Mr. John Collins, 2d.
1710. First   "   .... Capt. Abr. Fowler.
                                     Mr. James Hooker.
 "   Second "   .... Capt. Abr. Fowler.
                                     Mr. Andrew Ward.
1711. First   "   .... Mr. Andrew Ward.
                                     Mr. John Collins, 2d.
 "   Second "   .... Capt. Abraham Fowler.
                                     Mr. Caleb Leete.
1712. First   "   .... Capt. Abraham Fowler.[1]
                                     Mr. James Hooker.
 "   Second "   .... Mr. James Hooker.
                                     Capt. Andrew Ward.
1713. First   "   .... Mr. James Hooker.
                                     Mr. Caleb Leete.
 "   Second "   .... Mr. James Hooker.
                                     Capt. Andrew Ward.

---

[1] Capt. Abraham Fowler having been chosen Assistant, did not serve as Representative.

1714.	First Session,	....	Capt. Andrew Ward.	
			Mr. Caleb Leete.	
"	Second	"	....	Capt. Andrew Ward.
			Mr. Caleb Leete.	
1715.	First	"	....	Capt. Andrew Ward.
			Mr. Peter Talman.	
"	Second	"	....	Capt. Andrew Ward.
			Mr. Peter Talman.	
1716.	First	"	....	Capt. Andrew Ward.
			Lieut. Janna Meigs.	
"	Second	"	....	Mr. James Hooker.
			Mr. Caleb Leete.	
1717.	First	"	....	Mr. C. Leete.
			Capt. Janna Meigs.	
"	Second	"	....	Capt. Andrew Ward.
			Mr. Caleb Leete.	
1718.	First	"	....	Mr. Caleb Leete.
			Capt. Janna Meigs.	
"	Second	"	....	Mr. Caleb Leete.
			Mr. Benjamin Hand.	
1719.	First	"	....	Mr. Caleb Leete.
			Mr. Joseph Stone.	
"	Second	"	....	Mr. Benjamin Hand.
			Mr. Caleb Leete.	
1720.	First	"	....	Mr. Caleb Leete.
			Mr. Joseph Hand.	
"	Second	"	....	Mr. James Hooker.
			Mr. Benjamin Hand.	
1721.	First	"	....	Mr. Caleb Leete.
			Mr. Andrew Ward.	
"	Second	"	....	Mr. Caleb Leete.
			Mr. Joseph Stone.	

1722.	First Session,	....	Mr. Caleb Leete.
			Mr. Joseph Stone.
"	Second "	....	Mr. Caleb Leete.
			Mr. Joseph Stone.
1723.	First "	....	Mr. James Hooker.
			Mr. Caleb Leete.
"	Second "	....	Mr. Joseph Stone.
			Mr. Peletiah Leete.
1724.	First "	....	Mr. Caleb Leete.
			Mr. Joseph Stone.
"	Second "	....	Mr. Caleb Leete.
			Mr. Joseph Stone.
1725.	First "	....	Mr. Caleb Leete.
			Capt. Andrew Ward.
"	Second "	....	Mr. Caleb Leete.
			Capt. Andrew Ward.
1726.	First "	....	Capt. Janna Meigs.
			Capt. Andrew Ward.
"	Second "	....	Mr. Caleb Leete.
			Mr. Peletiah Leete.
1727.	First "	....	Mr. Caleb Leete.
			Mr. Peletiah Leete.
"	Second "	....	Mr. Caleb Leete.
			Mr. Peletiah Leete.
1728.	First "	....	Mr. Samuel Hill.
			Mr. Benj. Hand.
"	Second "	....	Mr. Samuel Hill.
			Mr. Benj. Hand.
1729.	First "	....	Mr. Samuel Hill.
			Mr. Benj. Hand.
"	Second "	....	Mr. Samuel Hill.
			Mr. Benjamin Hand.

166   HISTORY OF GUILFORD.

1730.	First Session, ...	Mr. Samuel Hill.
		Mr. Benj. Hand.
"	Second "	Mr. Samuel Hill.
		Mr. Benj. Strong.
1731.	First "	Mr. Samuel Hill.
		Mr. Benjamin Strong.
"	Second "	Mr. Samuel Hill.
		Mr. Benjamin Hand.
1732.	First "	Mr. Samuel Hill.
		Mr. Benj. Hand.
"	Second "	Mr. Sam. Hill.
		Mr. Benj. Hand.
1733.	First "	Mr. Sam. Hill.
		Mr. Thos. Hotchkins.
"	Second "	Mr. Sam. Hill.
		Mr. Thos. Hodgskins.
1734.	First "	Mr. Sam. Hill.
		Mr. Thos. Hotchkiss.
"	Second "	Mr. Sam. Hill.
		Mr. Thos. Hodgskins.
1735.	First "	Mr. Sam. Hill.
		Mr. Thos. Hotchkiss.
"	Second "	Mr. Sam. Hill.
		Mr. Peletiah Leete.
1736.	First "	Mr. Sam. Hill.
		Mr. Peletiah Leete.
"	Second "	Mr. Sam. Hill.
		Mr. Timothy Stone.
1737.	First "	Mr. Sam. Hill.
		Mr. Timothy Stone.
"	Second "	Mr. Sam. Hill.
		Mr. Timothy Stone.

HISTORY OF GUILFORD.

1738.	First Session,	....	Mr. Peletiah Leete.
			Mr. Sam. Hill.
"	Second "	....	Mr. Peletiah Leete.
			Mr. Sam. Robinson.
1739.	First "	....	Peletiah Leete.
			Samuel Hill.
"	Second "	....	Samuel Hill.
			Timothy Stone.
1740.	First "	....	Caleb Leete.
			Peletiah Leete.
"	Second "	....	Samuel Hill.
			Timothy Stone.
1741.	First "	....	Samuel Hill.
			Timothy Stone.
"	Second "	....	Samuel Hill.
			Timothy Stone.
1742.	First "	....	Samuel Hill.
			Benjamin Hand.
"	Second "	....	Samuel Hill.
			Benjamin Hand.
1743.	First "	....	Samuel Hill.
			Benjamin Hand.
"	Second "	....	Samuel Hill.
			Benjamin Hand.
1744.	First "	....	Samuel Hill.
			Benjamin Hand.
"	Second "	....	Timothy Stone.
			Sam. Robinson.
1745.	First "	....	Sam. Hill, *Speaker*.
			Timothy Stone.
"	Second "	....	Sam. Hill.
			Timothy Stone.

1746.	First Session,	....	....	Sam. Hill, *Speaker*.
				Timothy Stone.
"	Second	"	....	Samuel Hill.
				Timothy Stone.
1747.	First	"	....	Samuel Hill.
				Timothy Stone.
"	Second	"	....	Timothy Stone.
				Sam. Robinson.
1748.	First	"	....	Samuel Hill.
				Timothy Stone.
"	Second	"	....	Samuel Hill.
				Timothy Stone.
1749.	First	"	....	Timothy Stone.
				William Ward.
"	Second	"	....	Samuel Hill.
				Timothy Stone.
1750.	First	"	....	Andrew Ward.
				Sam. Robinson.
"	Second	"	....	Sam. Hill.
				Timothy Stone
1751.	First	"	....	Sam. Hill.
				Timothy Stone.
"	Second	"	....	Samuel Hill.
				Timothy Stone.
1752.	First	"	....	Sam. Hill.
				Timothy Stone.
"	Second	"	....	Timothy Stone.
				Sam. Robinson.
1753.	First	"	....	Timothy Stone.
				Sam'l Robinson.
"	Second	"	....	Timothy Stone.
				Sam'l Robinson.

1754.	First Session,	....		Andrew Ward.
				Nathaniel Ruggles.
"	Second	"	....	Timothy Stone.
				Andrew Ward.
1755.	First	"	....	Andrew Ward Jr.
				Sam'l Robinson.
"	Second	"	....	Timothy Stone.
				Sam'l Robinson.
1756.	First	"	....	Timothy Stone.
				Sam'l Robinson.
"	Second	"	....	Sam'l Robinson.
				Timothy Stone.
1757.	First	"	....	Sam'l Robinson.
				Timothy Stone.
"	Second	"	....	Sam'l Robinson.
				Timothy Stone.
1758.	First	"	....	Sam'l Robinson.
				Timothy Stone.
"	Second	"	....	Sam'l Robinson.
				Timothy Stone.
1759.	First	"	....	Andrew Ward.
				James Robinson.
"	Second	"	....	Timothy Stone.
				Edmund Ward.
1760.	First	"	....	Timothy Stone.
				Edmund Ward.
"	Second	"	....	Timothy Stone.
				Edmund Ward.
1761.	First	"	....	Timothy Stone.
				Nathaniel Hill.
"	Second	"	....	Timothy Stone.
				Nathaniel Hill.

170   HISTORY OF GUILFORD.

1762.	First Session,	....	Timothy Stone.
			Nathaniel Hill.
"	Second "	....	Timothy Stone.
			Sam'l Robinson.
1763.	First "	....	Sam'l Robinson.
			Nathaniel Hill.
"	Second "	....	Timothy Stone.
			Nathaniel Hill.
1764.	First "	....	Timothy Stone.
			Nathaniel Hill.
"	Second "	....	Timothy Stone.
			Nathaniel Hill.
1765.	First "	....	Timothy Stone.
			Nathaniel Hill.
"	Second "	....	Nathaniel Hill.
			Nathaniel Ruggles.
1766.	First "	....	Nathaniel Hill.
			Nathaniel Ruggles.
"	Second "	....	Nathaniel Hill.
			Nathaniel Ruggles.
1767.	First "	....	Nathaniel Hill.
			Josiah Meigs.
"	Second "	....	Nathaniel Hill.
			John Elliott.
1768.	First "	....	Nathaniel Hill.
			Joseph Pynchon.
"	Second "	....	Nathaniel Hill.
			John Burgis.
1769.	First "	....	Nathaniel Hill.
			Joseph Pynchon.
"	Second "	....	Nathaniel Hill.
			John Burgis.

1770.	First Session,	....	John Elliott.	
			John Burgis.	
"	Second	"	....	Nathaniel Hill.
			John Elliott.	
1771.	First	"	....	Nathaniel Burgis.
			Andrew Ward.	
"	Second	"	....	Jno. Burgis.
			Nathaniel Hill.	
1772.	First	"	....	Andrew Ward.
			John Burgis.	
"	Second	"	....	S. Brown.
			Andrew Ward.	
1773.	First	"	....	S. Brown.
			Andrew Ward.	
"	Second	"	....	S. Brown.
			Andrew Ward.	
1774.	First	"	....	John Burgis.
			J. Redfield.	
"	Second	"	....	John Burgis.
			Andrew Ward.	
1775.	First	"	....	John Burgis.
			Andrew Ward.	
"	Second	"	....	John Burgis.
			S. Brown.	
1776.	First	"	....	Andrew Ward.
			John Burgis.	
"	Second	"	....	N. Stone.
			Nathaniel Ruggles.	
1777.	First	"	....	N. Stone.
			Nathaniel Ruggles.	
"	Second	"	....	Andrew Ward.
			John Burgis.	

1778.	First Session,		....	Andrew Ward.
				Samuel Robinson.
"	Second	"	....	Andrew Ward.
				Samuel Robinson.
1779.	First	"	....	Samuel Lee Jr.
				N. Stone.
"	Second	"	....	John Burgis.
				N. Stone.
1780.	First	"	....	John Burgis.
				Andrew Ward.
"	Second	"	....	John Burgis.
				Andrew Ward.
1781.	First	"	....	John Burgis.
				Andrew Ward.
"	Second	"	....	
				Andrew Ward.
1782.	First	"	....	John Burgis.
				Andrew Ward.
"	Second	"	....	John Burgis.
				Andrew Ward.
1783.	First	"	....	John Burgis.
				Augustus Collins.
"	Second	"	....	Andrew Ward.
				John Burgis.
1784.	First	"	....	Augustus Collins.
				Samuel Lee.
"	Second	"	....	John Burgis.
				Andrew Ward.
1785.	First	"	....	Andrew Ward.
				Samuel Lee.
"	Second	"	....	John Burgis.
				Samuel Lee.

1786. First Session,............ John Burgis.
                                  Andrew Ward.
  "   Second   "   .... John Burgis.
                                  Samuel Lee.
1787. First   "   .... John Elliott.
                                  Andrew Ward.
  "   Second "   .... John Burgis.
                                  John Elliott.
1788. First   "   .... John Burgis.
                                  Andrew Ward.
  "   Second "   .... John Burgis.
                                  Andrew Ward.
1789. First   "   .... John Elliott.
                                  Andrew Ward.
  "   Second "   .... Andrew Ward.
                                  John Elliott.
1790. First   "   .... Andrew Ward.
                                  John Elliott.
  "   Second "   .... Andrew Ward.
                                  John Elliott.
1791. First   "   .... Andrew Ward.
                                  John Elliott.
  "   Second "   .... Andrew Ward.
                                  John Elliott.
1792. First   "   .... Augustus Collins.
                                  Samuel Lee.
  "   Second "   .... Andrew Ward.
                                  John Elliott.
1793. First   "   .... Augustus Collins.
                                  Andrew Ward.
  "   Second "   .... Andrew Ward.
                                  John Elliott.

1794.	First Session,	....	Andrew Ward.	
			William Brown.	
"	Second "	....	Andrew Ward.	
			William Brown.	
1795.	First "	....	Andrew Ward.	
			N. Rossiter.	
"	Second "	....	Augustus Collins.	
			William Brown.	
1796.	First "	....	Andrew Ward.	
			John Elliott.	
"	Second "	....	Andrew Ward.	
			William Brown.	
1797.	First "	....	Andrew Ward.	
			Augustus Collins.	
"	Second "	....	N. Rossiter.	
			Jonathan Todd.	
1798.	First "	....	N. Rossiter.	
			Andrew Ward.	
"	Second "	....	N. Chidsey.	
			Rufus Norton.	
1799.	First "	....	Augustus Collins.	
			Samuel Lee.	
"	Second "	....	Augustus Collins.	
			Samuel Lee.	
1800.	First "	....	Augustus Collins.	
			Samuel Robinson.	
"	Second "	....	Augustus Collins.	
			Samuel Lee.	
1801.	First "	....	Augustus Collins.	
			N. Rossiter.	
"	Second "	....	N. Rossiter.	
			Augustus Collins.	

1802.	First Session,	....	N	. Rossiter.
			Augustus Collins.	
"	Second "	....	Augustus Collins.	
			N	. Rossiter.
1803.	First "	....	Augustus Collins.	
			N.	Rossiter.
"	Second "	....	Augustus Collins.	
			N. Rossiter.	
1804.	First "	....	Augustus Collins.	
			N	. Rossiter, 2d *clerk*.
"	Second "	....	Augustus Collins.	
			N	. Rossiter, 1st *clerk*.
1805.	First "	....	Augustus Collins.	
			Nathaniel Griffing.	
"	Second "	....	Augustus Collins.	
			Nathaniel Griffing.	
1806.	First "	....	Augustus Collins.	
			Nathaniel Griffing.	
"	Second "	....	Augustus Collins.	
			Samuel Robinson.	
1807.	First "	....	Nathaniel Griffing.	
			Joseph Elliott.	
"	Second "	....	Augustus Collins.	
			Nathaniel Griffing.	
1808.	First "	....	Augustus Collins.	
			Nathaniel Griffing.	
"	Second "	....	Augustus Collins.	
			Joseph Elliott.	
1809.	First "	....	Augustus Collins.	
			Joseph Elliott.	
"	Second "	....	Augustus Collins.	
			Joseph Elliott.	

176 HISTORY OF GUILFORD.

1810.	First Session,	....	Augustus Collins.
			Nathaniel Griffing.
"	Second "	....	Augustus Collins.
			Joseph Elliott.
1811.	First "	....	Augustus Collins.
			Joseph Elliott.
"	Second "	....	Augustus Collins.
			Nathaniel Griffing.
1812.	First "	....	Augustus Collins.
			Nathaniel Griffing.
"	Second "	....	Augustus Collins.
			Nathaniel Griffing.
1813.	First "	....	Augustus Collins.
			Nathaniel Griffing.
"	Second "	....	Augustus Collins.
			Nathaniel Griffing.
1814.	First "	....	Nathaniel Griffing.
			Jonathan Todd.
"	Second "	....	Nathaniel Griffing.
			Jonathan Todd.
1815.	First "	....	Joseph Elliott.
			Samuel Robinson.
"	Second "	....	Joseph Elliott.
			Samuel Robinson.
1816.	First "	....	Joseph Elliott.
			Samuel Robinson.
"	Second "	....	Nathaniel Griffing.
			Samuel Robinson.
1817.	First "	....	Samuel Robinson.
			Benjamin Baldwin.
"	Second "	....	Nathaniel Griffing.
			Samuel Robinson.

1818. First   "   ....   Nathaniel Griffing.
                                      Samuel Robinson.
  "   Second "   ....   Nathaniel Griffing.
                                      William Todd.

Constitution of the State adopted in 1818.

NATHANIEL GRIFFING, } *Delegates to Cons. Convention.*
WILLIAM TODD.   }

After 1818 there was but one Session of the General Assembly each year.

1819.   ....   Nathaniel Griffing.
                                           William Todd.
1820.   ....   Nathaniel Griffing.
                                           William Todd.
1821.   ....   Nathaniel Griffing,
                                           William Todd.
1822.   ....   Nathaniel Griffing.
                                           William Todd.
1823.   ....   Nathaniel Griffing.
                                           William Todd.
1824.   ....   Nathaniel Griffing.
                                           William Todd.
1825.   ....   Nathaniel Griffing.
                                           Sam. Robinson.
1826.   ....   Nathaniel Griffing.
                                           Abel Rossiter.
1827.   ....   Nathaniel Griffing.
                                           William Todd.
1828.   ....   Nathaniel Griffing.
                                           Abel Rossiter.

1829.	....	Nathaniel Griffing.
		William Todd.
1830.	....	Nathaniel Griffing.
		George Landon.
1831.	....	Nathaniel Griffing.
		Abel Rossiter.
1832.	....	Nathaniel Griffing.
		Joel Tuttle.
1833.	....	Nathaniel Griffing.
		Abel Rossiter.
1834.	....	Joel Tuttle.
		Abraham S. Fowler.
1835.	....	Nathaniel Griffing.
		Abel Rossiter.
1836.	....	George Landon.
		Nathaniel Griffing.
1837.	....	George Landon.
		Henry Elliott.
1838.	....	Joel Tuttle.
		John H. Bartlett.
1839.	....	George A. Foote.
		Marcus B. Bartlett.
1840.	....	George A. Foote.
		Samuel C. Johnson.
1841.	....	George A. Foote.
		Samuel W. Dudley
1842.	....	No representatives chosen.
1843.	....	No representatives chosen.
1844.	....	No representatives chosen.
1845.	....	No representatives chosen.
1846.	....	Reuben Stone.
		William Hale.

1847.	Reuben Stone.
	William Hale.
1848.	Reuben Stone.
	Jasper Monroe.
1849.	Reuben Stone.
	Franklin C. Phelps.
1850.	Julius A. Dowd.
	Lewis Griswold.
1851.	Russel Benton.
	James A. Norton.
1852.	Henry Fowler, 2d.
	Lewis Griswold.
1853.	Samuel W. Dudley.
	Henry Fowler.
1854.	Edward L. Leete.
	Leverett Griswold.
1855.	George A. Foote.
	Amos Fowler.
1856.	John Hale.
	Calvin M. Leete.
1857.	George A. Foote.
	Sam. W. Dudley.
1858.	Albert B. Wildman.
	Benjamin Corbin.
1859.	Ralph D. Smith.
	T. Rossiter.
1860.	Sherman Graves.
	John Hale.
1861.	Richard Bartlett.
	Stephen R. Bartlett.
1862.	Calvin M. Leete.
	John Griswold.

1863.	....	John H. Bartlett.
		Saml. W. Dudley.
1864.	....	John H. Bartlett.
		Henry E. Norton.
1865.	....	Samuel W. Dudley.
		Edward L. Leete.
1866.	....	Henry Fowler of Rich.
		Gen. Edw. M. Lee.
1867.	....	Gen. Edw. M. Lee.
		David B. Rossiter.
1868.	....	Rev. E. Edwin Hall.
		Eli Parmelee.
1869.	....	Julius A. Dowd.
		Stephen R. Bartlett.
1870.	....	Edward R. Landon.
		Hethcote G. Landon.
1871.	....	Henry Benton 2d.
		John R. Rossiter.
1872.	....	Albert B. Wildman.
		Charles F. Leete.
1873.	....	Henry Fowler.
		John R. Rossiter.
1874.	....	H. Lynde Harrison.
		George B. Spencer.
1875.	....	H. Lynde Harrison.
		John R. Rossiter.
1876.	....	H. Lynde Harrison.
		John Wm. Norton.
1877.	....	H. L. Harrison, *Speaker*.
		David Bartlett.

At a court for the jurisdiction held April, 1644, after appointing the magistrates for the other plantations of the colony, "It was ordered that for the more comfortable carrying on the affairs at Guilford *'till they have a magistrate* there, the free burgesses may choose among themselves four deputies and form a court," which it seems they did, but the next year a magistrate seems to have presided.

The Treasurers for the Plantation until the Union with Connecticut.

Thomas Jordan,............................ 1643 to 1650.
Robert Kitchel,......... .... 1650 to 1652.
Thomas Jordan, reëlected,............ 1652 to 1654.
Robert Kitchel, reëlected,............. 1654 to 1656.
William Leete,............................ 1656 to 1657.
Abraham Cruttenden,................... 1657 to 1660.
Thomas Cook,................... .... 1660 to 1662.
Robert Kitchel, reëlected,............. 1662 to 1664.

The Marshals from the Settlement until the Union with Connecticut.

Thomas Jones,................... .... 1643 to 1652.
John Fowler,............................... 1652 to 1661.
John Scranton,............................ 1661 to 1662.
William Seward,.......................... 1662 to 1664.

Town Clerks Since the Settlement of the Town.

1. Governor William Leete,......... 1639 to 1662.
2. George Bartlett, ... 1662 to 1665.
3. Samuel Kitchell, ... 1665 to 1668.
4. William Johnson, ... 1668 to 1673.
5. John Graves,.................... 1673 to 1685.
6. Josiah Rossiter,[1].............. 1685 to 1706.
7. Joseph Dudley, ... 1706 to 1707.
8. Josiah Rossiter rechosen, ... 1707 to 1716.
9. John French,.................... 1716 to 1717.
10. Samuel Hill, ... 1717 to 1720.
11. Andrew Ward, ... 1720 to 1721.
12. Samuel Hill, rechosen, ... 1721 to 1752.
13. Nathaniel Hill, ... 1752 to 1771.
14. Ebenezer Parmelee, ... 1771 to 1776.
15. Thomas Burgis, Jr., ... 1776 to 1799.
16. John H. Fowler,................ 1799 to 1801.
17. Samuel Fowler, ... 1801 to 1835.
18. Reuben Stone,.................. 1835 to 1838.
19. Joel Tuttle,................... 1838 to 1843.
20. Henry W. Chittenden,........... 1843 to 1848.
21. Edward R. Landon,.............. 1848.

---

[1] Nov. 10, 1687; John Collins, Sen., was empowered to assist Mr. Rossiter in the work of recording during the time of the providential weakness of Mr. Rossiter.

APPENDIX.

A.

The Articles of Confederation for the Jurisdiction of New Haven.

At a General Court held at New Haven for the Jurisdiction, the 27th of October, 1643.

PRESENT.

Magistrates.	Deputies.
THEOPHILUS EATON, Governor.	GEORGE LAMBERTON, New Haven.
STEPHEN GOODYEAR, Deputy.	JOHN ASTWOOD, } Milford.
THOMAS GREGSON.	JOHN SHIRMAN,
WILLIAM FOWLER.	WILL. LEETE, } Guilford.
EDWARD TAPP.	SAM: DISBROUGH,
	RICH: GILDERSLEEVE, } Stamford.
	JOHN WHITMORE,

1. It was agreed and concluded, as a fundamental order not to be disputed or questioned hereafter, that none shall be admitted to be free burgesses in any of the plantations within this jurisdiction for the future, but such planters as are members of some or other of the approved churches in New England, nor shall any but such free burgesses have any vote in any election (the six present freemen at Milford enjoying the liberty with the cautions agreed).[1] Nor shall any power or trust in the ordering of any civil affairs be at any time put into the hands of any other than such church members, though as free planters all have right to their inheritance and to commerce, according to such grants, orders and laws as shall be made concerning the same.

2. All such free burgesses shall have power in each town or plantation within this

---

[1] Milford having previously admitted, as free burgesses, six planters who were *not* in church-fellowship, met some difficulty in securing admission into the confederation; but, having promised that these six should not hereafter be chosen as deputies or into any public trust, for the confederation, nor vote personally or by proxy at an election of magistrates, and that in the future no one would be made a free burgess but church members, it was received, October 23, 1643, as a member of the jurisdiction.

jurisdiction to choose fit and able men, from amongst themselves, being church members as before, to be the ordinary judges, to hear and determine all inferior causes, whether civil or criminal, provided that no civil cause to be tried in any of these plantation courts in value exceed twenty pounds, and that the punishment in such criminals, according to the mind of God, revealed in his word, touching such offences, do not exceed stocking and whipping, or if the fine be pecuniary, that it exceed not five pounds. In which court the magistrate or magistrates, if any be chosen by the free burgesses of the jurisdiction for that plantation, shall sit and assist with due respect to their place, and sentence shall pass according to the vote of the major part of each such court, only if the parties, or any of them, be not satisfied with the justice of such sentences or executions, appeals or complaints may be made from and against these courts to the court of magistrates for the whole jurisdiction.

3. All such free burgesses through the whole jurisdiction, shall have a vote in the election of all magistrates, whether governor, deputy governor, or other magistrates, with a vote for a treasurer, a secretary and a marshal, etc., for the jurisdiction. And for the ease of those free burgesses, especially in the more remote plantations, they may vote by proxy in these elections, though absent, their votes being sealed up in the presence of the free burgesses themselves, that their several liberties may be preserved, and their votes directed according to their own particular light, and these free burgesses may, at every election, choose so many magistrates for each plantation, as the weight of affairs may require, and as they shall find fit men for that trust. But it is provided and agreed, that no plantation shall at any election be left destitute of a magistrate if they desire one to be chosen out of those in church fellowship with them.

4. All the magistrates for the whole jurisdiction shall meet twice a year at New Haven, namely, the Monday immediately before the sitting of the two fixed general courts hereafter mentioned, to keep a court called the court of magistrates, for the trial of weighty and capital cases, whether civil or criminal, above those limited to the ordinary judges in the particular plantations, and to receive and try appeals brought unto them from the aforesaid plantation courts, and to call all the inhabitants, whether free burgesses, free planters or others, to account for the breach of any laws established, and for other misdemeanors, and to censure them according to the quality of the offence, in which meetings of magistrates, less than four shall not be accounted a court, nor shall they carry on any business as a court; but it is expected and required, that all the magistrates in this jurisdiction do constantly attend the public service at the times before mentioned, and if any of them be absent at one of the clock in the afternoon on Monday aforesaid, when the court shall sit, or if any of them depart the town without leave, while the court sits, he or they shall pay for any such default, twenty shillings fine, unless some providence of God occasion the same, which the court of magistrates shall judge of from time to time, and

all sentences in this court shall pass by the vote of the major part of magistrates therein, but from this court of magistrates, appeals and complaints may be made and brought to the general court as the last and highest for this jurisdiction; but in all appeals or complaints from, or to, what court soever, due costs and damages shall be paid by him or them that make appeal or complaint without just cause.

5. Besides the plantation courts and court of magistrates, there shall be a general court for the jurisdiction, which shall consist of the governor, deputy governor and all the magistrates within the jurisdiction, and two deputies for every plantation in the jurisdiction, which deputies shall from time to time be chosen against the approach of any such general court, by the aforesaid free burgesses, and sent with due certificate to assist in the same, all which, both governor and deputy governor, magistrates and deputies shall have their vote in the said court. This general court shall always sit at New Haven (unless upon weighty occasions the general court see cause for a time to sit elsewhere), and shall assemble twice every year, namely, the first Wednesday in April, and the last Wednesday in October, in the latter of which courts, the governor, the deputy governor and all the magistrates for the whole jurisdiction with a treasurer, a secretary and marshal, shall yearly be chosen by all the free burgesses before mentioned, besides which two fixed courts, the governor, or in his absence the deputy governor, shall have power to summon a general court at any other time, as the urgent and extraordinary occasions of the jurisdiction may require, and at all general courts, whether ordinary or extraordinary, the governor and deputy governor, and all the rest of the magistrates for the jurisdiction, with the deputies for the several plantations, shall sit together, till the affairs of the jurisdiction be dispatched or may safely be respited, and if any of the said magistrates or deputies shall either be absent at the first sitting of the said general court (unless some providence of God hinder, which the said court shall judge of), or depart, or absent themselves disorderly before the court be finished, he or they shall each of them pay twenty shillings fine, with due considerations of further aggravations if there shall be cause; which general court shall, with all care and diligence provide for the maintenance of the purity of religion, and shall suppress the contrary, according to their best light from the word of God, and all wholesome and sound advice, which shall be given by the elders and churches in the jurisdiction, so far as may concern their civil power to deal therein.

Secondly, they shall have power to make and repeal laws, and, while they are in force, to require execution of them in all the several plantations.

Thirdly, to impose an oath upon all the magistrates, for the faithful discharge of the trust committed to them, according to their best abilities, and to call them to account for the breach of any laws established, or for other misdemeanors, and to censure them, as the quality of the offence shall require.

Fourthly, to impose an oath of fidelity and due subjection to the laws upon all the free burgesses, free planters, and other inhabitants within the whole jurisdiction.

Fifthly, to settle and levy rates and contributions upon all the several plantations, for the public service of the jurisdiction.

Sixthly, to hear and determine all causes, whether civil or criminal, which by appeal or complaint shall be orderly brought unto them from any of the other courts, or from any of the other plantations. In all which, with whatsoever else shall fall within their cognizance or judicature, they shall proceed according to the scriptures, which is the rule of all righteous laws and sentences, and nothing shall pass as an act of the general court but by the consent of the major part of magistrates, and the greater part of deputies. — *New Haven Colonial Records*, 1638–1649, pp. 112–116.

B.

Admission of Guilford into the Jurisdiction of Connecticut.

At the general assembly or court of election held at Hartford, October 9, 1662.

Several inhabitants of Guilford tendering themselves, their persons and estates, under the government and protection of this colony. This court doth declare that they do accept and own them as members of this colony, and shall be ready to afford what protection is necessary. And this court doth advise the said persons to carry peaceably and religiously in their places towards the rest of the inhabitants, that yet have not submitted in like manner. And also to pay their just dues unto the minister of their town; and also all public charges due to this day.— *Col. Rec. of Connecticut*, 1636–1665, page 387.

C.

Freemen of Guilford in 1669.

September 24, '69. A list of the freemen of Guilford, drawn up by the constable and townsmen according to the order of the court.

Mr. Leete,	Georg Hiland,
George Huburd,	Daniell Huburd,
Mr. Rositar,	John Bishup,
John Fowlar,	Thomas Chitendon,
William Johnson,	Thomas Mecoke,
John Scranton,	John Parmarly,
Thomas Cooke, Senior,	Abraham Cruttenden Jun.,
John Steuens,	Daniell Benton,
Edward Benton,	Thomas Cruttenden,
Abraham Crutenden Senior,	Daniell Euatts,
John Graue,	John Chittenden,

APPENDIX.

John Hobson,	Nathaniell Chittenden,
William Ston,	Richard Bristo,
John Ston,	Joseph Dudly,
William Seword,	Thomas Cooke Jun.,
Richard Gutrich,	Henery Crean,
John Johnson,	John Hill,
John Shedar,	John Nortun.

John Hobson, ⎫
John Graue,   ⎬ Townsmen.
Thomas Cooke, ⎭

John Stone, Constable.

Col. Rec. of Connecticut, 1665–1667, page 525.

D.

Permission to purchase Falcon Island.

At a General Court held at Hartford, October 18, 1677, the following permission was granted:

This court grants Mr. Andrew Leet liberty to purchase Falcon Island and Goose Island for himself and his heirs, which said islands lie before or near Guilford.— *Col. Rec. of Connecticut*, 1665–1677, page 325.

E.

Efforts made to create Guilford County.

A bill for making a new county to be called Guilford county, and to consist of Saybrook, Killingworth, Guilford, Durham and Branford, was passed in the lower house, October, 1718. *Journal L. H. Oct.* 22, 1718. The project was revived in October, 1728, and in May, 1736, when a bill to erect a new county, composed of the foregoing towns with Haddam, having been largely debated, passed the lower house. *Journals*, 1728, 1736, *Civil Officers etc.*, II, 331. Again, in May, 1744, and May, 1753, similar bills passed the lower house. *Civil Officers, etc.*, III, 62, 393. *Col. Rec. of Connecticut*, 1717–1725, Note to pages 141-2.

F.

St. Alban's Lodge No. 38, Free and Accepted Masons.

This lodge was instituted in colonial days by virtue of a charter issued by the Provincial Grand Master for North America, of which the following is an accurate copy:

John Rowe, Grand Master.

TO ALL AND EVERY our Right Worshipful and Loving Brethren, Free and Accepted MASONS now Residing or that may hereafter Reside in Guilford in the Colony of Connecticut in New England. *We John Rowe* Esquire, Provincial Grand Master of the Antient and Honourable Society of Free and Accepted MASONS for all North America, where no other Grand Master is Appointed,

Send Greeting.

WHEREAS, Application hath been made unto us by Timothy Ward, Bilious Ward, David Landon, Timothy Ludinton, Eber Waterhouse, Asher Fairchild, Benjamin Stone, Giles Trubee and William Johnson, Free and Accepted MASONS now residing in Guilford aforesaid; setting forth that they live at a great Distance from any regular Lodge, and are deprived of the Benefits of MASONRY on that account. Therefore humbly Request that they may be made a regular Lodge, and appoint our Brother Mr. Bilious Ward to be the first Master of the same, and do promise strictly to observe all the Laws and Regulations of MASONRY, and to the utmost of their Power Support and Contribute to the well being of the Craft.

NOW THEREFORE KNOW YE, That we of the great Trust, Power and Authority, reposed in us by his Grace the Most Worshipful *Henry Somerset*, Duke of Beaufort, etc., Grand Master of MASONS, have Constituted and appointed our Right Worshipful and well beloved Brother *Mr. Bilious Ward* to be the first Master of the Lodge at Guilford aforesaid, and do hereby impower him to Congregate the Brethren together, and form into a Regular Lodge, he taking Special Care that all, and every Member thereof, and all transient Persons admitted therein have been, or shall be regular made MASONS: and that he appoint two Wardens, and other Officers to a Lodge Appertaining for the due Regulation of said Lodge for One Year; at the end of which he shall Nominate a new Master to be approved by the Lodge, at least two thirds of the Members in his favour, and said new Master shall Nominate and Appoint two Wardens and a Secretary for the ensuing year, also a Treasurer, who must have the Votes of two-thirds of the Members in his favor; and so the same Course Annually.

AND WE DO HEREBY GIVE to said Lodge all the Privileges and Authority of other Regular Lodges, Requiring them to observe all and every of the Regulations contained in the Printed Book of Constitutions (except such as have been, or may be Repealed at any Quarterly Communication or other General Meeting of the Grand Lodge in London), to be kept and observed, as also all such other Rules and Instructions as may from Time to Time be transmitted to them by Us, or our Deputy, or Successors to either for the Time being; And that they do Annually send an Account in Writing to Us, or our Deputy, or Successors to either of Us for the Time being, of the Names of the Members of said Lodge, and their Place of Abode, with the Days and Place of Meeting, with any other things they may think proper to Communicate for the benefit of MASONRY; And that they do Annually keep the Feast of St. John the Baptist, or St. John the Evangelist,'or both, and Dine together on said Day or Days, or as near either of them as shall be most Convenient: And lastly, that they do Regularly Communicate with the Grand Lodge in Boston, by sending to the Quarterly Communications such Charity as their Lodge shall think fit, for the Relief of Poor Brethren, with the Names of those that Contributed the same, that in case any such may come to want Relief, they may have the preference to others.

GIVEN under Our Hand and Seal of MASONRY at BOSTON the 10th day of July A. D., 1771, and of MASONRY 5771.

RICHARD GRIDLEY, D. G. M.
JOHN CUTLER, S. G. W.
ABR'M SAVAGE, J. G. M.

BY THE GRAND
MASTER'S COMMAND,
Tho. Brown, Gr. Sec'ry.

In the early history of this Lodge, the convivial element seems not to have been lost sight of, and the account-books tell, we are informed, of taxes frequently levied at its meetings to meet the expense of *Flip* purchased for its members. Indeed the flip-mug, which was used on such occasions of solemn conviviality, is said still to be in existence, although no longer employed as in former days.

The regular communications of the Lodge are held on the first and third Monday nights of each month at Masonic Hall.

Past Masters of St. Alban's Lodge.

1771, 2, 3,	Billious Ward.
1774, 5,	Eli Foote.
1797,	Isaac Chalker.
1798,	George Cleveland.
1799,	Oliver Bray.
1800,	Jedediah Lathrop.
1801,	George Cleveland.
1802, 3	Joel Griffing.
1804, 5, 6,	Jeremiah Parmelee.
1807,	William Spencer.
1808, 9,	Peletiah Leete.
1810,	Thomas Powers.
1811,	Jeremiah Parmelee.
1812, 3,	Jedediah Lathrop.
1814,	Abraham I. Chittenden.
1815, 16,	Joseph Griffing.
1817, 18, 19,	Jedediah Lathrop.
1820, 1, 2, 3,	Amos Seward.
1824,	Merritt Foote.
1825, 6,	Jedediah Lathrop.
1827,	Amos Seward.
1851,	Charles A. Ball.
1852,	C. L. Crowel.
1853,	Charles W. Miller.
1854,	C. L. Crowel.
1855, 6, 7, 8, 9, 60, 1, 2,	Asahel B. Morse.
1863, 4, 5, 6,	Henry B. Stannard.
1867, 8, 9,	William T. Dowd.
1870, 1,	Henry B. Stannard.
1872, 3,	William T. Dowd.
1874, 5,	C. Henry Norton.
1876,	William T. Dowd.
1877,	C. Henry Norton.

The records of the lodge having been destroyed by the fire at Music Hall, 1862, the names of its masters from 1775 to 1797 cannot be furnished.
The charter was revoked in 1827, and the lodge resuscitated in 1851.

APPENDIX. 191

G.

Guilford's Roll of Honor.

This Roll contains the names of those persons from Guilford or accredited to the town, who, having served in the Union army, laid down their lives during the war, or subsequently, in consequence of injuries received in service.

Names.	Regiment.	Date and cause of Death.	Age.	Place of Burial.
Andrew Adams,	11 C. V.,	died July 27, 1864, of wounds.	20,	Guilford.
William Nelson Bartlett,	14 C. V.,	killed Aug. 15, 1864, at Deep Bottom, Va.,	18,	"
Charles H. Benton,	16 C. V.,	died Oct. 1, 1862, at Fairfax Seminary, Va.,	19,	"
Joel Canfield Benton,	14 C. V.,	died Oct. 20, 1862, of typhoid fever, at Harper's Ferry, Va.,	22,	Field of battle.
Joel Edward Benton,	14 U. S.,	killed June 27, 1862, at Fair Oaks, Va.,	41,	Guilford.
Raphael Ward Benton,	14 C. V.,	killed Sept. 17, 1862, at Antietam, Md.,	18,	N. Guilford.
Henry A. Beers,	11 C. V.,	killed June 18, 1864, at Petersburg, Va.,	18,	Guilford.
Chas. Augustus Bishop,	16 C. V.,	died Feb. 23, 1865, of consumption, Bedloe's Island, N. Y.,		
George W. Blake,	14 C. V.,	died at Salisbury, N. C.		
Lewis Wm. Blatchley,	15 C. V.,	killed March 8, 1865, at Kinston, N. C.	20,	Field of battle.
Ellis D. Bradley,		died May 15, 1864, of typhoid fever, at N. Guilford,	14,	N. Guilford.
Henry B. Bullard,	1 Lt. Batt.,	died Feb. 6, 1862, of disease, at Port Royal, S. C.,	26,	Port Royal.
Jno. Randolph Burgis,	9 C. V.,	died Sept. 14, 1862, of typhoid fever, at New Orleans,	29,	New Orleans.
Joseph Coan,	15 C. V.,	died Nov 7, 1862, of typhoid fever, at Fairfax Seminary, Va.,	28,	Nut Plains.
Fairfield Cook,	1 Lt. Batt.	died June 20, 1863, of fever, at Hilton Head, S. C.,	17,	Hilton Head.
Patrick Cox,	20 C. V.,	died Sept. 4, 1864, of wounds, at Chattanooga, Tenn.		
Moses G. Clements,	14 C. V.,	killed July 3, 1863, at Gettysburg, Pa.,	31,	Field of battle.
Nathan C. Clements,	14 C. V.,	died Jan. 30, 1864, of small pox, at Washington, D. C.,	36,	Washington.
John Nelson Davis,	15 C. V.,	died May 4, 1863, of small pox, at Arlington Heights, Va.,	14,	Arlington.
Samuel Richard Davis,	15 C. V.,	died July 6, 1863, of consumption, at Guilford,	22,	Guilford.
William Henry Dolph,	15 C. V.,	died April 17, 1863, of erysipelas at Suffolk, Va.,	34,	Suffolk.
Benjamin R. Dowd,	15 C. V.,	died Dec. 4, 1862, of disease, at Washington, D. C.		Washington.
Samuel Bradley Dunn,	13 C. V.,	died Oct. 2, 1864, of wounds, at Baltimore, Md.,	30,	Guilford.

Roll of Honor (continued).

Names.	Regiment.	Date and cause of Death.	Age.	Place of Burial.
Hy. Chittenden Dudley,	14 C. V.,	died Jan. 17, 1863, of typhoid fever, at Falmouth, Va.,	26,	Guilford.
Oliver Wolcott Evarts,	14 C. V.,	killed May 3, 1863, at Chancellorsville, Va.,	31,	Chancellorsville.
Edmund Irving Field,	14 C. V.,	killed Sept. 17, 1862, at Antietam, Md.,	22,	Antietam.
Geo. Augustus Foote,	14 C. V.,	died Nov. 13, 1869, of wounds (received Dec. 13, 1862), at Guilford,	34,	Guilford.
Douglas Fowler,	17 C. V.,	killed July 1, 1863, at Gettysburg, Pa.		
Richard H. Fowler,	27 C. V.,	died Dec. 17, 1862, of wounds at Fredericksburg, Va.	15,	Falmouth.
Emerson S. Fowler,	27 C. V.,	died Dec. 25, 1862, of typhoid fever at Falmouth, Va.,	45,	Washington.
Samuel Fowler,	27 C. V.,	died Jany. 9, 1863, of wounds, at Washington, D. C.,	33,	Guilford.
Wells Gilbert,	6 C. V.,	died Aug. 22, 1863, of chronic diarrhœa at Guilford.	20,	Winchester.
John L. Graham,	5 C. V.,	killed May 29, 1862, at Winchester, Va.,	20,	Field of battle.
Joseph A. Grosvenor,	16 C. V.,	killed Sept. 17, 1862, at Antietam, Md.,	24,	
Samuel E. Grosvenor,	16 C. V.,	drowned April 24, 1865, in the Potomac river,	23,	Field of battle.
Henry Harrison Hall,	10 C. V.,	died Aug. 16, 1864, of wounds at Deep Bottom, Va.,	22,	Guilford.
Wm. Henry Hubbard,	16 C. V.,	died Sept. 16, 1863, of diphtheria, at Portsmouth, Va.,	20,	Newbern.
H. Ellsworth Hull,	15 C. V.,	died Nov. 2, 1864, of yellow fever, at Newbern, N. C.,		Field of battle.
Richard Lawrence Hull,	14 C. V.,	killed Sept. 17, 1862, at Antietam,		
Saml. H. Hull,	1 Lt. Batt.,	died Feb. 1, 1876, of injuries received in service, at Guilford.		
Abraham Jackson,	29 C. V.,	died Oct. 24, 1864, of disease at Portsmouth Grove, R. I.	44,	Field of battle.
Harmon Barber Johnson,	15 C. V.,	killed March 8, 1864, at Kinston, N. C.,		
Joannes Lambric,	1 H. Art.,	died Jan. 15, 1865, of disease at Broadway landing, Va.	21,	Wilmington.
Charles Gilbert Lee,	16 C. V.,	died March 6, 1865, of starvation, at Wilmington, N. C.,		
Samuel Mason,	14 C. V.,	killed Oct. 27, 1864, at Hatcher's run, Va.		
Patrick Murphy,	5 C. V.,	killed Oct. 5, 1863, by a fall from cars.	28,	Florence.
Dennis F. Nettleton,	16 C. V.,	died Feb. 25, 1865, of starvation, at Florence, S. C.,	35,	
Francis Morgan Norton,	14 C. V.,	killed Feb. 6, 1864, at Morton's Ford, Va.,		
Jonathan G. Norton,	1 Lt. Batt.,	died Oct. 14, 1863, of typhoid fever, at Folly island, S. C.	36,	Leete's island.
John Norton,	21 C. V.,	died Dec. 25, 1862, of disease at Falmouth, Va.,	41.	
Joel Cruttenden Parmelee,	27 C. V.,	killed Dec. 13, 1862, at Fredericksburg, Va.,		

Roll of Honor (continued).

Names.	Regiment.	Date and Cause of Death.	Age.	Place of Burial.
Uriah Nelson Parmelee, Jr.	1 Cav.,	killed April 1, 1865, at Five Forks, Va.,	23,	Field of battle.
Alexander Peterson,	30 C. V.,	died Aug. 16, 1864, of wounds at Alexandria, Va.		
Miles G. Richardson,	14 C. V.,	died Nov. 2, 1862, of Hemorrhage, at Harper's Ferry, Va.,	20.	
Francis S. Scranton,	14 C. V.,	died Dec. 14, 1862, of wounds, at Fredericksburg, Va.,	25.	
Thomas Marvin Scranton,	14 C. V.,	died Jan. 3, 1863, of brain fever, at Washington, D. C.,	38.	
Abraham Tibbals,	10 C. V.,	died Aug. 6, 1862, of dysentery, at Newbern, N. C.,	36.	
Charles Tucker,	2 H. Art.,	died Jan. 2, 1865;		
Hezekiah Tuttle,	1 Lt. Batt.	died March 14, 1865, of consumption, at Hartford,	36.	
Toby Trout,	30 C. V.,	died April 15, 1865, of disease, at Alexandria, Va.		
Harvey S. Welton,	27 C. V.,	died July 14, 1863, of disease at Harper's Ferry, Va.,		Harper's Ferry.
Henry Wm. Wright,	54 Mass.,	died June 15, 1864, of consumption, at Guilford,	30,	Guilford.

H.

The Guilford Agricultural Society.

This society, composed largely of Guilford farmers and others interested in agriculture and horticulture, has been in existence about sixteen years, although only acting under a permanent organization since 1872, and incorporated in 1874. Its object is to awaken and promote an intelligent interest in agricultural and kindred pursuits.

It has held fourteen annual agricultural and industrial exhibitions, usually during the latter part of September or the beginning of October. These attract large numbers of visitors from Guilford and the adjoining towns, affording opportunity for an examination of the articles exhibited and a pleasant exchange of views on agricultural and industrial subjects. Competition at these exhibitions, or fairs, is ordinarily confined to Guilford and the neighboring towns.

The officers for 1877 were as follows:

President.
WILLIAM E. WEED.

Vice-Presidents.
JEROME COAN,   SIDNEY W. LEETE.

Secretary.
J. W. NORTON.

Treasurer.
GEORGE B. SPENCER.

Directors.

RICHARD H. WOODRUFF,	EVERETT L. DUDLEY,
RICHARD W. STARR,	DANIEL L. SPENCER,
LEWIS FOWLER,	ROGER C. LEETE,
ARTHUR S. FOWLER,	H. FRANCIS DUDLEY,
E. ROGER DAVIS,	WILLIAM H. LEE,
CHARLES L. BENTON,	HENRY H. GRISWOLD,
DUDLEY CHITTENDEN,	GEORGE W. DUDLEY,

WILBUR F. ROSSITER.

Chief Marshal.
RICHARD F. KELSEY.

APPENDIX.

I.

United Workers for Public Improvement.

This association, familiarly known by its initials as the U. W. P. I., was organized, February 9th, 1874. Its objects are defined in the constitution, as being the raising of funds to repair the walks, light the streets, improve the condition of the village Green, and extend the work of beautifying and improving the village as necessity may demand and funds shall permit. The active membership is composed of ladies and numbers one hundred and two; gentlemen are admitted to honorary membership, and thirty have availed themselves of the privilege.

The funds to carry out the general designs of the association are raised from the annual dues for membership, special subscriptions and donations, the proceeds of occasional concerts, lectures and exhibitions, the proceeds of ice cream festivals and restaurants improvised on stated public occasions.

It has caused to be erected eighty-eight lamp posts throughout the village and kept the same number of lights burning during nights requiring artificial illumination for the benefit of the traveler, supervised the preservation and improvement of the walks and grass of the village Green, and in a general way encouraged the planting of trees and ornamentation of the homes of the good people of Guilford. This has been done by personal as well as united efforts, in which the members have not hesitated to take hold of the work with their own hands. The annual raking of the Green in the spring by the ladies is quite a fête day, and is an occasion of much pleasure and satisfaction to all the citizens.

An auxiliary to the U. W. P. I., formed May 28, 1877, having as its object the charitable design of relieving suffering in the community, is expected to be a most active and useful branch of the association.

The officers of the U. W. P. I., elected February 9th, 1877, are as follows:

President.
Mrs. B. B. PARKHURST.

Vice Presidents.

Mrs. A. G. HULL,	Mrs. HENRY HALE,
" LYDIA COAN,	" EDWARD GRISWOLD,
" HARVEY LEETE,	" HART LANDON,
" A. A. STONE,	" R. L. FOWLER,
" CHARLES GRISWOLD,	Miss LIZZIE SPENCER.

Secretary and Treasurer.
Miss SARAH BROWN.

Executive Committee.

Mrs. RICHARD SPENCER,   Mrs. GEO. C. KIMBERLY,
 "   HY. E. NORTON,   "   N. F. LEETE,
 "   E. B. FOWLER,   "   JAMES COOK,
 "   H. D. CHITTENDEN,   "   AMOS CHITTENDEN.

Committee on the Village Green.

Mrs. RIPLEY BAYLIES,   Mrs. HELEN PARMELEE,
         Miss LYDIA D. CHITTENDEN.

Committee on Care of Lamps.

Mrs. E. B. FOWLER,   Miss NETTIE FOWLER,
 "   A. G. HULL,   Mrs. HY. E. NORTON.

The manuscript of the *History of Guilford*, prepared after many years of loving study of its old records and the lives of its early settlers by the late Judge Ralph D. Smith, with such annotations and additions as the editor was able to make, has been presented by his heirs to the U. W. P. I., with the hope that its publication would contribute to the fostering of a genuine pride in the citizens of a village that has borne an honorable name for two hundred and thirty-eight years, and that any profits resulting from its sale, would be applied to the ornamentation and improvement of old Guilford.

It is proper to add that Miss Nettie Fowler and Mrs. Ripley Baylies constitute the committee appointed by the association to secure subscribers and superintend the distribution of the book.

INDEX.

Adams, Andrew, 191.
Adams, Rev. Dr. Wm., 137.
Address to Guilford, an, 124, 125.
Agicomook, 9; or Stony creek, 73.
Agricultural society, 194.
Ahaddon, 70; alias Joshua, 71, 72.
Aiasomut, 70.
Ajicomick river, 65.
Albany, 97.
Alden, Miss Almira, 112.
Alderbrook cemetery, 112, 132, 141.
Alexandria, Va., 193.
Allen's American Biographical Dictionary, 69.
Allyn, John, 80.
Alms house, 58.
Ambler, Rev. John L., 118.
American Biographical Dictionary, Allen's, 69.
American Peace Society, corresponding secretary of, 113.
Amherst college, 99.
Andrews, Joseph, 85.
Andross, E., 160.
Andross, Edmund, 20.
Andross, Major, 123.
Antietam, Md., 191, 192.
Apostle to the Indians, 132.
Appendix, A, 183–186; B, 186; C, 186, 187; D, 187; E, 187; F, 188, 189, 190; G, 191, 192, 193; H, 194; I, 195, 196.
Aquaihamish, a blind Indian, 70.

Arlington, 130.
Arlington Heights, Va., 191.
Articles of agreement, 66–68; of confederation for the jurisdiction of New Haven, 183-186.
Ashawmutt, 67.
Ashford, 99.
Asia Minor, U. S. consul to, 136.
Assembly, no meeting of, 160.
Assoweion, 70.
Astor, John Jacob, 132.
Astor, William B., 132.
Astwood, John, 183.
Athamonassett river, 63, 71.
Athens, Ga., college at, 128.
Athol, Mass., 113, 114.
Attestation, An, to the Church History of New England, 93.
Atwater, Ira, 87.
Austin, Francis, 16.
Austin, Stephen, 16.
Austin, city of, 16.
Avon, 42.
Ayres, W. H., 85.

Backus, Dr. Chas., of Somers, 97.
Bacon, Rev. Leonard, D.D., 141.
Baily, John, 28.
Baldwin, 32.
Baldwin, Abraham, 128.
Baldwin, Rev. Abraham C., 83, 84, 118.
Baldwin, Benjamin, 176.

INDEX.

Baldwin, Rev. David, 108.
Baldwin, Judge Henry, 97.
Baldwin, John, 20, 23, 24; took the oath of fidelity, 20.
Baldwin, Nathaniel, 30, 105.
Baldwin, Samuel, 28.
Baldwin, Rev. Dr. Theron, 137.
Baldwin, Timothy, 30.
Baldwin, Wm. W., 147.
Baldwin county, Ga., 129.
Ball, Charles A., 190.
Banks, Rev. Geo. W., 6, 85, 115, 142.
Baptist church organized, 110.
Baptists, number in Guilford, 1838, 116.
Barber's Conn. Hist. Collections, 49, 101.
Barker, Elizur, 144.
Barker, Jacob, 132.
Barker, S. A., 146.
Barker, Samuel, 144.
Barker, Samuel A., 111.
Barnes, Timothy, 50.
Barnum, Henry S., 85.
Bartlett, Augustus E., 149.
Bartlett, Daniel, 30.
Bartlett, David, 180.
Bartlett, Ebenezer, 105.
Bartlett, Edwin W., 150.
Bartlett, George, 13, 25, 30, 105, 110, 119, 154, 156, 157, 182.
Bartlett, J. H., 146.
Bartlett, John, 119, 157.
Bartlett, John 2d, 147.
Bartlett, John H., 110, 178, 180.
Bartlett, Joseph, 107.
Bartlett, Marcus B., 178.
Bartlett, Nathaniel, 149.
Bartlett, Richard, 148, 179.
Bartlett, Stephen R., 150, 179, 180.
Bartlett, William Nelson, 191.
Basaltic cliffs, 44.
Bayley, John, 29.
Baylies, Mrs. Ripley, 196.

Beattie, John, 41, 148.
Beaufort, Henry Somerset, Duke of, 188.
Beckwith, Mathew, 29.
Bedloe's island, N. Y., 191.
Beecher, Dr. Lyman, 97.
Beers, Henry A., 191.
Bellamy, Mathew, 25, 81.
Belleville ave. Congregational church, 115.
Bennett, Rev. Lorenzo T., D.D., 6, 109, 142.
Benton, Amos N., 147.
Benton, Andrew, 27.
Benton, Andrew J., 142.
Benton, Charles H., 191.
Benton, Charles L., 194.
Benton, Dan., 24.
Benton, Daniel, 27, 107, 186.
Benton, Edward, 13, 15, 24, 27, 186.
Benton, Henry 2d, 180.
Benton, Joel Canfield, 191.
Benton, Joel Edward, 191.
Benton, Joseph, 30.
Benton, Lot, place, 87.
Benton, Raphael Ward, 191.
Berkshire county, Mass., 32.
Berlin, 143.
Bethlehem, Conn., 115.
Betts, Thomas, 13, 14, 25, 59.
Birch, Heman, 137.
Bishop, Charles Augustus, 191.
Bishop, Ebenezer, 30, 108.
Bishop, David, 105.
Bishop, E. C., 20.
Bishop, Enos, 48.
Bishop, James, 154.
Bishop, John, 9, 10, 12, 23, 28, 52, 54, 59, 62, 65, 66, 151, 186.
Bishop, John jr., 25, 27.
Bishop, John sen., 13, 15, 27.
Bishop, Martin C., 150.
Bishop, Samuel, 30.

INDEX. 199

Bishop, widow Susanna, 29.
Bishop, Stephen, 14, 15, 25, 27, 78, 79.
Blackley, Samuel, 14.
Blake, Rev. E. A., 111.
Blake, George W., 191.
Blanford, Mass., 99.
Blatchley, Lewis Wm., 191.
Blatchley, Samuel, 26 ; lots and accommodations, 23.
Bloody cove, 47.
Bluff head, 43, 45.
Booth, Wilson, 87.
Boreman, William, 14, 15, 26, 27 ; died, 26.
Bowers, John, 19, 93.
Bowers, Rev. John, 27.
Bowers, Mr., 94.
Boston, 18, 38, 39, 93.
Bowdoin college, 118.
Boynton, Rev. George M., 115.
Bradley, Abraham 3d, 124.
Bradley, Ellis D., 191.
Bradley, Nathan, 21 ; account of, 21, 22.
Bradley, Stephen, 21, 74.
Bradley, Capt. Stephen, 162.
Bradley, Lieut. Stephen, 161.
Bradley, Sergt. Stephen, 72, 73, 77.
Brainerd, Rev. Israel, 97.
Brainerd, Mr., 104.
Branford, 7, 9, 22, 26, 27, 32, 43, 47, 116, 142, 143, 144, 187; bounds, 77; Menunkatuck Indians at, 11.
Bray, Oliver, 190.
Bray, Thomas R., 149.
Bray, Thomas Wells, A. M., pastor of the Third church in Guilford, 96.
Bray, Rev. Thomas Wells, 117.
Brewer, Rev. Daniel, 102.
Bridgeport, 142.
Bridgeport, Conn., 118.
Bridge street, 18.
Bristo, Richard, 187.

Bristow, Richard, 13, 24, 59.
Bristol, England, 19.
British parliament, member of, 121.
British ship, a, in the sound, 49.
Broad street, 18.
Broadway landing, Va., 192.
Brooklyn, N. Y., 84, 115.
Brookfield, 137.
Brooks, David, 42.
Brown, S., 171.
Brown, Miss Sarah, 195.
Brown, Tho., 189.
Brown, William, 174.
Browne, Mr., 129.
Brownell, Rt. Rev. Dr. Thomas Church, 109.
Bryan, Alex., 154.
Bryant, William Cullen, 134.
Buildings, number of, in the village, 1838, 35.
Bullard, Henry B., 191.
Burgess, Rev. Nathan B., 108.
Burgess, Thomas, 105.
Burgis, John, 146, 170, 171, 172, 173.
Burgis, John, bill of mortality kept by, 39, 40.
Burgis, Deacon John, 145.
Burgis, Jno. Randolph, 191.
Burgis, Thomas, 110, 182.
Burgis, Deacon Thos. jr., 145.
Burton, 121.
Bushnell, Elizabeth, 20.
Bushnell, Francis, 12, 13, 20, 26.
Bushnell, Rev. Dr. Horace, 137.
Butcher, Daniel, 26.
Butler, Rev. David, 108.
Butler, William Allen, 134.
Byfield, Maj., 90.

Caffinch, Jno, 65, 66.
Caffinge, John, 9, 10, 15, 28, 62.
Caldwell, Charles, 28.

INDEX.

Calumet, the, editor of, 113.
Cambridge, 121.
Camp distemper, 40.
Canaan, 32.
Canada, threatened invasion from, 131.
Canfield, Joel, 42.
Canfield, Dr. Joel, 146.
Cape Breton, 48.
Centennial celebration, 141.
Central Park, N. Y., 134.
Cincinnati, O., Second Presbyterian church, 112.
Chalker, Alexander, 13, 25.
Chalker, Isaac, 190.
Chamish, 70.
Chancellorsville, Va., 192.
Charles I, 120.
Charleston, N. H., 32.
Charleston, S. C., 93.
Chatfield, Francis, 12, 15.
Chatfield, George, 14, 15, 25, 27.
Chatfield, Thomas, 13, 15, 26.
Chatham, 143.
Chatham, Conn., 113.
Chatham, N. Y., 117.
Chattanooga, Tenn., 191.
Chester Factory, Mass., 118.
Chew, Mr. Joseph, 49.
Chicago, 112.
Chidsey, Joseph, 30.
Chidsey, N., 174.
Chidsey, Nathan, 149.
Chipman, Elizabeth Grey, 113.
Chipman Lineage, the, 114.
Chipman, Mr., publications of, 114.
Chipman, Richard Harrison, 114.
Chipman, Deacon Richard M., 113.
Chipman, Rev. Richard Manning, 113.
Chitendon, Thomas, 186.
Chittenden, Abraham, 105.
Chittenden, Abraham I., 190.
Chittenden, Deacon Abram, 145.
Chittenden, Mrs. Amos, 196.
Chittenden, Anson, 106.
Chittenden, Rev. Charles, 111.
Chittenden, Daniel, 146.
Chittenden, Dudley, 194.
Chittenden, Ebenezer, 130.
Chittenden, Ebenezer 2d, 130.
Chittenden, Gov., 151.
Chittenden, Mrs. H. D., 196.
Chittenden, Henry W., 83, 84, 146, 182.
Chittenden, John, 72, 186.
Chittenden, Sergt. John, 78, 79.
Chittenden, John B., 106.
Chittenden, Levi, 119.
Chittenden, Miss Lydia, 196.
Chittenden, Mrs. Mary G., organ presented by, 88.
Chittenden, Nathaniel, 187.
Chittenden, Samuel, 105.
Chittenden, Simeon, 119.
Chittenden, Deacon Simeon, 149.
Chittenden, Simeon B., 83, 84.
Chittenden, Hon. Simeon B., 142.
Chittenden, Thomas, 27, 72, 130.
Chittenden, William, 9, 10, 12, 23, 25, 27, 52, 54, 59, 61, 62, 65, 66, 130, 151, 153, 154, 155, 156.
Chittenden county, 32 ; landing, 8.
Christ church, 109.
Christian Indian burying ground, 69.
Church of England, 108 ; Liturgy of, 108.
Clams, fisheries of, 8.
Clapboard hill, 38, 43 ; district, 82, 83.
Claremont, N. H., 32.
Clark, Joseph, 30.
Clark, Sylvanus, 144.
Clark, Thos., 24.
Clarke, Thomas, 20.
Clay, Joseph, 27.
Clements, Moses G., 191.
Clements, Nathan C., 191.
Cleveland, George, 190.

INDEX. 201

Coan, Abraham, 110, 146.
Coan, Jerome, 150, 194.
Coan, Joseph, 191.
Coan, Mrs. Lydia, 195.
Coasting trade, vessels employed in, 33.
Cohabit, 29, 30.
Colchester, 42.
Collins, Augustus, 172, 173, 174, 175, 176.
Collins, Gen'l Augustus, 149.
Collins, Charles, 110.
Collins, Daniel, 30, 104.
Collins, John, 22, 23, 28, 30, 78, 79, 81, 108.
Collins, John sen., 172.
Collins, Mr. John 2d, 163.
Collins, Lewis, 42.
Collins, Samuel, 108.
Collins, Timothy, 104.
Collins, Wm. R., 119.
Colonial Records, 157.
Colonial Records of Connecticut, 181, 187.
Columbia college, N. Y., 133.
Combination, the, 152.
Commonasnock, 70.
Cone, Henry D., 85.
Congregational church, 35; ancient, removed, 38; Harwinton, Conn., 113; West Hartford, 114; Bethlehem, Conn., 115; Newark, N. J., 115.
Congregationalists, 57; number in Guilford, 1838, 116; in North Guilford, 1838, 120.
Connecticut, 29, 43, 46, 93, 112, 121; Halleck's poem, 6; Western Reserve, Ohio, 33; guest from, 37; general assembly of, 39; river, 39, 44, 46, 47; Historical Collections, Barber's, 49; colony of, 51; path, 68, 71; charter granted by general court, 77, 80;

Connecticut, first meeting house in, with a steeple, 87; Home Missionary Society, 97; Journal, the, 101; extract from, 49; and New Haven colonies united, 156; admission of Guilford into the jurisdiction of, 186.
Constitutional convention, delegates to, 177.
Continental army, chaplain in, 128.
Cook, Fairfield, 191.
Cook, James, 196.
Cook, Thomas, 13, 157, 181.
Cook, Wequash, 69.
Cooke, Thomas, 12, 24.
Cooke, Thomas, sen., 186.
Cooke, Thomas, jr., 187.
Cooper, the novelist, 72.
Corbin, Benjamin, 179.
Corson, Rev. Levi H., 109.
Corwin, James, 107.
Cosster's, Mrs., physics and physical drugs, 41.
Cotton, Mr., 90, 91, 93.
Cotton, John, 19, 93.
Cotton, Rev. John, 93.
County court in Hartford, one of the first judges of, 28.
County court for New Haven county organized, 154.
Court of probate, first judge of, 27.
Covenant, signed on shipboard, 11, 12.
Cox, Patrick, 191.
Crampton, Dennis, 21, 27.
Crane, Henry, 23; removed to Killingworth, 23.
Crane, Jasper, 154.
Crean, Henry, 187.
Cromwell, Jane, 120.
Cromwell, Lord Protector Oliver, 120.
Cromwell, Oliver, relative of, 17.
Cromwell's parliament, 121.

Crooked Lane, 28, 124, 126, 127.
Crooper hill, 77.
Crosswell, Rev. Dr. Hairy, 109.
Crowel, C. L., 190.
Cruttenden, Abraham, 12, 27, 78, 79, 181.
Cruttenden, Abraham jr., 14, 24, 27, 186.
Cruttenden, Abraham sen., 13, 15, 24, 27, 186.
Cruttenden, Isaac, 27.
Cruttenden, Rev. Richard, 119.
Cruttenden, Samuel, 107.
Cruttenden, Thomas, 27, 186.
Curtis, Rev. William B., 119.
Cutler, Mr., 129.
Cuyler, John, 189.

Daggett, Judge, 137.
Daniels, Joseph L., 85.
Darken, Rev. Edward, 109.
Darwin, Ephraim, 28, 29.
Dartmouth college, 113.
Davis, Edwin O., 106.
Davis, John, 107.
Davis, John Nelson, 191.
Davis, Samuel Richard, 191.
Davis E. Roger, 194.
Day, Rev. T. L., 85.
Day, Rev. Theodore L., 100, 142.
Death, the advantage of the Godly, a discourse on, 95.
Decoration day, corner stone of monument laid, 51.
Deep Bottom, Va., 191, 192.
De Forrest, Judge Robert E., 142.
Denison, Richard, 42.
Deputies, list of, 155, 156.
Derby, 27, 94.
Desborough, Mr., 32, 51, 54.
Desborough, Samuel, 59.
Desborough, Mr., 152.

Disborough, Samuel, 25, 41, 120, 121, 145, 151, 153, 155, 183.
Disborough, Samuel, terryer of, 61.
Disborow, Elizabeth, divorced wife of Thomas Relf, 16.
Disborow, James, 120.
Disborow, Maj. Gen. John, 120.
Disborow, Mr., 18, 25.
Disborow, Samuel, 12, 17, 18, 68, 69, 89, 120.
Disbrow, Samuel, 59.
Discourse on Ecclesiastical Prosperity, 114; on Free Discussion, 114; on Maintenance of Moral Purity, 114.
Divinity school at New Haven, 114.
Dodd, Stephen, 28.
Dolph, William Henry, 191.
Dover, N. H., 112.
Douglass, Rev. ———, 111.
Dowd, Benjamin R., 191.
Dowd, Henry, 13, 15, 24.
Dowd, Hy., 27.
Dowd, J. A., 148.
Dowd, Julius A., 116, 179, 180.
Dowd, Julius N., 82.
Dowd, William T., 190.
Dowde, Henry, 12.
Dudley, Abraham, 106.
Dudley, Asher, 116.
Dudley's, David, dwelling house, 8.
Dudley, Everett L., 194.
Dudley, George W., 194.
Dudley, H. Francis, 194.
Dudley, Hy. Chittenden, 192.
Dudley, Joseph, 81, 162, 182, 187.
Dudley, Sergt. Joseph, 162.
Dudley, Martin, 104.
Dudley, Mr., 82.
Dudley, Oliver, 149.
Dudley, Samuel W., 119, 149, 178, 179, 180.
Dudley, Selah 119.

INDEX. 203

Dudley, W. C., 147.
Dudley, Wm., 12, 13, 24, 30, 119, 149.
Dudley, Wm. M., 149.
Dudley's creek, 8.
Dunn, Samuel Bradley, 191.
Dunk, Thomas, 16.
Durham, 7, 32, 45, 142, 187; turnpike, 45.
Dutchman's coat, 10.
Dutton, Rev. Aaron, 88, 98.
Dutton, Dorcas S., 99.
Dutton, Rev. Dr., 83.
Dutton, Mary, 99.
Dutton, Mr., 104.
Dutton, S. W. S., D.D., 104.
Dutton, Rev Samuel W. S., 99.
Dutton, Thomas, 104.
Dutton, Deacon Thomas, 98.
Dutton, Rev. Thomas, 99.
Dutton, Rev. Thomas Rice, 118.
Duty of Living and Dying to the Lord, funeral sermon, 96.
Dwight, Dr., 57.

East creek, 34, 43, 45.
East end point, 78.
East Granby, Conn., 113.
East Greenwich, in Kent, 79.
East Guilford, 8, 29, 30, 48, 50, 81, 130, 131.
East Haddam, 117.
East Hampton, 26.
East Hampton, Long Island, 27.
East Haven, 9, 30, 47; heights, 50; Menunkatuck Indians at, 11.
East Riding of Long Island, 26.
East river, 8, 9. 10, 18, 43, 45, 46, 66, 67, 68, 71, 73, 74, 81.
Easton, Pa., 137.
Eaton, Gov., 120.
Eaton, Theophilus, governor, 183.
Eddy, Rev. Henry, 118.

Edinburgh, 120.
Eliot, Jared, 104.
Eliot, John, 161.
Eliot, Rev. John, 132; pastor of Roxbury, 94.
Eliot, Joseph, 94.
Eliot, Mary, 132.
Eliot, Mr. 94.
Elliot, Lucius, 117.
Elliott, 32.
Elliott, Aaron, 144.
Elliott, Henry, 149, 178.
Elliott, James, 81.
Elliott, John, 144, 170, 171, 173, 174.
Elliott, John, A. M., pastor of a church in E. Guilford, 97.
Elliott, Joseph, 19, 27, 41, 48, 145, 175, 176.
Elliott, Mr, 81.
Elliott, Reuben, 92, 144, 145.
Elliott, Samuel, 92, 146.
Elliott, Whitney, 149.
Elliott, Wyllys, 17, 92, 149.
Elizabethtown, 81.
Ellington, Conn., 114, 115.
Ellsworth, Oliver, 114.
Ely, Hon. Smith, jr., 134.
England, 18, 20, 21, 22, 23, 25, 28, 51, 89, 91, 120, 121, 145.
English, 42, 47; settlement commenced, 9; coats, 9; planters of Menunkatuck, 10, 65, 66, 67, 68; of America, 19; soldiers, 46; magistrates, 68.
Ephraim's rocks, 29.
Episcopal church, 100; in process of erection, 35; taken down, 38; in New Haven, 109; wardens, 110; congregation, 108.
Episcopalians, number in Guilford, 1838, 116; in North Guilford, 1838, 120; of Stratford, 129.

Essex, England, 23, 29.
Essexborough, 38.
Ettisley, manor of, in Cambridgeshire, 120.
Euatts, Daniell, 186.
Europe, 99, 114, 132.
Evain, Scotland, 28.
Evangelical (Congregational) church, 113.
Evarts, Daniel, 27.
Evarts, John, 13, 24, 25, 27.
Evarts, Oliver Wolcott, 192.
Everest, Jacob, 29.

Fairchild, Asher, 188.
Fairchild, Joy H., 104.
Fairchild, Lewis, 50.
Fairchild, William, 50.
Fairfax seminary, Va., 191.
Fairfield, 23.
Fairfield, Conn., 113.
Fairfield, Illinois, 33, 106.
Fair Oaks, Va., 191.
Fair street, 18, 22, 29.
Falcon island, 66; permission to purchase, 187.
Falmouth, Va., 192.
Farmer's wharf, 45.
Farmington, 28, 117.
Fener, Joseph, 81.
Fenn, Benj., 154.
Fenwick, George, 10, 62, 64.
Fenwick, Mr., 10, 66, 91.
Field, David, 50.
Field, Edmund Irving, 192.
Field, Edmund M., 149.
Field, Rev. Julius, 111.
First church, persons who have entered the ministry from, 104; names of deacons, 105, 106.
First Congregational church, 82, 112; North Branford, Conn., 114.

First Society, 8, 18, 30, 31, 32, 34, 36, 37, 42, 43, 45, 81, 82, 103.
Fishing, advantages for, 9.
Fitch, Samuel, 42.
Five Forks, Va., 193.
Flip, taxes levied to meet expense of, 189; mug, still in existence, 189.
Florence, S. C., 192.
Folly island, S. C., 192.
Foote, Anson, 42.
Foote, Dr. Anson, 146.
Foote, Eli, 190.
Foote, George A., 110, 178, 179.
Foote, Col. George A., 146.
Foote, Geo. Augustus, 192.
Foote, Merritt, 190.
Fourth church, list of deacons in, 107.
Fourth Society in Guilford, 100, 103; last clergyman settled over, 103.
Fowlar, John, 186.
Fowler, 32.
Fowler, Abraham, 145, 161.
Fowler, Capt. Abr., 162, 163.
Fowler, Ensign Abr., 161.
Fowler, Lieut. Abr., 162.
Fowler, Abraham S., 178.
Fowler, Ammi, 149.
Fowler, Amos, 179.
Fowler, Rev. Amos, 96.
Fowler, Andrew, 104.
Fowler, Rev. Andrew, 108.
Fowler, Arthur S., 194.
Fowler, A. S., 146.
Fowler, David S., 149.
Fowler, Douglas, 192.
Fowler, Mrs. E. B., 196.
Fowler, Emerson S., 192.
Fowler, Henry, 148, 179, 180.
Fowler, Henry 2d, 179.
Fowler, Henry, of Rich., 180.
Fowler, Henry C., 35.

INDEX.   205

Fowler, John, 13, 18, 24, 54, 105, 154,
    156, 157, 158, 181.
Fowler, Dea. John, 158, 159.
Fowler, John H., 104, 182.
Fowler, Joseph, 30.
Fowler, Judge, 18.
Fowler, Lewis, 194.
Fowler, Louis, 150.
Fowler, Mr., 97, 104.
Fowler, Miss Nettie, 196.
Fowler, Noah, 147.
Fowler, Oliver B., 34.
Fowler, Mrs. R. L., 195.
Fowler, Richard, 149.
Fowler, Richard H., 192.
Fowler, Samuel, 30, 182, 192.
Fowler, Maj. Samuel, 144, 145.
Fowler, Stephen, 149.
Fowler, Victor, 149.
Fowler, William, 183.
Fredericksburg, Va., 192, 193.
Freemen, names and date of admission as,
    12, 13.
French, John, 182.
French, Thomas, 14, 15, 24, 27, 59.
French war, second, 48.
Frisbie, Russell, 22, 147.

Gallagher, Rev. C. W., 111.
General assembly, 177.
General court, deputies to assist, when
    chosen, 53; deputies to, from Guil-
    ford, 157, 177.
Georgia, 38, 112, 128.
Gettysburg, Pa., 191, 192.
Gibbon, 85.
Gilbert, Dorcas S., 99.
Gilbert, Rev. Edwin R., of Wallingford,
    99.
Gilbert, Wells, 192.
Gildersleeve, Rich., 183.
Glastonbury, 108.

Gneiss rock, 44.
Goffe, Gen., 122.
Goffe, Judge, 116.
Goldam, Henry, 15, 25.
Goldsmith, 85.
Goldsmith, Alvah B., 144, 146.
Goldsmith, Elder Alvah B., ordained,
    110.
Goldsmith, Joshua, 111.
Goodrich, Richard, 26.
Goodwin, Mr., 90.
Goodyear, Stephen, deputy, 183.
Goose island, 187.
Gordon, Charles E., 85.
Gordon, Mary, 112.
Goshen, 52.
Graham, Rev. John, 100.
Graham, John L., 192.
Granite rocks, 44.
Graue, John, 186, 187.
Graves, John, 20, 24, 105, 106, 158,
    182; town clerk, 20.
Graves, Capt. John, 161.
Graves, Deacon John, 78, 79, 160.
Graves, Ens. John, 158, 159, 160.
Graves, Sherman, 83, 84, 179.
Graves, Deacon William, 77.
Great Barrington, Mass., 118.
Great harbor, 47.
Green, Dr. Ashbel, president of Prince-
    ton college, 102.
Green, Samuel, 93.
Green, the, 18, 38, 82.
Greene, Gen., 12.
Greenfield Hill, Fairfield, Conn., 115.
Greenville, N. Y., 33, 303.
Greenwich, Conn., 81.
Gregson, Thomas, 183.
Gridley, Richard, 189.
Griffin, Henry, 111.
Griffing, Jasper, 29, 92.
Griffing, Joel, 190.

Griffing, Joel L., 42.
Griffing, Joseph, 190.
Griffing, Judge, 18.
Griffing, Nathaniel, 83, 121, 145, 175, 176, 177, 178.
Griffing, Judge Nathaniel, 92.
Griffing, Robert, 119.
Griffing, Mrs. Sarah, 83.
Griswold, Amos jr., 148.
Griswold, Mrs. Charles, 195.
Griswold, Mrs. Edward, 195.
Griswold, George, 144, 146.
Griswold, Geo. C., 148.
Griswold, H. B., 148.
Griswold, Henry H., 194.
Griswold, John, 179.
Griswold, Leverett, 116, 147, 179.
Griswold, Lewis, 147, 179.
Griswold, Sherman, 104.
Griswold, Thomas, 28.
Griswold's rocks, 17.
Grosvenor, Mr., 118.
Grosvenor, Joseph A., 192.
Grosvenor, Samuel E., 192.
Grove Hall Female Seminary, New Haven, 99.
Guildford, 12; capital of Surry, 12.
Guilford, 6, 7, 10, 12, 14, 15, 17, 19, 21, 22, 23, 25, 26, 27, 28, 29, 30, 34, 37, 41, 42, 43, 44, 47, 48, 49, 51, 52, 54, 58, 66, 71, 73, 74, 75, 76, 81, 85, 91, 92, 93, 94, 95, 96, 97, 100, 101, 102, 106, 108, 122, 142, 143, 144, 191, 192, 193; sketch of the history of, 5; poet, the, 6; harbor, 7, 45, 46; First Society, 8, 86; present town of, purchased, 9; articles given for, 9; borough, 9, 36, 45; great plains south of, 93; Johnsons, ancestor of, 20; Savings Bank, the, 35; its officers, 35; point, 36; Fourth Book of Deeds, 37; road through, 38;

Guilford, turnpike, 45; oysters, 46; account of a military expedition from, 49; Booke of the more fixed Orders for the Plantation, 62; records, 73, 80; article in, 9; charter granted to, 77, 78; Institute, 83; trustees of the, 83, 84; Bible to be used in, 84; principals of, 85; library, 85; parish, rector of, 109; Third church, 112; first white person born in, 122; district, probate court for, 127; light battery, salute by, 141; judges and clerks of, 144; list of magistrates and justices, from 1644 or 1645, 145–148; plantation called, 152; deputies from, 153; deputies to general court from, 183; admission of, into the jurisdiction of Connecticut, 186; freemen of, list of, 186; county, efforts made to create, 187; roll of honor, 191, 192; agricultural society, 194; 193; officers, 194.
Guilford, Vt., 32.
Gurnsey, Mr., 118.
Gutrich, Richard, 187.
Gutridge, Richard, 12.
Gutteridge, Richard, 13.
Guttridge, Richard, 24.

Hackinsack, N. J., 42.
Haddam, 40, 49, 97, 142.
Hadley, Mass., 116.
Hale, Henry, 110.
Hale, Mrs. Henry, 195.
Hale, John, 111, 147, 179.
Hale, William, 111, 147, 178, 179.
Hall, Eber, 50.
Hall, Rev. E. Edwin, 83, 84, 99, 180.
Hall, Henry Harrison, 192.
Hall, Henry L., 104.
Hall, Hiland, 50.
Hall, James D., 116.

Hall, Jno., 22, 107.
Hall, Thomas, 105.
Hall, William, 13, 24, 26, 30.
Halle, William, 12.
Halleck, 6.
Halleck, Fitz Greene, 132, 133, 134, 135.
Halleck, Israel, 132.
Halleck's Connecticut, 55.
Halleck's Life, 85.
Hammonassett, 18, 19, 76; river, 7, 8, 10, 11, 62, 63, 66, 77; source discovered, 21; Indians at Killingworth, 11; land, right in sold out, 64.
Hand, Benjamin, 164, 165, 166, 167.
Hand, Joseph, 27.
Harbor street, 20, 166.
Harman, Nathan, 26.
Harper's Ferry, Va., 191, 193.
Harrison, Elizabeth (Bunnel), 114.
Harrison, Rev. Fosdic, 114, 118.
Harrison, H. Lynde, 148, 180.
Harrison, Judge H. Lynde, 142.
Harrison, Mary, 114.
Hart, Augustine, 85.
Hart, Ebenezer, 49, 50.
Hart, George, 146.
Hart, Richard E., 148.
Hart, Thomas, 50, 106.
Hartford, 14, 20, 23, 28, 38, 109, 122, 145, 156, 157; court of election held at, 186; general court held at, 187.
Harvard college, 94.
Harwinton, Conn., 113, 114.
Hatcher's run, Va., 192.
Hawkhurst, England, 26.
Hawks, Rev. William N., 109.
Hayes, Gen. Rutherford B., president of the U. S., 134.
Hebert, Ebenezer, 137.

Hebron, 42.
Hendrick, W. F., 35.
Higginson, Francis, 14, 92; first pastor at Salem, Mass., 14.
Higginson, John, 12, 14, 25, 65, 89, 92.
Higginson, Rev. John, 17.
Higginson, Mr., 18, 80, 81, 89, 92, 93.
Higginson, Rev. Mr., 14.
Higginson, Hon. Stephen, 93.
Higginson, Thomas, 81.
High street, 116.
Highland, George, 14, 15, 24, 27.
Hiland, George, 186.
Hill, Franklin M., 110.
Hill, George, 136; sonnet by, 132.
Hill, George 2d, 150.
Hill, Henry, 127, 144, 145.
Hill, John, 24, 187; a carpenter, 20.
Hill, Michael, 37.
Hill, Nathaniel, 227, 144, 145, 169, 170, 171, 182.
Hill, Samuel, 144, 165, 166, 167, 168, 182.
Hill, Col. Samuel, 127, 144, 145.
Hilton Head, 191.
Hinman, Hon. Edward, 137.
History of Connecticut, 90.
History of Guilford, 96; manuscript of, presented to the U. W. P. I., 196.
History of Harwinton, Conn., 114.
History of New England, Palfrey's, 16.
History of the Judges, 120.
Hitchcock, Judge, 137.
Hoadley, John, 89.
Hoadley, John, 12.
Hoadley, Mr., 118.
Hobson, John, 187.
Hobson, Samuel, 30.
Hodely, John, 13, 32, 153.
Hodgkin, John, 23, 27, 29.
Hodgskins, Thos., 166.

Hogeboom, Judge Henry, 137.
Holmes, Oliver Wendell, poem by, 133.
Hooker, James, 27, 105, 127, 144, 145, 162, 163, 164, 165.
Hooker, Judge, 127.
Hooker, Mr., 90, 92.
Hopson, Samuel, 149.
Hosford ——, 42.
Hotchkin, 29.
Hotchkin, Beriah, 104.
Hotchkin, Rev. Beriah, 102.
Hotchkin, Joseph, 50.
Hotchkin, Mr., 103.
Hotchkin, Thomas, 50.
Hotchkins, Thos., 166.
Hotchkiss, 29.
Hotchkiss, Eber S., 147.
Hotchkiss, T. D., 147.
Hotchkiss, Thos., 166.
Howard, Rev. William, 119.
Howlett's, 18.
Hoyt, James P., 85.
Hoyt, Jonathan, 27, 29.
Hubball, Richard, 23, 24, 27; admitted a planter, 23.
Hubbard, Bela, D.D., 104.
Hubbard, Rev. Bela, D. D., 108.
Hubbard, Daniel, 33.
Hubbard, Sergt. Daniel, 78, 79.
Hubbard, George, 12, 14, 23, 54, 145, 153, 155, 156, 157.
Hubbard, Grove, 149.
Hubbard, John, 30.
Hubbard, Mr., 36.
Hubbard, Sam. F., 149.
Hubbard, Wm. H., 110.
Hubbard, Wm. Henry, 192.
Huburd, Daniell, 186.
Huburd, George, 186.
Hudson, 103.
Hues, Richard, 14, 15.
Hughes, John, 12.

Hughes, Richard, 25, 27.
Hull, Alfred, G., 35, 116, 147.
Hull, Mrs. A. G., 195, 196.
Hull, H. Ellsworth, 192.
Hull, Richard Lawrence, 192.
Hull, Sam'l H., 192.
Hull, Zadoc, 110.
Hungry hill, 38.
Hunt, Robert, 147.
Hunting, advantages for, 9.
Hutchinson, Elisha, 42, 146.
Hyde Park, Mass., 113.

Idol, stone supposed to have been an, 11.
Illinois, University of, 99.
Indian, 69; inhabitants, 9; war, land granted to soldiers in, 48.
Indians, 42, 47; town inhabited by, 8; nothing certain known concerning, 11; fortification for protection against, 16; of America, 19; names of, 70; progress of the gospel among, 91; apostle to the, 94, 132.

Jackson, Abraham, 192.
Jamaica, L. I., 81.
Jamaica, N. Y., 99.
James the 2d, 75, 80.
Joans, Thomas, 12.
Johnson, Dr., 130; ancestor of, 10.
Johnson, Harmon Barber, 192.
Johnson, John, 14, 15, 16, 24, 26, 187.
Johnson, John G., 149.
Johnson, Mr., 129.
Johnson, Nathaniel, 108.
Johnson, Samuel, 33, 81, 105, 129, 130; cloth dressing carried on by family of, 33.
Johnson, S. C., 146.
Johnson, Samuel C., 178.
Johnson, Samuel, D.D., 104, 108, 129, 130.

INDEX.

Johnson, Walter, Esq., 92.
Johnson, William, 20, 24, 27, 105, 129, 157, 158, 159, 161, 182, 186, 188.
Johnson, Deacon William, 77, 78, 79, 159, 160, 161.
Johnson, Dr. William, 81.
Johnson, Sergt. Wm., 158.
Jones, Samuel, 25.
Jones, Thomas, 13, 25, 181.
Jones, William, 76, 154.
Jones's bridge, factory near, 134.
Jordan, Anne, 20.
Jordan, John, 10, 15, 20, 54, 66, 68.
Jordan, Thomas, 13, 25, 32, 69, 123, 153, 154, 155, 180.
Josephus, 85.
Journal L. H., 187.
Judgment and Mercy, etc., a funeral sermon, 95.
Jurdon, John, 12.
Justices in North Guilford parish, 149, 150.

Kellogg, Rev. Nathan, 111.
Kelsey, A., 111.
Kelsey, Alvah, 147.
Kelsey, Richard F., 194.
Kelsey, William, 146.
Kelsey, William S., 20.
Kent, 79; adventurers from, 11; county of, 22.
Kent, England, 26.
Kennilworth, 77.
Keyhow, alias James the Brother, 76.
Killingworth, 7, 8, 19, 23, 26, 28, 29, 30, 32, 85, 142, 143, 144, 187; Hammonassett Indians at, 11; Town Records, 19; harbor, 8; line, 21.
Kimball Union Academy, 113.
Kimberly, Abraham, 29.
Kimberly, Erastus C., 110.

Kimberly, George C., 110.
Kimberly, Mrs. Geo. C., 196.
King Philip, war against, 48.
King's (Columbia) college, president of, 129.
Kingsnorth, Daniel, 22, 22.
Kingsnorth, Henry, 12, 13, 22, 24; his will, 22.
Kingsnorth, James, 22.
Kingsnorth, John, 22.
Kingsnorth, Mary, 22.
Kinston, N. C., 191.
Kirtland, George, 42.
Kitchel, Rev. Cornelius L., 85, 99.
Kitchell, Joanna or Hannah, 81.
Kitchell, Robert, 9, 10, 12, 18, 23, 27, 36, 52, 54, 59, 65, 66, 81, 151, 153, 155, 156, 181.
Kitchell, Samuel, 27, 70, 71, 182.
Koukeshihu, 70.

Labore, Anthony, 42.
Lamberton, ship, 16.
Lamberton, George, 183.
Lambric, Joannes, 192.
Lancasterian method adopted, 82.
Landon, David, 188.
Landon, E. R., 144, 146.
Landon, Edward R., 6, 35, 138, 141, 144, 146, 180, 182.
Landon, George, 178.
Landon, Mrs. Hart, 195.
Landon, Hethcote G., 180.
Last of the Mohicans, The, 72.
Lathrop, Jedediah, 110, 190.
Lathrop, John Hiram, LL.D., 137.
Leake and Watt's Orphan Asylum, N. Y., 40.
Lee, Charles Gilbert, 192.
Lee, Edward, 27.
Lee, Edward M., 148.
Lee, Gen. E. M., 142, 180.

INDEX.

Lee, Samuel jr., 172, 173, 174.
Lee, William H., 194.
Lee, Lieut. Wm. H., 141.
Leet, Andrew, 187.
Leet, Mr., 63.
Leete, Abner, 50.
Leete, Albert A., 106, 147.
Leete, Ambrose, 105, 107.
Leete, Andrew, 72, 73, 74, 76, 77, 78, 79, 123, 145, 159.
Leete, Anna, 122.
Leete, Benjamin, 30.
Leete, Caleb, 163, 164, 165, 166.
Leete, Calvin M., 179.
Leete, Charles F., 180.
Leete, Daniel, 49, 107.
Leete, Edward L., 84, 106, 147, 179, 180.
Leete, John, 122.
Leete, Gov., 61, 64, 120, 122; his family, 20.
Leete, Mrs. Harvey, 195.
Leete, Mr., 18, 51, 152, 186.
Leete, Mrs. N. F., 196.
Leete, Peletiah, 50, 107, 165, 166, 167, 190.
Leete, Peletiah 2d, 101.
Leete, Roger C., 194.
Leete, Rowland, 50.
Leete, Rufus N., 147.
Leete, Samuel, 111.
Leete, Sidney W., 194.
Leete, Simeon, 47, 50.
Leete, Solomon, 49; his house burned, 49.
Leete, Theodore A., 104.
Leete, William, 9, 10, 12, 13, 23, 52, 54, 59, 62, 65, 66, 70, 71, 76, 89, 121, 127, 151, 152, 153, 154, 155, 159, 160, 181, 183.
Leete, William jr., 104.
Leete, Gov. William, 145, 182.

Leete's island, 43, 46, 49, 50, 83, 192; cemetery at, 39; granite quarry at, 41.
Leicester, Eng., 92.
Leverett, Mass., 99.
Library formed, 85.
Light, The, Appearing More and More, 91.
Lindsley, John, 14, 26.
Lisbon, Conn., 113.
Litchfield, 32, 108; county, 32.
Littlefield, 105.
London, 11, 17, 25, 81, 90, 91, 92.
Long hill, 38, 43.
Long Island, 49, 107; East Riding of, 26; sound; 7, 39.
Loper, Henry, 110, 146.
Loper, Samuel W., 142.
Lord James the second, of England, 80.
Louisburg, 48.
Loyselle, Miss Ruth, 110.
Ludington, Timothy, 50, 188.
Lyme, 69, 85.
Lyon, Rev. Chas. W., 111.
Lyons, Rev. Mr., missionary, 108.

Mack, Eli T., 85.
Madison, 7, 8, 18, 21, 29, 30, 31, 37, 58, 63, 106; church, 21; (East Guilford), 143, 144.
Magistrates and justices, list of, 145–148.
Magnalia, 90.
Maine, 38.
Marietta college, 99.
Marvin, David, 42.
Maryland, 142.
Mason, Samuel, 192.
Masonic Hall, 189.
Masons, free and accepted, St. Alban's lodge of, 188, 189.
Massachusetts, 19, 92, 135.
Mateowepesack, 71.

Mather, Cotton, 19, 90, 93.
Mather, Dr. Increase, 94.
Mather, Mr., 94.
Maycock, Thomas, 74.
Meacock, Thomas, 20, 27, 72, 73, 77, 161; admitted a planter, 21.
Mecoke, Thomas, 186.
Medicines, faith in quack, 41.
Mediterranean, 136.
Meigs, Lieut. Janna, 164, 165.
Meigs, Capt. Jehiel, 50.
Meigs, John, 19, 24, 25, 28, 50, 78, 79, 105.
Meigs, Josiah, 170.
Meigs, Lieut. Col., 49.
Meigs, Capt. Phineas, 50.
Meigs, Tryal, 28.
Meishunok, 70.
Memoir of Eli Thorp, 114.
Menunketuck, 8, 66, 67; sachem squaw of, 9, 75; English planters of, 10, 65; Indians at Branford and East Haven, 11; or West river, 45; lands called, 62; Indian inhabitants of, 65; named Guilford, 152.
Mepham, John, 12, 15, 64, 87.
Mequunhut, 70.
Merwin, Clarina B., 115.
Merwin, Rev. Samuel, 115.
Merwin, Susan T., 115.
Messanamuck, 66.
Metuckquashish, 70.
Methodist Episcopal church, 85, 111; clergymen in charge, 111.
Methodists in Guilford, 1838, 116; in North Guilford, 1838, 120.
Middlebury college, Vt., 112.
Middlefield, 32.
Middle Haddam, 110.
Middletown, 45, 47, 111, 142, 143; parishes of, 32.
Midlothian, 121.

Milford, 12, 14, 20, 51, 52, 54, 136, 152; deputies to general court from, 183.
Milledgeville, Ga., 129.
Miller, Charles W., 148, 190.
Mills, Thomas, 15.
Mipham, John, 153, 155.
Mohegan Indians, 68; sachem, 72.
Mohegans, sachem of, 10, 74; Uncas, sachem of, 46.
Monroe, Beverly, 35.
Monroe, Jasper, 147, 179.
Moore, Jairus P., 85.
Moosamattuck, 66.
Moose hill, 43, 83; cemetery at, 39.
Morse, Asahel B., 190.
Morse, Seth, 50, 107.
Morse, John, 50.
Moriton, N. H., 113.
Morton's Ford, Va., 192.
Mt. Pleasant, N. Y., 106.
Munson, Judge, 138.
Munger, John, 50.
Munger, Nicholas, 25, 27.
Munger, Wait, 50.
Murdock, Dr. James, 97.
Murray, Bridgeman, 50.
Murray, Jonathan, 50.
Murray, Rev. W. H. H., 51.
Murphy, Patrick, 192.
Music hall, 34; fire at, 190.
Muttomonossuck, 66.
My Peace I give unto you, etc., 93.

Naish, Thomas, 12.
Nathan's pond, 21.
National Freedman's Relief Commission, 113.
Naushuter, 76.
Nausump, 75.
Nausup, an Indian, 72; alias Quatabacot, deed of sale from, 73, 74, 75, 76.

Nebeserte, 68.
Neck, the, 11; Indians found on the, 11; land in the. 64; called the, 69; river, 8; plains, 21.
Nettleton, Dennis F., 192.
Newark, N. J., 23, 81, 115.
Newbern, N. C., 192, 193.
New Concord, N. Y., 117.
New England, 11, 22, 38, 55, 90; colonists, 58; tribes, first convert among, 69.
N. E. Hist. and Gen. Reg., 141.
New Hampton, N. H., 117.
New Haven, 9, 11, 19, 21, 22, 35, 37, 38, 39, 42, 43, 45, 62, 72, 81. 87, 89, 91, 93, 94, 99, 100, 108, 109, 112, 122, 152; and New London Railway Co., chartered, 39; New London and Stonington Railroad, 39; ancient colony of, 51; colony, 55, 120, 121; government of, 52; East Consociation, 112; county, 122, 123, 124, 127; justices of county court of, 127; and New London Railroad, 138; Town and Colony Records, 152; general court held at, 183; deputy to general court from, 183; articles of confederation for the jurisdiction, of, 183, 186.
New Haveners, 51.
New London, 35, 38, 39, 49; and Stonnington rail road, 138.
Newman, Mr., his barn in New Haven, 51; agreement made in confirmed, 62.
Newman, Robt., 65.
New Orleans, 191.
New York, 38, 39, 42, 113, 115, 132; city, 34, 40; New Haven and Hartford rail road Co., 39; northern parts of, destitute of religious instruction, 103; conference, 111;

New York, statue of Halleck presented to, 134.
Newtown, Conn., 102.
Niantic, Indians, sachem of, 69; river, 96.
Noble, 120.
Northampton, Mass, 94.
Northamptonshire, Eng., 20.
North Becket, 18.
North Branford, Conn., 114, 115; First Society of, 143.
North Bristol, 8.
Northfield, Litchfield co., Conn., 119.
Northford, 120, 142.
North Guilford, 8, 16, 29, 30, 31, 32, 36, 37, 43, 44, 45, 48, 108, 116, 117, 128, 191; cemetery at, 39; library formed in, 86; church, list of deacons, 119; parish, justices in, 149, 150.
North Killingworth, 108.
North Madison, 8, 31, 37, 45.
North Society, 37.
Norton, 32.
Norton, Alfred, 149.
Norton, C. Henry, 190.
Norton, Francis Morgan, 192.
Norton, Miss Grace, 19.
Norton, Henry E., 116, 138, 180.
Norton, Horace, 146, 147.
Norton, Mrs. Hy. E., 196.
Norton, James A., 147, 179.
Norton, J. W., 194.
Norton, John, 187, 192.
Norton, Jonathan G., 192.
Norton, John William, 106, 180.
Norton, Rufus. 174.
Norton, Thomas, 12, 15, 26.
Nothingarians in Guilford, 1838, 116.
Norwalk, 14, 25.
Norwich, 24, 38, 84.
Nut plains, 18, 191; cemetery, 39; Upper, 83; Lower, 83.

INDEX.   213

Oberlin college, 118.
Ockley, 90.
Old Society, 37.
Oliver, Andrew, Esq., 92.
Oneida (collegial) institute, 113.
Oneida county, N. Y., 103; missionary to, 97.
Onion river, Vt., 130.
Orange, south parish of, 129.
Orthodox or Trinitarian, 83.
Osborn, Walter, 146.
Our Saviour's Dying Legacy of Peace to his Disciples, etc., 93.
Oyster river, corn mill on, 26.
Oysters, 46; fisheries of 8.

Palfrey's History of New England, 16.
Pardy, Joseph, 75.
Paris, N. Y., 33, 105.
Park, Edward, 29.
Parkhurst, Mrs. B. B., 195.
Parks, Nathaniel, 30.
Parmalee, Eli, 85.
Parmarly, John, 186.
Parmelee, Ebenezer, 86, 182.
Parmelee, Ebenezer jr., 144.
Parmelee, Eli, 106, 180.
Parmelee, George, 59.
Parmelee, Mrs. Helen, 196.
Parmelee, Jeremiah, 190.
Parmelee, Joel Cruttenden, 192.
Parmelee, U. N., 148.
Parmelee, Uriah Nelson, jr., 193.
Parmelin, John, 12.
Parmelin, Jno. jr., 13, 24.
Parmelin, John sen., 13, 24.
Parsons, General, 49.
Pashquishook, 10.
Pasquishunk, 69.
Pauquun, 70.
Pease, Rev. Hart, 111.
Peck, Rev. Jeremiah, 81.

Pequot, 69.
Pequots, conquest of the, 11; battle with, 46.
Pesuckapaug pond, 74, 77.
Petersburg, Va., 191.
Peterson, Alexander, 193.
Phelps, F. C., 111.
Phelps, Franklin C., 147, 179.
Philadelphia, 100, 101; First Congregational church, 112.
Philip, King, 48.
Physic and physical drugs, Mrs. Cosster's, 41.
Physicians, list of, 42.
Piermont, N. H., 112, 117.
Pierson, 181.
Pillsbury, Rev. Benjamin, 111.
Pistapaug pond, 7.
Pitman, Jonathan, 81.
Plaine, William, 15.
Plane, William, 12.
Planters, meeting of, 151.
Plantation, town clerk of the, 20; treasurers for, 181.
Plum-gut, 49.
Plutarch, 85.
Plymouth, Mass., 93; pastor of the church at, 19.
Point House, 36.
Ponaim, 70.
Pope, 85.
Population, entire, 31; in Madison and Guilford, 31; increase for ten years, 31.
Poquain, 68.
Pork and pease, 17.
Port Royal, S. C., 191.
Portsmouth, Va., 192.
Portsmouth Grove, R. I., 192.
Potomac river, 192.
Powers, Thomas, 110, 190.
Presbyterian cloak, 101; churches, but few, 103.

214 INDEX.

Princeton college, 102.
Princeton, N. J., 113.
Productions, principal, 44.
Protector, Richard, 121.
Protestant Episcopal church, 35.
Prudden, Mr., 14, 21, 51.
Puritan, 121.
Puritans, 57, 63.
Pynchon, Joseph, 29, 145, 170
Pynchon, Thomas Ruggles, 42.

Quakers, 55.
Quatabacot, alias Nausup, 73, 74, 75, 76.
Quillipeak, 62.
Quillipiack, 67.
Quillipiag, 69.
Quinnipiack, 11.
Quissuckquonoh, 70.
Quonopaug pond, 44, 45.

Ramshorn, Toby, 101.
Rawson, Rev. James, 111.
Records, 15, 21, 59; names of planters in original, 13, 14.
Redfield, Ebenezer, 61.
Redfield, J., 171.
Redfield, Jared, 42.
Redfield, John, 42.
Reformed Dutch churches, but few, 103.
Relf, Thomas, divorced from his wife, 16.
Review of the More Fixed Laws, etc., 151.
Reynolds, Gideon Perry, 42.
Richards, Rev. John, of Waterbury, 117.
Richardson, Miles G., 193.
Richmond, 32.
Richmond, Mass., 107.
Richmond, Va., 110.
Ripley, Erastus L., 147.
Riverdale, N. Y., Presbyterian church, 115.

Robinson, Henry, 104.
Robinson, Rev. Henry, 142.
Robinson, James, 169.
Robinson, Jon'n, 30.
Robinson, Samuel, 146, 167, 168, 169, 170, 172, 174, 175, 176, 177.
Robinson, Col. Samuel, 106, 145.
Robinson, Thomas, 28.
Rogers, Seth H., 42.
Roman catholics, first met as a religious body, 116.
Root, Rev. David, 112.
Rose, Joel, 119.
Rositar, Mr., 186.
Rosse's meadow, 77.
Rossiter, Col. Abel, 149, 177, 178.
Rossiter, Benjamin, 119, 149.
Rossiter, Bray, 41.
Rossiter, Dr. Bray, 26.
Rossiter, Bryan, 23, 41, 42.
Rossiter, Dr. Bryan, 18, 61, 93, 123; joined the settlers in Guilford, 18; sworn as a freeman, 18.
Rossiter, David B., 180.
Rossiter, Dr., 93.
Rossiter, Joanna, 93.
Rossiter, Johannah, 19.
Rossiter, John, 24, 26.
Rossiter, John R., 119, 149, 180.
Rossiter, Josiah, 61, 72, 73, 74, 76, 77, 78, 79, 123, 145, 160, 161, 162, 182.
Rossiter, Mr., 123, 182.
Rossiter, N., 174, 175.
Rossiter, Nathaniel, 127, 145.
Rossiter, T., 179.
Rossiter, Theophilus, 30, 119.
Rossiter, Deacon Theophilus, 149.
Rossiter, Timothy, 149.
Rossiter, Wilbur F., 194.
Rowe, John, 188.
Roxbury, Conn., 114.

INDEX.

Roxbury, Mass., 94.
Ruggles, Mr., characteristics of, 94.
Ruggles, Nathaniel, 42, 169, 170, 171.
Ruggles, Dr. Nathaniel, 105, 145.
Ruggles, Thomas, 104.
Ruggles, Thomas jr., 104.
Ruggles, Rev. Thomas, 94.
Ruggles, Rev. Thomas jr., 95.
Russel, Col. Edward, 144.
Russel, Rev. John, 116; protector of the regicides, 116.
Russel, Mr., 117.
Russel, Samuel, 116.
Russel, Rev. Samuel, 116.
Rutland, Vt., 118.
Ruttawoo, 9; (East river), 45, 65, 70, 73.

Sabine, William, 50.
Sachem's head, 43, 45, 46, 47, 49, 83; origin of the name, 46; house 46; destroyed by fire, 46.
Sachem squaw, purchase from the, 65.
Sag Harbor, 49; return of prisoners at, 49.
St. Alban's lodge free and accepted masons, 188, 189; past masters of, 190.
St. John's church, 110
St. John the Baptist, feast of, to be kept, 189.
St. John the Evangelist, feast of to be kept, 189.
Salem, Mass., 14, 17, 92, 93, 111; Atheneum at, 93.
Salisbury, 32, 130.
Sandemanian sentiments, 102.
Savage, Abr'm, 189.
Savage's Winthrop's New England, 69.
Sawpitts farm, 92.
Sawpitts, granite quarry opened at, 40.
Sawpits-quarry wharf, 45.
Saxton, Abel, 50.
Saxton, Simeon, 50.

Saybrook, 10, 16, 21, 32, 48, 65, 42, 69, 81, 85, 93, 142, 143, 181; fort, 14; chaplain at, 92.
Schermerhorn, J. W., 34.
School, districts, 83; furniture, manufacture of, 34.
Scituate, Mass., 100.
Scott, Sir Walter, 134,
Scotland, one of the nine counsellors of, 120.
Scranton, Francis S., 193.
Scranton, Col. Ichabod, 48.
Scranton, Jared, 149.
Scranton, John, 13, 24, 43, 156, 158, 181, 186.
Scranton, Joseph A., 150.
Scranton, Samuel, 146.
Scranton, Thomas Marvin, 193.
Scriptures acknowledged as the rule of procedure, 51.
Seabrooke, 64.
Sebequenach, 71.
Second Presbyserian church of Philadelphia, 100; Washington, D. C., 114.
Sergeant, John, 28.
Seward, Amos, 3, 137, 146, 190.
Seward, Edwin H., 104.
Seward, Jason, 106.
Seward, Lieut. John, 162, 163.
Seward, Mr., died, 20.
Seward, Rachel Stone, 137.
Seward Timothy, 58.
Seward, William, 19, 24, 27, 104, 105, 181, 187; anecdote related of, 20.
Seward, Lieut. Wm., 41, 77, 78, 79, 158, 160.
Sewers, Edward, 14, 15, 26, 27.
Seymour, 138.
Shakespear, 85, 134.
Shambisqua, 75.
Shaumpishuh, sachem squaw, 9, 35, 47, 65, 72.

Sheader, John, 14, 24, 27, 187.
Sheafe, Jacob, 89, 155; moved to Boston, Mass., 14.
Sheldon, Winthrop D., 85.
Shells, masses of, 9.
Shelly, Shubel, 28.
Shepard, Mr., 69.
Shipman, Elias, 42.
Shirman, John, 183.
Sibley's Harvard graduates, 81, 93.
Shoreline Sentinel, the, 35.
Slocum, John P., 85.
Small pox, 40.
Smollett, 85.
Smith, Grace, 136.
Smith, Justin W., 42.
Smith, John, 136.
Smith, Judge, 138.
Smith, Lovine (Hebert), 136.
Smith, Mary D., 137.
Smith, Mr., 118.
Smith, R. D., 82.
Smith, Ralph D., 5, 83, 84, 144, 146, 179, 196; manuscript left by, 5.
Smith, Ralph Dunning, 136–141; his children, 137; judge of probate court, 137; manuscripts left, 140.
Smith, Richard, 136.
Smith, Richard Edward, 137.
Smith, Sarah Spencer, 137.
Smith, Tabor, 20.
Smith, Thomas, 23, 27.
Smith, Walter Hebert, 137.
Smith, Rev. William S., 85, 99.
Soil, richness of increased, 42.
Society for the Propagation of the Gospel in Foreign Parts, 108, 129.
Some Helpes to Stirre up to Christian Duties, etc., 90.
Somers, 97.
Somers, William, died, 15.

Somerset, Henry, Duke of Beaufort, 188.
Sound, the, 8, 9; fine prospect of, 17.
Southbury, Conn., 136, 137; first pastor of the church in, 100.
Southold, Long Island, 29, 52.
South Lane, 20, 21.
Southmayd, Miss Dorcas, 98.
Spencer, Daniel L., 194.
Spencer, George B., 110, 180, 194.
Spencer, Henry R., 147.
Spencer, Miss Lizzie, 195.
Spencer, Mrs. Richard, 196.
Spencer, Samuel C., 146.
Spencer & Sons, 34.
Spencer, William, 146, 190.
Springfield, 29, 102.
Sproat, Dr., 101, 102.
Sproat, Rev. James, D.D., 100.
Stamford, 28, 52, 54, 114; annexed to New Haven, 152; deputies to general court from, 183.
Stannard, Henry B., 190.
Stanton, Dr., 90.
Stanton, John A., 147.
Staplehurst, 22.
Starr, Comfort, 28, 106.
Starr, Deacon Comfort, 146.
Starr, Edward C., 104.
Starr, Jehosaphat, 28.
Starr, John W., 104.
Starr, Richard W., 194.
Starr, William, 106, 145.
State street, 28.
Steiner, Dr. Lewis H., 137.
Steiner, Hon. Lewis H., 142.
Steuben county, N. Y., 105.
Steuens, John, 186.
Stevens, John, 14, 15, 24, 27.
Stevens, Nathaniel, 50.
Stevens, Samuel, 50.
Stevens, Thomas, 14, 15, 26, 27.
Stevens, William, 15, 24, 27.

Stiles, President, 120, 121.
Stiles's History of the Judges, 122, 123.
Stillwater brook, 45.
Stillwell, Elizabeth, 20.
Stillwell, Jasper, 13, 17, 20, 25.
Stockbridge, 32.
Ston, John, 187.
Ston, William, 187.
Stone, 32.
Stone, Alvord A., 148.
Stone, Mrs. A. A., 195.
Stone, Benjamin, 188.
Stone, Daniel, 50.
Stone, John, 12, 13, 25, 78, 79, 187.
Stone, Joseph, 164, 165.
Stone, Joshua, 30.
Stone, Josiah, 30.
Stone, Leverett C., 147.
Stone, Medad, 124.
Stone, N., 171, 172.
Stone, Ens. Nathaniel, 162.
Stone, Reuben, 146, 178, 179, 182.
Stone, Samuel, 37.
Stone, Sam E., 147.
Stone, Rev. T. D. P., 84.
Stone, Timothy, 104, 145, 166, 167, 168, 169, 170.
Stone, Col. Timothy, 105, 127, 144, 145.
Stone, William, 12, 14, 15, 24, 27, 37.
Stone house, the noted, 16; description of, 16, 17; first marriage celebrated in it, 17; stone for, brought on hand-barrows by Indians, 17.
Stonington, 39.
Stony creek, 7, 9, 26, 42, 65, 66, 73, 74.
Stratford, 129, 130.
Strong, Benj., 166.
Strong, Lyman, 42.
Stout, Rev. E. F., 111.

Stoughton, Capt. Israel, 69.
Suffolk, 191.
Suksqua, 70.
Surrey, 90.
Surry, adventurers from, 11.
Swayne, Mr., 153.
Syracuse, 98.

Talcott, Alvan, 42, 83, 84.
Talcott, Dr. Alvan, 6, 82, 142.
Talcott, John, 48.
Talman, Ebenezer, 30, 37.
Tallman, Peter, 28, 164.
Tapp, Edward, 183.
Taunton, Mass., 102.
Taylor, Bayard, 132.
Taylor, Mr., 118.
Tennent, Gilbert, 101.
Terryers, book of the, 60.
Terryville in Plymouth, Conn., 114.
Texas, 16.
Theological seminary, Princeton, N. J., 113.
Third church, deacons of, 116.
Third Congregational church, 111; organized, 112; Guilford, 113, 115.
Thomaston, Conn., 99.
Thompson, Frederick S., 85.
Thompson, Major, 17.
Thompson, Major Robert, 92.
Thompson's heirs, attorney for, 92.
Tibbals, Abraham, 193.
Tinkard, Thos., 29.
Toby, old, 101.
Todd, Jonathan, 174, 176; A.M., pastor of the second church in Guilford, 95.
Todd, Dr. Jonathan, 131.
Todd, Rev. Jno., 132.
Todd, William, 131, 144, 145, 177, 178.
Torrington, Conn., 113.

Totoket, or Branford mountain, 43; one-eyed squaw of, 67; purchased from the Indians, 153.
Town, list of, 1825, 37; mill, 35; meeting, special, 41; Records, 41; clerks, list of, 182.
Travels, 57.
Treat, Robert, 48, 80.
Trinity college, Hartford, 109.
Trowbridge, John, 122.
Trowbridge, Thomas, 75.
Trout, Toby, 193.
Trubee, Giles, 188.
Trumbull, Dr., 21, 51, 90, 103.
Tucker, Charles, 193.
Tuckshishoagg, 66, 67, 68, 69; or Tuxis pond, 10.
Turner, Rev. Lawson, 111.
Tuttle, Hezekiah, 193.
Tuttle, Joel, 144, 146, 178, 182.
Tuxis pond, 62, 63; or Tuckshishoag pond, 10.
Tyler, Abraham, 48.
Tyler, William, 147.

Uncas, 10, 62, 66, 67, 70, 71, 74; sachem of the Mohegans, 46; grant of, 62; the Mohegan, 63; deed of sale from, 71; his mark, 72.
Union, Arkansas territory, 117.
Union college, 118.
Union library, 86.
Union school district, 83.
Union Theological Seminary, N. Y., 114, 115.
United States, oldest dwelling house standing in, 16; second chief justice, 114; senate, 128; consul to Asia Minor, 136.
United Workers for Public Improvement, 38, 195, 196; officers, 195, 196; Manuscript of the History of Guilford presented to, 196.

University of Illinois, 99.
University of New York, 113.
Usher, John, 93.

Vaill, Mr., 119.
Vaill, Rev. William Fowler, 117.
Vermont, 118; first governor of, 130.
Verona, N. Y., 33, 97.
Village, the, size and form, 37.

Wallingford, 7, 27, 99.
Wantumbeourn, 70.
Ward, Andrew, 28, 163, 186, 169, 171, 172, 173, 174, 182.
Ward, Andrew jr., 169.
Ward, Capt. Andrew, 81, 145, 163, 164.
Ward, Col. Andrew, 48.
Ward, Gen. Andrew, 127, 145.
Ward, Billious, 188, 190.
Ward, Edmund, 100, 104, 108, 169.
Ward, Gen. 48.
Ward, J. Wilson, 85.
Ward, Samuel, 50.
Ward, Thelus, 50.
Ward, Timothy, 188.
Ward, Tryal, 28.
Ward, William, 168.
Washington, 32, 124, 128, 136, 191, 192; Second Presbyterian church, 114.
Washington, Conn., 108.
Washington, Gen., 131.
Waterbury, 81, 117; Conn., First Congregational church, 112.
Waterhouse, Eber, 188.
Water street, 18.
Watertown, 98, 117.
Weed, William E., 194.
Weekwosh, 10, 11, 64, 66, 67, 68, 69; the Indian, 70; the purchase from, 69.

Weld, William E., 148.
Welton, Harvey S., 183.
Wequash, 69.
Weslyan university, 111.
Westfield, 32.
West Hartford, 114.
West Haven, 29, 129.
West India trade, 34, 47.
Westminster, general convention held at, 131.
Westmoreland, N. Y., 33.
Weston (Easton) academy, 137.
West river, 33, 34, 36, 43, 45, 122, 123.
West rock, 8.
Wethersfield, 14, 28, 93, 116, 153.
Wethersfield, Ill., 118.
Wetmore, Mr., 129.
Whalley, Gen., 122.
Whalley, Judge, 116.
Whedon, Luman, 82.
Where is the Lord God of Elijah, a funeral sermon, 97.
Whitcomb, R. W., 111.
White, Horace, Esq., 112.
Whitehall, council held at, 120.
Whitesboro, N. Y., 113.
Whitfield, Henry, 9, 12, 62, 65, 66, 68, 69, 70, 89.
Whitfield, Henry B. D., 90.
Whitfield, Rev. Henry, 40, 116.
Whitfield, John, 25, 32, 91.
Whitfield, Mr., 9, 10, 16, 17, 22, 25, 32, 35, 51, 62, 63, 64, 65, 80, 88, 91, 92, 120, 121; his company, 56.
Whitfield, Nathaniel, 18, 25, 27, 32, 91.
Whitfield's church, 121.
Whitmore, John, 183r
Whitmore, Rev. Zulva, 118.
Whitney, Eli, 130.
Whittier, John Greenleaf, poem by, 135.
Wicks, Rev. Henry, 84, 99.

Wilcox, Almon O., 148.
Wilcox, John R., 144.
Wilcox, Josiah, 27.
Wilcox, William T., 147.
Wilcoxon, Obadiah, 27.
Wildman, Albert B., 147, 179, 180.
Willard, Julius, 42.
Williams college, 99.
Williams, Elisha, A.M., rector of Yale college, 95.
Willis, N. P., 137.
Williston, Vt, 130.
Wilmington, N. C., 192.
Wilson, Edwin H., 85.
Wilson, Gen. James Grant, 133.
Wilson, Rev. John, 142.
Wilson, Rev. John S., 111.
Wilson's Halleck, 86.
Winchester, city of, 90.
Winchester, Va., 192.
Windsor, 19, 27, 29, 41.
Winthrop, Gov., 69.
Winthrop's New England, Savage's, 69.
Wise, Henry, 29.
Wolcottville, 113.
Wood, Fanny (Ellsworth), 114.
Wood, Rev. George Ingersoll, 114.
Wood, Hon. Joseph, 114.
Wood, Mr., 115.
Wood, kinds now to be found, 44.
Woodruff, Richard H., 194.
Wright, Benjamin, 14, 15.
Wright, Benj. sen., 24, 27.
Wright, Henry Wm., 193.
Wymond, Rev. R. W., 111.
Wyoming, Pa., 137.

Yale college, 94, 95, 96, 97, 98, 99, 100, 101, 102, 108, 109, 114, 115, 116, 117, 118, 119, 128, 132, 136, 173.
Yale theological seminary 115.

www.ingramcontent.com/pod-product-compliance
Lightning Source LLC
Chambersburg PA
CBHW050144170426
43197CB00011B/1961